MOSES TEGGART
Bard of the Boglands

An Anthology

JOHN R R WRIGHT

MOSES TEGGART
Bard of the Boglands

An Anthology

JOHN R R WRIGHT

Published by South Lough Neagh Publishing

© 2008 South Lough Neagh Regeneration Association

All rights reserved. No part of this publication may be reproduced, stored in a retrieval system, or transmitted in any form or by any means, electronic, mechanical, photocopying, recording, or otherwise, without the prior permission of the copyright holder.

Cover design & book layout by Creative Juices, Lurgan
Printed by W&G Baird, Antrim

ISBN 0-9549259-2-0

CONTENTS

Dedication X
Preface XI
Acknowledgements XIII
Foreword XIV
Editor's Notes XV
Moses Teggart: Bard of the Boglands 1
A Short Introduction to the Poetry of Moses Teggart 52

SCOTTISH POEMS

The Sands of Troon 70
At the Birthplace of Burns 71
Campsie Glen 73
The Bonnie Rose O'Airlie 75
Mirren 77
Her Lover's Lass 78
The Bonny Scotch Bluebell 79
Jenny's Hazel Een 80
Keepin' Tryst 81
Aboon Ben Lomond 83
Anither Year 84
Ailsa Craig 85
Burn's Great-Granddaughter 87
Rowanberries in Campsie Glen 89
The Luggie 90
The Bard Greet Himsel' on New Year's Eve 91
By the Banks of the River Wey 94
Lulworth Cove 96
The Wimplin' Luggie 98
Loch-na-Gar 99
Where the Bonnie Kelvin Winds 100
At New-Year's Time 102
Jenny Gow 104
In the Strathavon 106
The Rose O'Rochsilloch 108

AMERICAN POEMS

The Go-Ahead Yankee 109
Crowned with Glory 110
Dawn 111
The Old Moon and the New 112

Arrow-Wounds	113
Fate	114
The Woods in Winter	115
The Moon and the Soul	117
The Sky	118
Forebodings	119
Remembrance	120
Cast Down	121
Jenny Wren	122
The Scarlet Tanager	123
Under the Elms	124
The English Starling	126
The Jaguar in Forest Park	127
The Little Sprig of Green	129
Flora: A Lady Tree	130
At Dewy Dusk in August	132
Morning Song of the Wood Thrush	133
Humility in Song	134
Where Yellow Poppies Blow	135
Our Dumb Animals	136
To the City of Homes	137
Aella Green	139
Caged Skylarks in Forest Park	140
To the February Wind	141
The Peabody Elm	141
Five Unhappy Song Birds	142
A City Rowan Tree	143
The Blue Jay	145
A Giant's Hemlock	146
Snowbirds	147
The Chickadee	148
The Welcome of the Fields	149
Woodland Clover in March	151
Ursa Major	152
Lines to a Lonely Pine	153
The Redbreast's Vesper	154
In Carlo's Company	155
A Lover's Song to Spring	156
The Wind and the Leaves	157
Lenora	158
On the Lord's Day	160
The Harebell	160
The Red Pines	160
Distant Hills	161
The Wood Thrush and his Song	162

At Sunset	162
A November Hepatica	163
The Music of the Crows	164
The Wind and Brown Oak Leaves	165
The Music of Sorrow	166
Ames Hill	167
Innocence	169
To Spring	171
Listening to the Lark at Sunrise	171
To James Duncan	172
June	172
Autumn	173
The Daffodils	174
For the Last Time	175
Hero to Leander	176
The Vision and Penelope	179
The Dog Argos	181
Helen's Gift to Telemachus	183
Aurora to Tithonus	184

IRISH POEMS

The Old Stripper	186
Bringing Home the Cows	187
The Montiagh Moss	188
My School-Girl	190
Sweet-Brier	191
Home Thoughts from Abroad	192
The Reply to Mr Frank Burns, Rural Postman, Portadown, Ireland	193
O Fresh and Fragrant Roses	194
The Water Wagtail	196
Upon the Sally Tree	197
When the Skylark Soars and Sings	198
Childhood	199
Tartaraghan	200
Love in Spring	206
Bilzy	207
The Peasant Folks' Hallowe'en	211
Love in the Kail-Plat	213
The Boor-Tree	214
An Exile	215
The Boys an' the Bird-Creel	216
Spring in Ballinary	218
The Pearl of Portadown	220

The Flower of Derryane	222
The Skay	223
The Belle of Derrykeevin	225
The Lily of Lough Neagh	226
Dead at the Birches	228
The Bogland Farmer to his Wife	229
The House at the Head of the Town	231
The Braes of Ballinary	233
The Crabtree Loanin'	235
Memories of the Wee Mosscheeper	236
At the Mouth of the Old Turf Stack	237
The Belle of Ballinary	238
Liza and her Ploughboy	240
Mounthall	242
Ned and Mary	245
March in the Boglands	246
'Tis all for Thee	247
Remembrance	247
Solicitude	247
Night and Morn	248
Enduring Love	248
When the Bud is on the Thorn	249
A Birches Boy	251
Summer's Come! Summer's Come!	252
The Crabtree Chair	254
Coney Island	256
The Belle of Columbkill	258
Where Blue-Eyed Mary Dwells	260
The Chay Lady	262
Ben the Thatcher	264
The Cattle Come from the Hills	267
Above the Bogs in Ireland	269
The Sally Tree	270
The Ould Straw Stack	271
Lizzie Wall	272
The Blackthorn Blossom	274
The Whiterump	275
In Dear Old Ireland	276
The Turf Cutter	277
Where the Bog Bean Grows	279
The Voice of Mary	280
Lillian Martin	281
Light and Darkness: or The Birches Boy's Fate	282
The Belle of Derryagh	285
Up the Ramper	286

To the Robin Red Breast	287
Where Darling Sally Dwells	289
Brannon's Brae	290
A Lough Neagh Lament	293
A Little Thorn	295
A Change	295
The Lough at Derryadd	295
The Blackcap	297
Upon the Stubble Rigg	297
Liza	297
Bog Fir	298
In Milltown Churchyard	298
Over at Mitton's	299
Divided	300
The Stonechecker	302
Bella	302
The Turf Bummer	302
The Bluecap	303
On the Wee Green Ramper	303
A Black Frost	304
Wee Jerry	305
In the Big Moss	305
My Father's Birches	306
Treasure-Trove	306
The Meadowpipit	306
Yellow Broom	307
The Loved One	308
The Belle of Clonmacate	309
The Shovel and the Spade	311
Morn	312
Night	313
The Fisher Girl	314
The Old Stone-Breaker	315
A Monody for Mary	317
To be a Boy Again	318
Working and Dreaming	318
Summer Nights	319
Down the Long Road	319
Granda's Laburnum	321
Fine Grosbeaks	321
A Fine Crop of Turf	322
The Old Foot-Stick	323
Columbkill	324
How They Manage in Derryagh	325
The Blue Cornflower	325

The Bullfinch	325
The Spey-Wife	326
The Pewit	326
The Banshee's Lament	327
Our Bogland Home	329
Bonnie Mary of Drumcree	330
Pulling Flax	332
In the Town of Birr	333
The Rag Thorn	334
In Derrylileagh Wood	334
A Bogland Boy	335
At the Cross Roads	335
The Jacksnipe	335
A Bogland Custom	337
Sloes	337
Adown the Lane	337
The Wet-My-Lip	338
In the Potato Plots	338
Autumn's Self	339
Autumn in Derryagh	340
God's Harvest	341
A Wayside Flower	342
At the Hill Gap	342
The Plantation	344
Bleaching Flax	344
Love's Entreaty	345
Love in Derrykarn	346
Weaving and Wooing	346
Makin' Hay	347
Love for Betty	348
The Maid of Moyallon	349
A Dreaming Skylark	350
The Bleating of the Snipe	350
Daisies on the Brae	352
The Invitation	354
Love for Things of the Bogland	356
Run Like a Redshank	357
The Yellow Willy	358
Life in the Bog Plat	360
Bringing Home Turf	360
In the Bogland	361
Hedgerow Flowers	363
The Clay Island	363
The Old Limekiln	364
The Maid of Markethill	365

In Memory of Mother	366
In a Quaker Meeting-House	367
April in Erin	369
Mary Mitton	370
Blue-Eyed Melia Lappin	372
Home	374
November in the Bogland	375
Mary M'Anally	377
Granny Roe	379
Down in Maghery	380
The Milltown Maid	382
When Mother's Gone	383
Wintertime in Derryagh	384
On the Banks O' the Bann	386
Toby Hole	388
Bogland Stubble	391
The Wet Bogland	393
An Old World Summer House	394
When the Carts Come Home	395
The Old Cow Loanin'	396
The Bonnie Bogland Girl	397
Lovely Annie Barr	398
Gorse	399
Lines to a Skylark in Winter	400
Turf Smoke	401
The Home of Jenny Wren	401
To a Bogland Orchid	402
The Banshee	403
Montiaghs' Mary	403
Breaking-in Bogland	404
A Farewell	405

APPENDICES

Appendix A - Family Tree of the Teggarts, Ballinary, Co. Armagh	406
Appendix B - Family Tree of the Mittons, Ballinary, Co. Armagh	407
Select Glossary	408
Select Bibliography	416
Alphabetical Index of Poems	417

MOSES TEGGART

BARD OF THE BOGLANDS

Dedicated

to

My wife, Emily, the source of all my joy
and the inspiration for this book

May those who read with open mind
This bogland poet's prose and rhyme,
Find something there to stir the soul
And draw them back to former time,
When turf-light glow from cottage windows shone,
And every townland name was famed in song.

John R R Wright

PREFACE

Though the mighty poet dazzles with his art,
The sweet minor singer lives within the heart.[1]

Until very recently, Moses Teggart was a virtually unknown poet, especially in his native Ulster. Born in rural north Armagh around the middle of the nineteenth century, the 'Bard of the Boglands' spent much of his adult life in Scotland and latterly, the United States.

With the single but notable exception of the Dublin Victorian author and literary critic, D J O'Donoghue, none of his contemporaries, on this side of the Atlantic, appear to have recognised his poetical talent. It is somewhat ironic, though understandable, given the twenty years he spent in Massachusetts, that he was better known and more acclaimed in New England than at home.

A prolific poet - he is believed to have written nearly nine hundred poems - Teggart published around a third of this number in various American and Ulster newspapers. Unfortunately, the remainder have not survived the ravages of time and are presumed to have been destroyed by his widow in the months following his untimely death in 1909. However, the extant poems, now collected and published here for the first time in book form, are more than sufficient to illustrate the quality of his muse.

The book has taken some four years to compile but it has been very much a labour of love for the quality of his verse is such that he deserves greater recognition than has hitherto been the case. It was certainly his fervent wish that he might bring credit and fame to the Birches area of North Armagh where he was born:

> *The house and that hill unknown to fame,*
> *I would raise to some renown,*
> *Were the hopes realised to me come*
> *In the house at the head of the town.*[2]

It was an aspiration he continued to hold throughout his life. As one of his American friends averred, *"The verse he wrote, when collected into a volume - as he deemed they some time might be - would be a treasure of fine thought and lovely imagery."*[3]

The *'some time'* has now arrived - and though nearly a hundred years have elapsed since his demise, it is hoped that this publication of his verse will give a wider audience the opportunity to enjoy and appreciate his work and allow his poetic spirit to finally rest in peace.

---

[1] N A Sherman, *Our Minor Poets, Springfield Republican,* 26 July 1896.
[2] *Springfield Republican,* November 1899.
[3] *Springfield Republican,* 2 March 1909.

Judged by the most discerning of literary standards, Moses Teggart cannot be regarded as a great poet but, at his best, as he was in his vivid description of pastoral landscapes, his portrayal of ordinary country folk and his empathetic and observant depiction of the natural world, he can certainly be ranked alongside the best Ulster poets of his generation.

In an increasingly technological and materialistic world which all too often has little time for good literature, never mind poetry, it is hoped that the readers of this volume may find some verses that will appeal to their humanity and transport them back to a bygone age when the cottages of North Armagh resounded to the whirr of the spinning wheel, the clack of the loom and the chorus of rustic voices as every townland name was celebrated in song.

ACKNOWLEDGEMENTS

This book would never have seen the light of day without the assistance and encouragement of a great number of wonderful people. My special thanks goes to: Sharyn Cardaropoli, Maggie Humberston (Connecticut Valley Museum, Springfield MA) and Diane Hutchinson for freely giving of their time to undertake research in the United States; Canon Ted Fleming, Thomas J R Glenny, John Jackson, Victor and Anna Martin, Joan Proctor, Ruthanne Smith and James Tennyson for so generously sharing their unrivalled knowledge of the North Armagh area; Jim Lyttle for his photographic expertise; Rev David Hilliard, Rev Gerald Macartney and Trevor McNeice for providing access, respectively, to the church records of Tartaraghan, Milltown and Drumcree parishes; Beatrice Hayes and Francis Teggart for kindly donating copies of several Teggart poems; Ross Chapman, Kenneth and Phyllis Flannagan, and Hilda Trueman for the loan of photographs; my dear friend, Jack Gilpin, for his constant support and wise counsel; the staff of the Micrographics Department, Boston Public Library for their guidance and direction; the staff of the Irish Reference Library, Armagh for whom nothing was too much trouble; Lynda Steenson, Registrar of Births, Deaths and Marriages, Craigavon Borough Council, who responded to a series of enquiries with incredible patience, efficiency and good humour; my son, Bryan Wright, for demystifying the world of computer graphics. Above all, I wish to thank my wife, and typist, Emily, for her constant support and inspiration during the past four years. Without her perseverance and industry this book could not have been written.

South Lough Neagh Regeneration Association

Supporting community based events and entrepreneurial initiatives have been two of the main driving forces linked with the ongoing success of South Lough Neagh Regeneration Association.

Since its formation in 1993, this voluntary organisation in conjunction with various national and local funders has embarked on a wide range of social, land management, infrastructure, historical, literary, heritage and cultural projects which have been extremely beneficial to the area and which have been received with enthusiasm by the community.

The Association has recently been to the fore in delivering a series of community based cultural awareness programmes. One such programme resulted in the publication of the book *'Skimming the Surface'* featuring a wealth of local historical detail of the south shoreline and surrounding areas of Lough Neagh. The book *'Moses Teggart - Bard of the Boglands'* is an element of the ongoing (2008) cultural outreach and awareness programme.

South Lough Neagh Regeneration Association operates from its offices at Maghery Business Centre, Maghery Road, Dungannon. Its three office staff and twelve committee members gratefully acknowledge the support funding from the Heritage Lottery Fund for this project.

It is the continuing objective of South Lough Neagh Regeneration Association to reach out to all the members of the diverse community in which it serves, bringing everyone together to work harmoniously towards a better shared society.

As a voice from the past and a record of fast disappearing days, we are confident that this publication *'Moses Teggart - Bard of the Boglands'* will not only be enjoyed by all, but will serve as common uniting influence within our wider society to-day and in the future.

Joseph Corr
Chairman

South Lough Neagh Regeneration Association (2008)

EDITOR'S NOTES

It has been decided to group the poems thematically under three headings - Scottish, Irish and American - in the hope that such an arrangement would best enhance the readers' appreciation and enjoyment. The American section also includes, for convenience, a number of the poet's adaptations of classical Greek themes, which were first published in Massachusetts. Within each division the poems are arranged in chronological order.

As much of Teggart's verse was written in his native vernacular or in lowlands Scots (Lallans), a glossary has been provided for those words which many readers might otherwise find strange and puzzling.

Where a poem has been located in more than one newspaper, as was often the case, the date of the first appearance has been given as the date of publication.

Although Teggart's names for some North Armagh townlands differs slightly from those found in official ordnance survey records, his spelling has been preserved throughout.

In some instances, the poet's very individual, and often superfluous, punctuation has been simplified.

Whilst every effort has been made to identify persons mentioned in the poems, this has not always been possible. However, in those cases where identification has been established with reasonable certainty, the relevant information has been appropriately appended.

As Teggart's Irish verse represents almost two-thirds of his poetical output, this proportion has been reflected in the number of local poems selected for publication.

Townlands of Tartaraghan Civil Parish

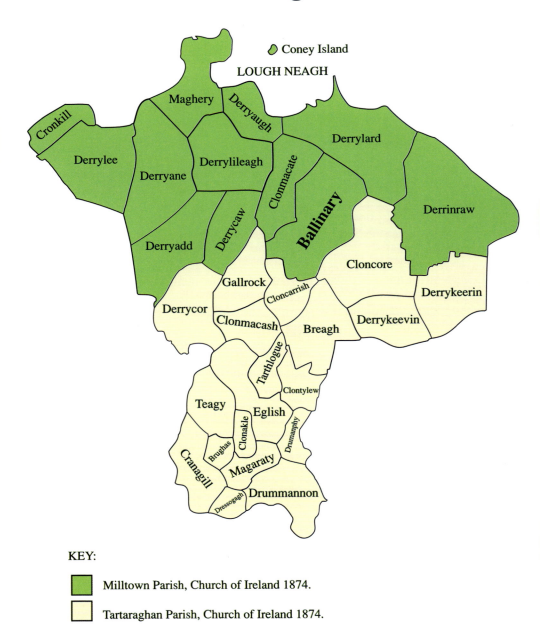

KEY:

- Milltown Parish, Church of Ireland 1874.
- Tartaraghan Parish, Church of Ireland 1874.

MOSES TEGGART: BARD OF THE BOGLANDS

A Bogland Boyhood in the Fields of Paradise[1]

It is the Year of Our Lord, 1853. In Europe the Ottoman Empire is preparing for the outbreak of hostilities with Russia, a conflict that was soon to involve both Britain and France in the so-called Crimean War; in the United States of America, Harriet Beecher Stowe's anti-slavery novel, *Uncle Tom's Cabin*, is enjoying record sales; in England minor earthquakes are shaking the southern and western counties; and in Ireland, the opening of the Boyne Bridge at Drogheda completes the rail link between Belfast and Dublin. However, none of these events was likely to have impinged upon the consciousness of the rural community that constituted the civil parish of Tartaraghan in north Co. Armagh.

Local events were of much more interest to the cotters and small farmers who comprised ninety-five percent of the parish population: the heavy and unexpected winter snowfalls that blanketed the district for nearly two weeks and made any sort of travelling well-nigh impossible; the severe flooding in the north of the parish resulting from the failure of the Lough Neagh drainage system to cope with excessive rainfall and swollen rivers; and the committal proceedings instituted against a local man at Clonmacate Petty Sessions for the alleged murder of a thirteen year old girl who was found dead in a bog hole. In fact, the hapless defendant, Thomas Murray, was eventually found to be innocent but only after three appearances in various courts.

For one local family however, the highlight of the year was the birth of a son, Moses, on 1 February. He was the second child of Moses and Charlotte Teggart of Ballinary. With an area of just over 600 acres, Ballinary was one of the largest townlands in the parish and was centrally situated in an area known as 'The Birches' - being so-called because of the prevalence of birch trees in the neighbourhood.[2]

Moses Teggart (Senior) was one of the many small tenant farmers living in Ballinary at the time. Indeed, to classify him as a farmer is something of an exaggeration, for his holding, at a fraction over three acres, was much too small for any meaningful agricultural activity. However, his position was little different from that of his neighbours, most of whom had less than five acres.[3] He provided for his family by growing vegetables, mainly potatoes and cabbages, cutting and selling turf from the adjacent moss and using his handloom to weave the yarn spun by his wife and daughters.[4] In later years, his economic position was considerably enhanced when he was appointed rural postman for the Milltown district of Tartaraghan parish.

---

[1] *'All around us in our childhood/ Lies the fields of paradise'*, Moses Teggart, *'Childhood'*, undated.

[2] According to Thomas Palmer, Clerk of Clonmacate Petty Sessions, the entire parish was once a birch forest in the early years of the nineteenth century, see *Bassett's Armagh Directory*, 1888.

[3] An analysis of Richard Griffith's, *Valuation of Tenements, Ballinary, Parish of Tartaraghan*, c.1864 reveals that over two-thirds of the tenants held five acres or less, and only an eighth had more than ten acres.

[4] The birth record for Moses (Junior) in Milltown Parish Church records Moses (Senior) as a weaver.

Birth Entry for Moses Teggart, Milltown Parish Church, 1853.

He must certainly have had a strong and robust constitution, for despite years of hard manual toil, often in cold and damp conditions, he was still able to deliver the district's mail until well into his seventies.[5] When he died, aged 88, on 26 March, 1913, he had exceeded the average life expectancy for males in the Tartaraghan district at that time, by nearly thirty years.[6]

Copy of Death Certificate, Moses Teggart (Senior), 1913.

He was one of the comparatively few people of his generation who could read and write. Even a quarter of a century after his birth, the proportion of the Tartaraghan population who could write their own name was still very low. An analysis of the marriage records in the parish church show that in 1850 just over a quarter of the participants were able to sign. Ten years later, this fraction had increased considerably but was still less than half.[7] Not only was he literate, Moses was also something of a poet. In 1886, he composed some verses to commemorate the opening of the newly built Clantilew Orange Hall:

---

[5] The 1901 census for Ballinary gives Moses' occupation as 'Auxiliary Postman'.
[6] See Rev W E C Fleming, *Tartaraghan Precinct North Armagh,* Dundalk, 2006, p.129.
[7] *Ibid*. In the adjacent Perpetual Curacy of Milltown, the comparative proportion for 1850 was somewhat higher, being just over a third.

> *Our Orange Hall 'tis opened now*
> *By loyal men and true,*
> *And for the future be it called*
> *The Hall of Clantilew.*
> *Its site has been well-chosen,*
> *O'er looking Lough Neagh Shore,*
> *And its massive walls will firmly stand*
> *Till time does be no more.*

The poem continues in similar vein for another seven verses - praising Ralph Smith Obre, the local landowner, for providing the site free of charge; congratulating Woods, the architect, on his design; and thanking a number of other local worthies for their generous donations to the building fund. Though interesting in its own right as an expression of Protestant religious and political views at the time, it is of little literary merit. Somewhat better was his poem, *'The Postman's Whistle'*, written just over thirteen years later. Largely autobiographical, it describes his experiences as a rural postman in the Milltown district of the parish. As door knockers were almost non-existent on cottage doors, the postman announced his arrival by *'a rousing wheep'* of his whistle:

> *The neat little whistle, the birling whistle,*
> >   *The whistle that Teggart delights to fill,*
> *Form Clonmacate until Milltown gate,*
> >   *And past the cabins of Columbkill.*

Despite the occasional metrical flaws, the poet does manage to convey his enthusiasm for the open air life and his pride in being physically able to deliver the mail even in adverse weather conditions:

> *Frost and snow, cannot him lay low,*
> >   *And long as the flesh and bone and gristle*
> *Together hold, like a warrior bold,*
> >   *May Teggart blow and birl his whistle.*

Particularly perceptive was his awareness that a letter could bring happiness or sadness to the recipient:

> *For a letter may hold an order for gold,*
> >   *Or the dun[8] may jag like a thorny thistle;*
> *Grief profound and a cheerful sound*
> >   *Both lie mute in the postman's whistle.*

---

[8] A letter that contains an importunate demand for payment of a debt or more generally, any kind of unwelcome correspondence.

Unfortunately, only a handful of his poems have survived the ravages of time, too few to allow for any definitive conclusion to be drawn on the overall literary merit of his muse, but it would seem that he was more of a 'versifier' than a true poet. At his best, he was capable of producing some striking descriptive phrases which show him to have had an observant eye for detail and a heightened sensitivity to the environment around him. All his poems are marred to some extend by technical weaknesses, but there is no doubt he was endowed with a feeling for words and a love of the natural world that he passed on to his son, Moses.

A life-long member of the Church of Ireland, whose adherents made up eighty percent of the Ballinary population, Moses was a regular worshipper at Milltown Church and following the emergence of the new Milltown Parish in 1871 he was elected a member of its inaugural Select Vestry.[9]

Milltown Parish Church.

He ensured that all his children attended Sunday school, even though it entailed a four mile walk in all sorts of weather. Much respected in the community for his integrity and uprightness of character, he was regarded as a patriarchal figure and the epitome of respectability. Though staunchly Protestant, he was no bigot. He was a welcome guest in many Catholic homes where he delighted in the music, the dancing and the craic. One of his closest Catholic friends was Edward Burns of Gallrock, a gifted musician and a well-known raconteur, in the locality. As Moses (Junior) was later to note, when he came across a photograph of the pair, there was a genuine affinity between them, based on mutual respect and appreciation of each other's talents:

> *The photograph it made me laugh*
>   *With joy on single card,*
> *Ta'en by the son (and finely done),*

---

[9] See Rev H W Coffey, *A History of Milltown Parish,* Portadown, 1950, p.8. The first rector of the parish was Michael Angelo Holden, 1874.

> *The sweet musician and the bard;*
> *The bond between you plainly seen*
> *'Tis brotherhood and kind regard.*[10]

Moses Teggart's character and Christian witness left an indelible mark on his family, especially on the young Moses, whose affection for his father went undimmed by the passage of years.

By all accounts, Moses' wife, Charlotte, was also much loved and respected by her close-knit family. Born to William and Mary McAnally in November, 1828, she was, like her husband, a member of the Established Church. Depicted by her son Moses as a God-fearing, industrious and caring mother, she would never go to bed at night until all her family were safely home:

> *As by her lamp she lone vigil kept,*
> *She many a garment made,*
> *Or while brothers and sisters soundly slept,*
> *For them and me she prayed.*
>
> *She never reproved me when I came,*
> *But softly unlatched the door—*
> *She was not a mother to chide or blame,*
> *But a welcome smile she wore.*[11]

Her sudden death, as a result of a heart attack, in November, 1881, prompted another of her sons, 13 year old Stuart, to compose some simple but poignant verses in her memory. Though tinged with Victorian sentimentalism, his poem, *'To Mama'* has an innocence and sincerity which seem entirely appropriate. In it he recollected her various kindnesses to him and recalled the many occasions on which she spoke to him of a loving Saviour and the certainly of eternal life for all believers:

> *I know she is in heaven now,*
> *On living waters fed,*
> *She ne'er did lock the cupboard door*
> *To keep me from the bread.*
>
> *She often used to talk to me*
> *Of Jesus and his love;*
> *So now she's gone to Jesus*
> *To dwell with Him above.*[12]

Moses, who was in Scotland at this time, travelled home for her funeral to Milltown churchyard. Not a November passed that he did not recollect that sad day and even twenty years later when he was in Massachusetts, she was still very much in his

---

[10] *'The Reply to Mr Frank Burns, Rural Postman, Portadown, Ireland. Written on receiving a souvenir from him'*, June 1894.

[11] *'In Memory of Mother'*, n.d., but probably written c.1890.

[12] Written on 23 November 1881.

thoughts. In one of his most eloquent and moving poems, *'A Lough Neagh Lament'* he recalled the sad occasion:

> *For there my darling mother sleeps,*
>   *And o'er her grassy pillow*
> *The dewy star of evening weeps,*
>   *Or beams upon the billow.*
> *There she at rest, all lowly laid,*
>   *Hears not the wan wave sobbing*
> *Around the blossom or the blade*
>   *That it of rest is robbing.*
>
> *Thou art my mourner, loved Lough Neagh,*
>   *Lone watch for me still keeping;*
> *Though from thy banks I'm far away,*
>   *I see and hear thee weeping.*
> *Tonight wan Memory walks the wave,*
>   *Of my repose me robbing;*
> *Lough Neagh and I beside one grave*
>   *Meet, and we both are sobbing.*[13]

Her passing was a traumatic event that marked a sea-change for all her family. Things in Ballinary were never to be the same again. Moses (Senior) was devastated by her sudden demise, and though he married again, some five years later,[14] he never forgot Charlotte. As was his wish, when he eventually died in March, 1913, he was laid to rest, not with his second wife, Mary, who predeceased him, but alongside Charlotte in Milltown Churchyard. As Moses (Junior) later admitted, her death deprived the family of that steadying influence that had safely guided them through all the adversities of life, and made home such a special place:

> *The stay she was of that loved home,*
>   *And now-both dusk and dawn,*
> *No more they charm us when they come,*
>   *Since mother's gone.*
>
> *It's dark, pitch dark the windows look,*
>   *And loveless seems the lawn;*
> *The music's flown, and closed the book*
>   *Since mother's gone.*[15]

'Home' was a stone-walled, lime-washed, straw-thatched cottage in that part of the townland known locally as *'the head of the town'*. The interior was comprised of four rooms with bare, uneven, clay floors. Each room had a small window that looked out on to a lane that ran parallel to the length of the cottage. Outside, on the

---

[13] *Springfield Republican,* November 1901.
[14] Moses Teggart married Mary Stapleton in Milltown Church, 22 July 1886. Though born in Co Armagh, her address at this time was given as Bayswater, London where she had been 'in service'. She died 22 December 1908 and was interred in Loughgall Old Cemetery.
[15] *'When Mother's Gone', Boston Pilot,* December 1906.

front wall, were climbing roses and in the garden, clumps of heather and ling mingled with rows of golden marigolds and red wallflowers. At the rear of the cottage was a small orchard of fruit trees and, as the emigrant poet later recalled, sister Mary's bower:

> *Beyond the house a fairy dell,*
> *With bird-song never dumb;*
> *And here are graftings loaded well*
> *With apple, pear and plum.*
> *Here, too, is Mary's flower-knot sweet*
> *And rich with mint and rose;*
> *Fond woodbine climbs about the seat*
> *In which she sits and sews.*[16]

There was also the essential plot for growing potatoes, oats and cabbages. A short, winding path, marked out by *'a row of stones, new lime-washed all'*, ran from the front door to the nearby lane.

There can be no doubt that this childhood home held a special place in the poet's heart, and though his description is somewhat rose-tinted and romanticised, viewed at a distance of over three thousand miles and nearly fifty years, the idyllic depiction is quite understandable. As he made clear on more that one occasion, there was certainly no place like home:

> *My native hill is heaven to me,*
> *And ere with death I parry—*
> *I hope my longing eyes shall see*
> *The Braes of Ballinary.*[17]

Young Moses was brought up in a loving and caring environment. His home may have lacked material comforts but it was a haven of happiness and security, a place of mirth and laughter, a bulwark against the malevolent winds of fate that blew from the windmills of the gods.

As a boy, Moses attended Cloncore (Lower) National School, a short distance from his Ballinary home. Erected by the Quaker, Thomas Charles Wakefield, in 1858, the 45 feet long building was of brick construction with a slated roof. When it opened its doors, early the following year, there was an unprecedented demand for places and it was massively over-subscribed. Three hundred applications were received but the school was only able to accept just over a third of that number. In actual fact, the school's capacity was rarely tested as parents often required their children, especially girls, to help with domestic chores, including spinning.[18] On many occasions the daily attendance was considerably less than half the number enrolled.[19]

[16] *'Our Bogland Home' Portadown News*, December 1902.
[17] *'The Braes of Ballinary'*, *Portadown News*, November 1899.
[18] Spinning was perceived as a female activity and was particularly labour intensive. It was estimated that it took four spinners to service one full-time weaver.
[19] The school was open around 240 days each year - a figure that would horrify the modern school child. For a more detailed account of the school's history, see Fleming, *op. cit.*, pp.272-78.

Moses' surname, misspelt as *Taggard*, first appears on the school register in January, 1860, together with that of his elder brother, William Francis. Though he was some nineteen months older than Moses, it would appear from their consecutive enrolment numbers, 96 and 97, that both boys started their education on the same day. With the help and encouragement of his literate father and stimulated by the high quality of instruction at Cloncore, the young Moses soon began to make a name for himself as something of a scholar.

Cloncore (Lower) National School.
Courtesy of the Rev W E C Fleming

Among those who took a particular interest in the new school was the then Rector of Tartaraghan, the Rev George Robinson.[20] An authority on botany and ornithology, he was a leading member of The Armagh Natural History and Philosophical Society and the Belfast Naturalist Field Club. He compiled many papers and pamphlets on natural history, including *'Our Summer Birds', 'The Advantages which Birds confer on Mankind'* (both Armagh, 1853) and *'The Occurrence of Rare Birds on Lough Neagh' since 1876* (Belfast 1884).[21] A regular visitor to the school, he would almost certainly have been aware of the academic promise shown by the young Moses and it is tempting to hypothesise, given the future poet's extensive knowledge of the flora, fauna and ornithology of his native parish, that he could well have imparted much of his enthusiasm and erudition to the fledgling scholar. By his own admission, Moses was, whilst still a young teenager, thoroughly conversant with the natural world of the boglands:

[20] George Robinson (1821-1893), Rector of Tartaraghan 1849-1882.
[21] See *Armagh Guardian*, 11 March 1853 and Fleming, *op. cit.*, p.159.

> *On Nature's wonders still intent,*
> > *And using well his eyes;*
> *He knows what drains the ducks frequent,*
> > *And every bird that flies.*
> *The flowers that in the hedges bloom,*
> > *To him they are a joy,*
> *And glad he is the earth has room*
> > *For him - the Bogland Boy.*[22]

To have acquired so much knowledge at so early an age, he would have required the assistance of an expert tutor and that *'expert'* was surely George Robinson. That the two were acquainted there can be little doubt. Many years later, in a poem written in praise of his native parish, Moses recalled these boyhood years and the esteem in which the rector was held:

> *And half a lifetime now away,*
> > *With memory's eyes I love to scan*
> *The face that in my childhood day*
> > *Was loved through all Tartaraghan.*[23]

When Moses was not at school he was expected to help out at home. He learnt to weave on his father's loom, but it was not something he liked doing. He was much happier out of doors, but even when he was assisting his father in cutting turf he found the process repetitive and boring:

> *When daddy's cuttin' turf, an' I*
> > *Am forkin' them away,*
> *How slow! how slow! the time goes by,*
> > *How burdensome the day.*[24]

His favourite chore was running messages for his mother. When provisions such as tea or sugar were needed, she would send him to Thomas Palmer's grocery and hardware shop in nearby Clonmacate or, if bread was required, to Mittons, their neighbours in Ballinary:

> *"Run like a redshank!" that's what she said*
> > *When she wanted her laddie to go*
> *In a hurry to Palmer's*[25] *or Mitton's for bread,*
> > *And the boy who never was slow*
> *Had his breeks rolled up to his knees, and then*
> > *Over the rampers he sped.*[26]

---

[22] 'A Bogland Boy', *Springfield Republican*, October 1902.
[23] 'Tartaraghan', *Springfield Republican*, February 1897.
[24] 'Working and Dreaming', *Springfield Republican*, July 1902.
[25] Combined Post Office and General Merchants owned by Thomas Palmer (1847-1909).
[26] *Bogland Blooms and Birds*, 'Run Like a Redshank', *Springfield Republican*, April 1904.

*Birches Post Office and General Store, c.1895.
The proprietor, Thomas Palmer, is seated far left.*

It was very likely, given his interest, and curiosity in the natural world around him, that the errands may have taken longer than his mother anticipated!

Back at school, Moses' intelligence and academic ability were formally recognised in 1867 when the principal, Robert Carson, appointed him as a monitor. It was an honour given only to the brightest of senior pupils and as the recipient was allowed, under supervision, to instruct some of the younger children, it was often regarded as the first step towards obtaining a recognised teaching qualification. For assisting the teacher in the classroom, Moses would have received a small monthly payment which would have risen, over time, as his experience increased.

It is not known how long Moses Teggart remained at Cloncore but at some time between the beginning of autumn 1867 and the end of January, 1868, he left the Birches to attend Belfast Model School, with the avowed aim of becoming a qualified teacher and thus eligible for appointment to any National School in Ireland. The school, opened in 1857, was the largest institution of its kind in Ireland and one of the most successful. Like other district model schools, it was under the control of the Commissioners for National Education, commonly referred to as the National Board. It was a non-denominational school and its principal objectives were *'to promote united education, to exhibit improved methods of literary and scientific instruction and to train young persons for the office of teacher.'*

Moses was particularly fortunate to have obtained a training place as a 'candidate teacher'. Selection was by means of public examination and was open, principally, to those who were paid monitors in local national schools, though provision was also made for the acceptance of local *'meritorious pupils'*. As a salaried monitor in Cloncore National School, he would have been eligible for selection, but he must also have excelled in the entrance examination as competition for training places was particularly keen. In keeping with its non-denominational policy, six of the eighteen candidates, accepted by the school, were Roman Catholic, six were

Presbyterian and the remaining six were a mixture of Anglicans and other Protestant dissenters. It speaks volumes for his ability that in spite of such a rigid and restrictive system, he was awarded a training place at the school.

Like all candidates he would have been required to

> ... know how to read well, to write a fair hand, to be able to construe any passage in the lesson books, to have a general knowledge of geography, to know the first two books of Euclid, to be able to solve questions in simple equations, to be acquainted with the simple rules of mensuration, to know a fair course of arithmetic, to be able to keep simple accounts, to have a general acquaintance with the National Lesson Books, and to exhibit a capacity and taste for teaching.[27]

In addition, all candidates were to be free of any disease or deformity which, should they be appointed to a school, would interfere with their usefulness as teachers. It was also stipulated that, at all times, they were required to *'keep themselves neatly and becomingly clad'*.

A candidate teacher's life was not an easy one. Teggart would have risen at 5.30 am, prepared the lessons for the day, listened to a lecture by the headmaster, before breakfasting and setting out for the Falls Road school. Around three o'clock, after a day's teaching, he would have returned to Balmoral for the afternoon meal. Following this, was a three mile walk and later in the evening further lectures and private study. In today's parlance, it was certainly *'no cushy number'*.

The Belfast Model was a comparatively new school when Moses Teggart arrived. Built at a cost of over £11,000, it was situated on a somewhat cramped site on the Falls Road. In fact, accommodation was so limited that the headmaster and male candidate teachers had to reside at the nearby new Model Agricultural School in Balmoral.[28]

As a trainee teacher, he would have received rigorous instruction in the school's broad curriculum which included not only reading, writing and arithmetic but also geography, geology, mechanics, natural history and, of particular significance in the light of his future employment, bookkeeping.

---

[27] Appendix to the *24th Report of the Commissioners for National Education, Ireland*, 1857, p.66.
[28] Built on the site now occupied by Musgrave Park Hospital, the accommodation block that once housed the young Teggart is still largely intact.

Musgrave Park Hospital, formerly the Balmoral Model Agricultural School.

Having successfully completed his two year course, Moses returned home in 1870 to take up a post as an assistant teacher in Tartaraghan No 1 National School, situated in the Presbyterian Meeting House in the most southerly part of Ballinary, known locally as 'Derrykiniff'.

Pupils of Tartaraghan No 1 School c.1925

Though the school was founded in 1824, it had encountered serious management problems in the early 1850s which lead to its closure in November, 1853. When it reopened in January, 1864, it had accommodation for some sixty to seventy pupils in two classrooms.[29] His stay there was brief, as an unexpected opportunity arose in Milltown National School, when the principal, Matilda Fleming, departed in 1871. Moses was appointed to the vacant position and remained there until 12 July, 1872 when he resigned to take up a teaching post in St Nicholas National School, Cove

---

[29] For additional information on the school see Fleming, *op. cit.*, pp.308-312.

Street, Cork - one of the largest schools in the country, with an enrolment of nearly 500 pupils. Established as a Church of Ireland School in 1822, it came under the auspices of the National Board in 1867.[30] Why he decided to move so far from home, it is impossible to say, but it seems likely that he made the decision with his heart rather than his head. Admittedly, the attendance at Milltown School at this time was precariously low and the building itself was in a poor state of repair, but his sudden departure appears to have been prompted by his on-going but troubled courtship of local beauty, Jane (Jenny) Mitton, the daughter of Ballinary neighbours, James and Rebecca Mitton. Born on the 22 May, 1855 she also had attended Cloncore National School before going on to board at Brookfield School, some seventeen miles away near the small village of Moira.

Brookfield School, c.1900.

This school which was opened in 1846 was a Quaker Foundation for the children of those families who were nominally members of the Society of Friends but had, for some reason, failed to maintain the high standards of morality and behaviour expected of them. As one source expressed it:

> *There were many families claiming to be Friends who had lost all right to that claim or any of the privileges which it confers . . . although, these had forfeited their membership, friends were not entirely clear of responsibility towards their offspring.[31]*

---

30 The school closed on 30th September 1957 when its 14 pupils transferred to Christchurch National School in the adjoining parish, see *Cork Evening Echo*, 1 October 1957.
31 Committee of Management, Brookfield School, *Brookfield Agricultural School: Its Origin and History*, Belfast, 1890, p.5.

The Mittons were one such family. James and Rebecca were married in Armagh Registry Office in March, 1855 following the birth of their son John in England, to where the couple had eloped a year previously. Needless to say, the local Society of Friends in Richhill was not amused.[32]

Getting accepted for a Brookfield education was not a simple matter. The prospective pupil had to be recommended by a local representative from the Society and satisfactory written answers had to be received to questions posed by the institution's management committee - perhaps the most important being, *'What claim has the child upon the school?'* Jane was fortunate that her representative or *'correspondent'*, to use the Society's terminology, was Ephraim Allen,[33] a highly influential Friend and one of the original founders of the school. Admitted to Brookfield on 10 June, 1869, she would have been subject to a strict and rigorous daily regime:

> *In summer the girls rise at half-past five, and attend to milking and other household duties, after which half-an-hour of Scriptural instruction follows before breakfast at seven o'clock. Other household matters then claim their attention, and in the discharge of these duties they go two and two, an older and a younger child, the older girl being responsible for the work. School commences at nine o'clock, and continues (except for a few minutes at ten for lunch) until forty minutes past eleven, when a number, whose duty it is, goes to assist in serving dinner at midday, the others spending the few minutes in recreation. After dinner they help in the necessary clearing up, and that duty satisfactorily performed, they go to the play-ground until half-past one, when the ring of the school-bell calls them for two hours of work, which requires scissors, needles, thimbles, etc., instead of books and slates.*
> *At half-past three there is recreation and a slight repast. School-work is resumed at half-past four until forty minutes past five, when there is a break, as in the morning, for dairy work, and the final preparation preceding supper, which is served at six. The usual routine after meals succeeds, and another turn in the play-ground and some fifty minutes' study complete the day's work, before assembling for family worship.[34]*

---

[32] A number of Ulster Mittons, including some from Co Armagh, frequently found themselves at odds with their religious fraternity. Between 1701 and 1833 there were sixteen occasions on which particular individuals had been 'disowned' by the Society of Friends.

[33] One of the most prominent and respected members of the Richhill Meeting, Co Armagh. Born in 1828, he published two volumes of verse, *The Song of the Cradle*, (1912) and *Allan's Poetical Works*. Appointed a Justice of the Peace in 1895, he died in 1916.

[34] Committee of Management, Brookfield School, *op. cit.*, pp.58-59.

The young Teggart could not have seen all that much of Jenny during these years as she only returned to Ballinary in the school holidays. Perhaps, it was a case of absence making the heart grow fonder, for it seems more than coincidental, that he relinquished the principalship of Milltown School to take up an assistant teacher post two hundred and sixty miles away in Cork city, at precisely the same time as Jenny Mitton moved to Waterford to enter 'service' with a well-to-do Quaker family, A A Nicholson's of Catherine Street.[35]

Former residence of the Nicholson Family, Catherine Street, Waterford.

There is certainly no doubt of his warm feelings for her. In his poem *'Over at Mitton's'*, he recalled the friendship between their respective families and his infatuation for the charismatic Jane:

> *Over at Mitton's - our neighbours white house*
> *The words how familiar to me!*
> *For in childhood if only the cat caught a mouse*
> *We were sure to run over to see.*
>
> *'Jane' to her people but 'Jenny' to us,*
> *A sweet little Quakerness she,*
> *Blue-eyed and red lipped and bewitching, and thus*
> *A mark for Dan Cupid and me.*

---

[35] She may well have acted as a nanny to the Nicholson children, twins Alfred and Rebecca (born July 1867), Maria (born July 1869) and Francis (born July 1872).

Mittons' house, Ballinary, as it is today.

However, the romance was not destined to flourish. Perhaps, Jane did not respond to his advances or possibly, the distance between Cork and Waterford, over sixty miles, was just too far for the relationship to prosper. It also appears that Jane, may not have remained in Waterford with the Nicholsons for more than a year and a half as the family relocated to Limerick in 1874 and eventually emigrated to Pennsylvania two years later. It seems likely that she returned to Ballinary around the middle of 1874 and remained there until she too emigrated to the United States in early 1875. Recorded as a seamstress of 236 Shawmut Avenue, Boston, Jane met and married thirty-three year old New Yorker, James F Doran, on 21 December, 1880.[36]

---

[36] The marriage (No 3416) took place at the residence of Baptist pastor, the Rev Orrin Thomas Walker, in Dudley Street, Boston, see *Boston Vital Records, Marriages 1880*.

COPY OF RECORD OF MARRIAGE	

I, the undersigned, hereby certify that I am the Secretary of State; that as such I have the custody of the records of marriage required by law to be kept in my office; that among such records is one relating to the marriage of

James F. Doran and Jennie Milton

and that the following is a true copy of so much of said record as relates to said marriage, namely:

Date of Marriage: December 21, 1880   **Place of Marriage:** Boston

——GROOM——

Name: James F. Doran
Age: 32   **Color:** White
Residence: Boston

Number of Marriage: 1st   **Single, Wid, or Divorced:** ---
Occupation: Car builder
Birthplace: New York City
Name of Father: Jackson E. Doran
Mother's Maiden Name: Sarah J. ---

—— BRIDE ——

Name: Jennie Milton
Age: 23   **Color:** White
Residence: Boston

Number of Marriage: 1st   **Single, Wid, or Divorced:** ---
Occupation: ---
Birthplace: Ireland
Name of Father: James Milton
Mother's Maiden Name: Rebecca ---

Name and official station of person by whom married:
          Rev. O.T. Walker   Boston
Date of Record: 3416

Copy of Marriage Record, James F Doran to Jennie Mitton, Boston, 1880.

Although her memory was to continue to haunt him for the rest of his life, Moses was never to see her again. Jane, for her part, made one last journey to see her aged parents at Ballinary in the late summer of 1889[37] but, by this time, Moses was in Massachusetts. By this date also, the Dorans had moved from Boston to the township of North Greenbush, Rensselaer County, New York. James, like his father, was a master cabinetmaker who specialised in fitting-out railway carriages and streetcars. His business prospered and a few years later the couple were able to purchase a small farm about fifteen miles distant, in the hamlet of Brookview near Schodack. James died in April, 1906, leaving Jane to run the farm with the help of a herdsman, Joseph Brands, a German immigrant. Eight years later, they were married.

---

[37] Accompanied by her father-in-law, Jackson Doran, she also spent some time visiting his relations in Scotland. They returned to the United States aboard the SS Pavornia, arriving in Boston on 14 October.

Affidavit for Licence to marry, Joseph Brands to Jane Doran, Schodack, NY, 1912.

She continued to reside at Brookview until her death, aged 82, on Thursday, 3 August, 1939,[38] following which she was interred, with her first husband, James, in Albany Rural Cemetery.[39]

---

[38] See *The Knickerbocker News*, Albany 4 August 1939.
[39] Section 104, Lot 548.

The Doran Grave, Albany Rural Cemetery.

Eighty-six year old Connie Stammel, a present day resident of Brookview, recalled visiting the Brands' home when she was a young girl:

> *The elderly couple only used the first floor of their house, but were quite happy for my friend and I to roam the whole place. I remember being mightily impressed with the dumb waiter that connected the kitchen to the upper floors. There was also a long hallway and beautifully carved bookcases with glass doors. Jane had a music box, with large metallic discs, which she often played. I remember her being a very friendly old lady who would sometimes give us a ride in her panelled station wagon.[40]*

The Brands' residence, Brookview, NY.

---

[40] In conversation with Diane Hutchinson of Schodack, 20 January 2006.

In Green Caledonia

In 1875, following Jane's emigration the disconsolate and lovesick Moses left Ireland for Scotland. Perhaps he felt that, with Jane gone, the Irish sky did not seem as blue or the grass as green. In the immediate aftermath of her departure, a return to Ballinary was not really an option. The townland would almost certainly have evoked too many painful and unsettling recollections: his frequent visits to her home; their daily walks across the fields to Cloncore School; the innocent childhood games they played along bogland rampers; the stolen night-time kisses in secluded lanes and the numerous occasions on which he helped her carry water from the well near his home.

As he readily acknowledged in a poem written at the time, but not published till much later, her departure was a defining moment in his life. Never again would he see her sitting at the fireside with a kitten on her knee or meet with her below the sally trees. The youthful days of *'love, innocence and spring'* were gone forever:

> *But cold below the sally trees*
> *One hearth's no longer bright,*
> *My blue-eyed love on foaming seas*
> *Is far from home tonight.*[41]

Once in Scotland, Moses used his bookkeeping skills to obtain a position with the Inland Revenue Commissioners as a Ride Officer for the Falkirk area, which covered east Stirlingshire and east Dunbartonshire.[42] It was whilst working there that he came into contact with Janet Main,[43] a native of Edinburgh and the daughter of fellow civil servant, William Main. She lived at 73 Park Road, just a short distance from his lodgings at 42 Arlington Street in the Kelvingrove area of the city. Less than two years later, the pair were married in her home on 5 January, 1877 by Church of Scotland minister, the Very Rev Dr Donald MacLeod,[44] incumbent of the nearby Park Church.

---

[41] *'A Change'*, Springfield Republican, November 1901.

[42] His salary of £110 per annum was considerably higher than that paid to the average schoolteacher at this time.

[43] Born in Musselburgh, Edinburgh, in 1844, Janet was some nine years older than Moses.

[44] Born 1831, Donald MacLeod was minister at Park Church, Glasgow, from 1869 to his death in 1916. He was Convenor of the Church of Scotland's Home Missionary Society (1888-90) and Moderator of the General Assembly (1895-96). By all accounts, a stout, jolly man with an affable personality.

Copy of Marriage Certificate, Moses Teggart to Janet Main, Glasgow, 1877.

Cowgate Street, Kirkintilloch, Dunbartonshire, c.1930.
The Teggarts lived at 109 - third window in white building, left of centre.

Whilst there is no evidence that Moses was known to the Reverend before the marriage, it is certainly possible that the two were acquainted previously. It was around this time that Moses first began writing poems and the cleric was already noted in the Glasgow area as an enthusiastic patron of the Arts, especially painting, sculpture, music and poetry. As such, he may well have taken a paternal interest in the young poet. The two witnesses at the marriage ceremony were Ellen MacTaggart of Stirling, friend of the bride, (born 1847) and James Duncan (born 1854). The latter, a close acquaintance of the groom, was held in particularly high esteem by the young poet, as he later acknowledged:

> *O Mage of my young manhood! whose ripe mind,*
> > *Though in moons younger, was with knowledge stored,*
> > *And wise in counsel, thou who in soul adored*
> *Beauty and truth: . . .*
> *Friend Duncan: Dost thou not whiles backward glance*
> > *And muse upon the great life we lived then?*
> > *Dost thou not sometimes see the countenance*
> *Of him who, in love, slow-weilding now this pen,*
> *Still think'st of thee, as knight of old romance,*
> > *A very prince among the sons of men?*[45]

After the marriage the couple set up home at 109 Cowgate Street, one of the main thoroughfares in Kirkintilloch, just seven miles north east of Glasgow.

A keen rambler, Moses often spent his weekends walking the banks of the nearby River Kelvin or its tributary the Luggie. On occasions, he would venture even further afield through the villages of Milton of Campsie and Lennoxtown to the solitary, unspoilt uplands and glens of the Campsie or Kilsyth Hills. He also took the opportunity, on at least two occasions, to visit the homeland of Scotland's national poet, Robert Burns. It was during these early post-marriage years that he wrote so many of his best Scottish poems. Influenced by 'the Ayrshire ploughman', he penned a number of delightful lyrics praising the charms of certain local lassies he had encountered on his travels, including Jenny Gow, Elizabeth Mirren and the anonymous 'Roses' of Rochislloch and Airlie. Though some were written in English, others were composed in Lallans, the dialect of the Scottish Lowlands, and the medium used by Burns. All these lyrics, as the two extracts below illustrate, have a freshness and a vitality that the master would have appreciated:

> *Here where the wimplin' Kelvin winds*
> > *So noiselessly along.*
> *It music only makes for minds*
> > *In love wi' silent song.*
> *Wi' perfect faith it seems to pause*
> > *Below the hazel bough.*
> *An' hark, as if it waitin' was*
> > *For red-lipped Jenny Gow.*[46]

---

[45] C H Barrows, *The Poets and Poetry of Springfield in Massachusetts*, 'To James Duncan', Springfield, 1907, p.157.

[46] 'Jenny Gow', *Springfield Republican*, September 1906.

I hae seen ye wi' the shepherd lad
Below the hawthorn tree,
An' the faithful collies barkit glad
Sic a bonnie sight tae see!
It may gien ye joy the mirth ye had,
But it wasna sae wi' me.
Weel, ma heid is whirrin',
But here's tae ye, Mirren,
An, your saft an' sweet blue ee.[47]

---

[47] 'Mirren', Springfield Republican, February 1896.

The Land of the Goldenrod[48]

Moses left the Civil Service in 1888 and returned home for a short while before emigrating to America. He was not accompanied by his wife, Janet. It would appear that their marriage had run into difficulties in the mid 1880s, resulting in a deterioration in the relationship and ultimately, in separation. She remained in Scotland, working as a housekeeper for a well-to-do family in West Princess Street, Kelvin, just a few hundred yards from her original lodgings in Park Road.[49] She resided in the area until her demise on 20th January, 1903. Interestingly the official cause of death was given as *'gastro intestinal catarrh - long time chronic alcoholism!'* It is possible that her alcoholic addiction may have been a prime cause of the separation, but such speculation must be treated with care, as it is equally likely that it was the breakdown of the marriage that led to her craving for alcohol. He arrived in Philadelphia on 6 March, 1889, on board the Allan Line steamship, the Carthaginian.[50]

The S. S. Carthaginian.

Why he went to Philadelphia is something of a mystery, as he wasted no time in making straight for Boston. It is possible, but rather unlikely, that he was still pursuing Jane Mitton. He would have been aware that she had gone there, but he surely knew also that she had married years ago and was now living elsewhere. Whatever his reason, he did not remain in the city for long before moving almost sixty miles west to the small town of Warren. Here, he found employment at the Fanny Jane Woollen Mill, first as a labourer, and later, as a bookkeeper.

---

[48] A particular favourite of the poet, the goldenrod is a yellow flowering plant found in abundance throughout large areas of North America, especially Massachusetts, Kentucky, Nebraska and South Carolina. According to American folklore it is regarded as a symbol of good fortune.

[49] *Census of Scotland, 1891 Glasgow.* Intriguingly, but erroneously, her marital status was recorded as 'widow'.

[50] Built by the Gowan Shipbuilding Company, the ship was launched on 9 October 1884. Owned by the Allan Line of Liverpool, it sailed regularly to Nova Scotia, Montreal, New York, Boston and Philadephia. In 1917, it hit a mine off the northern coast of Donegal and sank near the island of Inishtrahull.

Fanny Jane Woollen Mill, Warren, MA, c.1910.

Once again, his motive for moving to that part of Massachusetts can only be surmised, but in the light of future events, it seems almost certain that he was heading for Palmer,[51] a further eight miles distant. A rapidly growing township, with a population of just under six thousand, Palmer had attracted an ever increasing number of emigrant workers from all over Ireland, and especially from Moses' own area of North Armagh.

Main Street, Palmer, MA, c.1900.

---

[51] Situated on the Chicopee River, Palmer was founded by Englishman, John King in 1716. A considerable number of Scots-Irish Presbyterians settled there in 1727 and in the mid-nineteenth century its many cotton and woollen mills continued to draw Ulster emigrants from all religious persuasions. The 1900 census indicated that almost 15% of the township's families were of Irish origin, a proportion which included a considerable number from North Armagh.

Many former residents of Tartaraghan and Milltown had already found there an enthusiastic demand for their weaving skills in the woollen and cotton mills that characterised the district. Amongst those of the Birches diaspora who had made their way to the township were David Ritchie, William Vennard, Samuel Turkington, Abraham Swaine, John Matchett, John McAdam, William Simmons, Mary Clifford, James Cole, George Greenaway and Edward Henderson.[52] In 1887, the latter, together with his wife and family had settled in Three Rivers, one of the four villages that together made up the Palmer community. A carpenter from Gallrock, Tartaraghan, he had married Margaret Warden in 1857. The union was blessed with fourteen children though only ten lived into adulthood. Most of the surviving family were boys but there were two girls - Elizabeth and Margaret Anne. The latter, born in November, 1861, attracted the attention of Moses when he met up with her at the Fanny Jane Mill in the winter of 1889. Undoubtedly, he knew of her previously, as the Hendersons had lived in Ballinary for a short time in the early 1870s. Indeed, it is even possible that Margaret was the real reason why he came to Massachusetts. Past acquaintanceship may well have accounted for the ensuing whirlwind courtship that culminated in their marriage in Palmer's Second Congregational Church on 1 May, 1890.[53]

Second Congregational Church, Palmer, MA, 1907.

Just over a year later on the 9 May, Margaret gave birth to a baby girl, also called Margaret, in West Warren Hospital. Unfortunately, the birth was not without its

---

[52] Many others were to follow in the next decade including William James Mitton, Jane's youngest brother, and his wife, Rebecca Castles from Cloncore, Milltown.

[53] See *Massachusetts' Vital Records, 1841-1910*, Vol 406 p.493. The above, gives the groom's age as 30 and the bride's as 25 - both are inaccurate. Their real ages on this date were 37 and 28 respectively. The record also indicates that this was Moses' first marriage, which clearly it was not.

complications and ten days later, mother Margaret died from puerperal fever[54] and was buried in Four Corners Cemetery on the outskirts of Three Rivers. Baby Margaret's fate is unknown. Whilst there is no record of her death, she is not to be found in either the 1900 or 1910 Palmer census. Given the fact that Moses was still employed at Fanny Jane Mill, it would seem very possible that the child, had she lived, would have been reared by her grandmother, Margaret. However, the 1900 census does not record the existence of any child in the Henderson home. The baby could also have been adopted, but given the proximity of the grandmother this would have been a very unlikely scenario. It would seem almost certain therefore, that she died at birth or shortly afterwards.

As might be expected, the death of his wife and baby daughter left Moses depressed and desolate. He wrote nothing between mid May and mid July and published only three poems in the remaining months of the year. His melancholy mood was reflected in the sombre and pensive lyric, *'The Moon and the Soul'*, which he wrote in early September. In it he muses on death but draws some comfort from his Christian belief that it is not an end but merely a beginning to a new and better life:

> *How different is the fate of man*
> > *Who, here on earth sojourning,*
> *Spins round the sun a little span,*
> > *And then with grief and mourning*
> *Goes out in darkness, - bitter ban-*
> > *From which there's no returning.*
>
> *Yet not a star in all the skies*
> > *However, old and hoary,*
> *Can tell when e'er the mortal dies,*
> > *The opening of the story*
> *That shall begin when'er our eyes*
> > *Shall see the King of Glory.*[55]

The following year, he left Palmer for the city of Springfield, just fourteen miles south. At this time, it had a population of just over 50,000 and was rapidly expanding.[56] Situated on the Connecticut River, just a few miles north of the border between Connecticut and Massachusetts, it was the third largest city in the state. It was, in this period, one of the most beautiful cities in America. As one historian somewhat poetically declared:

> *. . . it was beautifully born. Conceived in sunshine and brought forth in verdure . . . the little old house which two and a half centuries ago was the germ of the present city . . . was even then surrounded by rare and wonderful charms.*[57]

---

[54] A serious form of septicaemia contracted by a woman during or shortly after childbirth. Usually attributable to unsanitary conditions.

[55] *Springfield Republican,* September 1891.

[56] Thirteen year later, in 1905, the population had increased by nearly half to 73,484 and by 1910 it had grown again to almost 89,000.

[57] E C Gardner, *Springfield Present and Prospective,* Springfield, 1905, p.1.

Dubbed *'The City of Homes'*, and rightly so, for it had many imposing and elegant Victorian mansions situated in leafy avenues and spacious boulevards. In addition to many splendid, neo-classical churches, schools and municipal buildings, the city had several theatres, a museum, an opera house and one of the best libraries in the country.

Public Library, Springfield, 1901 - typical of many of the imposing civic buildings erected in the city in the second half of the 19th century.

With the exception of Boston, it was the most cultured and progressive city in New England. The advantages of the city were admirably summarised by two of its most prominent citizens, Judge Copeland and Edwin Dwight:

> *Where else in the broad earth can be found a more beautiful stream than the Connecticut, a more beautiful valley than its waters or a more beautiful background to rise up and meet the sky? Where can we find more beautiful homes? Above all, where have education, religion, refinement, taste and all the elements of an elevated civilization been more prospered than here? There is a church on every hill, a schoolhouse in every valley, a lyceum in every neighbourhood, a newspaper in every house, while colleges and seminaries and academies can be seen from each other's spires.[58]*

---

[58] *Ibid.*, p.117.

When Moses arrived in the spring of 1892, he was offered employment with the recently founded *Connecticut Valley Poetical Advertiser* at 182 State Street. As its title implies, this journal was almost entirely written in verse, and distributed free to nearly every household in the greater Springfield area. The proprietor and editor of the publication, George Reuben Burleigh,[59] was not only a successful businessman but also a poet of some repute. Sometimes known as *'The Poet Laureate of New England'*, he acquired a degree of notoriety for his sartorial style; never appearing in public without his long, black Prince Albert coat and tall, silk hat. He had a prodigious memory and allegedly, could recite poems for hours without repetition. A close friend of Longfellow,[60] he was personally acquainted with many other writers and poets then living in New England.

It is very possible that the two men met at one or other of the literary soirées or clubs which were a feature of Springfield society at the time. As the literary editor of the Springfield Republican noted:

> *We have many a club, of women or of men, who are esteemed to have a literary outlook on life . . . they read Browning, Tennyson, Walt Whitman and Emerson . . . and also Thoreau . . . sometimes Aristotle or even Plato is ventured on.*[61]

However they met, Burleigh would have recognised Moses as a kindred spirit and it is hardly surprising that he offered him a position as bookkeeper for the *Advertiser*.

For whatever reason, his position with Burleigh only lasted a year. It was a sign of things to come. In the sixteen years he spent in Springfield, Moses had six different employers and moved lodgings on no less than ten occasions. During these nomadic years his longest period of employment was four years, as a bookkeeper, with F A Grant Brothers, a firm of wholesale confectioners on Main Street. Amongst the other businesses which made use of his bookkeeping expertise were the Springfield Printing and Binding Company, J F Lawson, specialists in parquet flooring, and Forbes and Wallace, the largest retail store in the city.[62]

---

[59] Born in Palmer, 2 October 1853, the son of Benjamin Abelard Burleigh and Hannah Cook Smith, he married Mary Snelgrove 1 June 1876. He died 27 December 1912 and was buried in Palmer's Oak Knoll Cemetery.
[60] Henry Wadsworth Longfellow (1807-1882), American poet best known for *'The Song of Hiawatha'* and *'Paul Revere's Ride'*. He spent most of his adult life in Cambridge, MA.
[61] Gardner, *op. cit.*, p.59.
[62] Founded in 1874, the *'Harrods'* of Springfield, offered acres and acres of merchandise and in 1905 it was estimated that twenty times the population of Springfield (almost 1,500,000) went through its door every year. It was a shoppers' paradise with goods on sale from every quarter of the globe. The store finally closed, after trading for a hundred years, in 1974.

Forbes & Wallace Store, Main Street, Springfield, c.1900.
(Courtesy Connecticut Valley Museum)

Though at heart he was, and remained, 'a Birches boy', Moses came to have great affection for Springfield. Forced by economic necessity to live in a succession of lodgings, he nevertheless found the city much to his liking. After nine years of residing at ease under an alien sky he wrote approvingly of his adopted home:

> *Foremost of all the cities fair*
> *   Sung to by the Connecticut,*
> *Thou, Springfield, for all time, dost wear*
> *   The crown of beauty! Nature put*
> *It long since on thy lovely brows.*
> *   And while thy river onward foams*
> *To thee I fain would pay my vows,*
> *   Queen city of time-honoured homes.*[63]

Moses' warm personality, lively intelligence and poetic ability ensured that he soon made many friends amongst the city's literary grandees, in particular, he was on especially good terms with three of Springfield's most influential writers - Aella Green, Charles Barrows and Charles Goodrich Whiting.

---

[63] *'To the City of Homes', Springfield Republican,* November 1901.

Aella Green was a country boy, a fact that would have endeared him to Moses. He was born in Chester, Massachusetts in 1838 and died in Springfield on 8 January, 1902.[64] After serving in the Civil War, he became a reporter for a number of local newspapers. He also published several volumes of verse, as well as a series of novellas, portraying Yankee life in small, rural towns. Like Moses, he liked to write about ordinary country folk engaged in everyday tasks. His most famous poem, and probably his best, is *'Where the Noble Have Their Country'*. It had a strong Christian ethos, celebrating the glories of God's handiwork and looking forward to a life after death when *'. . . earth's toiling is forgotten/In the restfulness of bliss.'*

In this *'land beyond the sun'* there will be magnificent forests, resonating to the songs of birds and the tinkling of mountain streams. There will be banks of luxuriant wildflowers, their fragrance, borne on a gentle breeze, wafting through verdant glades. It is a utopian vision with which Moses could certainly have identified. When Green died, Moses paid a moving tribute to his close friend, noting his love of nature and the certainty of his place in heaven:

> *Much given far afield to roam,*
> *Admiring Nature's plan,*
> *The wilds to thee were like a home—*
> *Unspoiled by errant man.*
>
> *The silent heart is not the end,*
> *Love journeys on and on;*
> *'Where the noble have their country,' friend,*
> *'Tis there that thou art gone.*[65]

Another of Moses' literary friends in Springfield was Charles Barrows, lawyer, poet and historian. Born in August, 1853, he was just a few months younger than Moses. A devout Christian and a regular worshipper at Olivet Congregational Church, he was revered for his contributions to several educational and community projects. He also took a keen interest in the Arts, especially literature, and was always ready to pass on words of encouragement and advice to young writers.

Charles H Barrows, 1853-1918.
(Courtesy of Connecticut Valley Museum)

---

[64] In his obituary, published in the *Springfield Republican* on 20 January 1902, the writer referred to his reverence for Christian values and his ability to see hidden beauty in the commonplace: *'If human nature was always a precious revelation; if you knew there really is a faith that cannot die; that there is fight even in a dove; if the roughness of a diamond dimmed it not for you - then Aella Green and you were kindred spirits.'*

[65] *'Aella Green', Springfield Republican,* January 1902.

At his funeral service, 16 October, 1918, the Rev Claude Butterfield commented on his willingness to help others:

> *Through extensive travels he had a wide field of acquaintanceship and his home was both the haven of those the world calls great and those whom the world forgets. Diplomats, poets, musicians, hymn writers, lecturers, students, all treasured his friendship and will mourn his passing.*[66]

Barrows was a particular admirer of Teggart's verse and when he published his best known book, *'The Poets and Poetry of Springfield in Massachusetts'* (1907), it contained many of his friend's poems, including the classically inspired *'The Vision and Penelope'* and *'Helen's Gift to Telemachus'*, as well as several sonnets and a sprinkling of 'Irish' lyrics. The latter included the superb description of the Birches landscape in October, *'Autumn in Derryagh'* and the enchanting eulogy to the virtuous, but unnamed, local lass, *'The Belle of Ballinary'* - surely one of the best of a series of poems addressed to various young ladies from Milltown parish. Some measure of the extent of Barrows' appreciation of Teggart's poetry can be gained by the fact that the number of pages in the anthology devoted to his work was almost twice that given to any of the other thirty-four poets.

The emphasis on Moses' contribution is even more remarkable given the author's predilection for indigenous writers:

> *It is to be regretted that of the whole list of Springfield poets, by right of residence, there are not more whose roots started in her soil. Is it true that poets are country born, and that the commercialism of cities, while it may grant them recognition, is not favourable to their birth and early development? If otherwise, why have we not more true verse to show, native born, in this city of seventy-five thousand?*[67]

Perhaps when he penned these words he had Moses in mind, for the Armagh man was very much a country boy whose fame, such as it presently is, is largely due to his association with the city of Springfield. Ballinary nurtured the poet but it was the Massachusetts city which brought him the recognition he so desperately craved and so clearly deserved.

Though Aella Green and Charles Barrows were special friends, neither was as close to Moses as the journalist and author, Charles Goodrich Whiting.

Charles Goodrich Whiting, 1842-1922
(Courtesy of Connecticut Valley Museum)

---

66 *Springfield Republican*, 17 October 1918.
67 *Op.cit.*, p.22.

Springfield Republican Offices, c.1880.

Born in St Albans, Vermont on 30 January, 1842, he was employed as a reporter on the *'Springfield Republican'* from 1868 before being promoted to literary editor in 1874. It was his influence that ensured the publication of so many of Moses' poems in the newspaper's columns between 1892 and 1909.

There was an obvious 'meeting of minds' between the two men as Whiting shared Moses' love of nature and poetry. For many years, his nature editorials were eagerly received by a devoted readership who identified with his pantheistic philosophy and appreciated his ability to describe *'the fury of wind and storm, the coming and going of birds and flowers, the fulfilment of the harvest and to find in them the immanent divinity of the universe.'*[68] Like Barrows, Whiting went out of his way to encourage the literary talent of Springfield. He organised meetings on Sunday afternoons for aspiring artists and writers and, as one observer noted, there were many who owed him a great debt of gratitude for his sage advice and enthusiastic support:

> *It was as literary editor that he endeared himself to many a young writer, poet or artist, for he had a ready sympathy for them. He quickly saw the good qualities of their work . . . and by his excellent criticism and editing he brought out the best that there was in them, and I think there is many a writer today whose first efforts he edited and printed, who will remember him with honour and affection.*[69]

Both men were keen ramblers and Moses often accompanied his friend on long walks in Springfield's four hundred acre Forest Park or even further afield, in weekend excursions over the wooded slopes of Mount Holyoke and Mount Tom, a few miles north of the city. The latter was a particularly favourite location for Moses and he wrote several poems in praise of the red pines on its wooded slopes and the many varieties of flowers that populated it winding paths. After the monotonous grind of pouring over endless columns of figures in account ledgers, the escape to the great outdoors refreshed and stimulated him both mentally and physically. Some sense of the exhilaration and pleasure he derived from his walks on the mountain can be gained from a few verses he composed on Mount Tom, one November evening in 1905:

---

[68] *Springfield Republican*, 21 June 1922.
[69] Clementine Dawes Nahmer, Letter to *New York Times*, 3 July 1922. A similar view of Whiting's literary influence can be found in Barrows, *op. cit.*, p.97.

Oh happy, happy sunset hour!
    Oh day of days divine!
Sleep sweet the modest mountain flower,
    And dream thou mountain pine!

For through soul love the dream survives,
    Yet are there moments blest
When sunset dreams are for true lives
    Eternities of rest.[70]

He experienced similar feelings of elation on another occasion when he stood on the summit and viewed the distant panorama in front of him:

Distant hills so blue, so blue
    Just pleasant journeys from
This mighty peak, this wonder view
    The Nebo, this Mount Tom.
Here well might man, some Lord's day on
    Enraptured takes his stand,
And view these hills, till distance gone,
    Laughed back the promised land.[71]

Spectacular vista, as seen from the summit of Mount Tom, 1905.

---

[70] *Memories of Mount Tom - 'At Sunset'*, Springfield Republican, November 1905.
[71] *Memories of Mount Tom - 'Distant Hills'*, Springfield Republican, November 1905.

Some two months later, Moses again eulogised the glory of the mountain, singling out a particular day when, in Whiting's words, *'the crows were crying overhead and sweeping in salient and re-entrant curves, until they melted into the distance and were gone.'*[72] Recalling the incident, Moses noted that the crows' song, like the singing of Wordsworth's solitary reaper, remained in the mind long after the event:

> *And now at dawn, at close of day,*
> *Or when the winds repose,*
> *Still hear we miles and miles away*
> *The music of the crows.*[73]

Whiting, an expert botanist, and ornithologist was equally enamoured of all the species of flora and fauna to be found on the mountain - the bright berries of the black alder, the white and red clover, the marsh marigolds, the evening primroses, the hepaticas, the wild geraniums, the asters, the goldenrods and numerous other varieties of trees and shrubs.

For both men, however, nature in all it myriad forms had a deeper, mystical significance. Influenced by the legacy of New England Transcendentalism,[74] Whiting believed that the most important truths derived not from books and observation but from the intuition, as opposed to reason, within each being. Such truths could only be gained from a direct relationship with God and was not dependent on the dictates of past authorities and institutions or in the existence of any intermediaries. Put simply, he believed in the concept of the Oversoul, a kind of cosmic unity between man, God and nature. Recalling a visit to the summit of Mount Tom in the winter of 1902, Whiting observed:

> *It is the soul that beholds and not the show that is beheld which counts . . . That ineffable, incomprehensible, intolerable, eternal Divinity is here, taking the little human soul into its own vast being, and making it one with him. On a mountain top dwells the vast Oversoul, and man accepts his place, and is silent.*[75]

Moses, too, was influenced to some extent by the writings of such prominent transcendentalists as Thoreau and Emerson. He would have read with particular interest the latter's seminal essay on *Nature* (1836) in which Emerson described the advantages of seeking true solitude, going out into nature and leaving behind all distracting activities as well as society. Indeed, Emerson suggested that if a man wished to be really alone he should look at the stars, *'for the rays that come from these heavenly worlds will separate between him and what he touches.'* The night sky had a particular fascination for Moses too, for when he gazed at the stars he was acutely aware of his separation from the material world. The stars were created to allow man to perceive, in Emerson's phrase, *'the perpetual presence of the sublime'*. They never lost their power to move Moses, for whom they were an ever constant

---

[72] C H Whiting, *op. cit.*, p.262.
[73] *More Mount Tom Memories*, 'The Music of the Crows', *Springfield Republican,* January 1906.
[74] A philosophical religious, social and literary movement which was at its height between 1830 and 1860, although it continued to be influential until well into the 1890s.
[75] C G Whiting, *Walks in New England*, London & New York, 1903, p.265.

reminder of God's power and presence in the world. On a memorable night spent on the slopes of Mount Holyoke, he was awe-struck by the incredible myriad of stars in the darkening sky:

> *I know it now, I feel it still,*
> > *I see it with my spirit's eye,*
> *The truth they told me when a child—*
> > *That God was in the sky.*
>
> *And when the night, with stars, and none,*
> > *Would to my sight the blue deny,*
> *O spirit mine rest thee in peace,*
> > *Thy God is in the sky.*[76]

On another similar occasion, whilst living in Palmer, he mused on the power of the December night sky to lift the immortal soul:

> *And 'tis midnight now and the sky is naked,*
> > *While the King himself wide watch doth keep*
> *O'er a million stars and the moon that waked,*
> > *And smiled ere she sank into sounder sleep.*[77]

Though he occasionally drew on the transcendentalist vocabulary, whilst referring to the *'Master Spirit'* and *'Supreme Being'*, Moses was probably more of a pantheist than a transcendentalist. Whereas the latter believed that God stood outside and independent of the universe of which He is the creator, pantheists asserted that He dwelt in the world in which human beings and nature are thought to be aspects of an all inclusive divinity. As he once expressed it:

> *In all things sees he good at hand,*
> > *In grass and waving trees,*
> *In all that lovelier makes the land,*
> > *God's immanence he sees.*[78]

Though there can be no doubt that Moses, influenced by the overt pantheistic and transcendental views of Whiting, accepted some of the elements of each philosophy, he never wrote anything which would have been regarded, then or now, as contradictory to Christian principles. It is true that he did reject institutionalised religion, preferring to seek God in nature and not from a pew, but there is nothing in all his canon of prose and verse that would have disturbed the faithful of Milltown parish.

Much as he liked Springfield, Moses' thoughts were never too far away from home and those friends he had left behind. In the latter part of 1904 his mind turned again

---

[76] *'God is in the Sky'*, *Springfield Republican*, June 1908.
[77] *'The Sky'*, December 1891. Teggart wrote numerous other poems that were inspired by the starry heavens including, *'A Falling Star'*, July 1891, *'Ursa Major'*, September 1904, *'Stars Seen and Unseen'*, March 1907 and *'Life Abounding'*, *Springfield Republican*, January 1908.
[78] *'The Fuller Life'*, *Springfield Republican*, September 1907.

to the Mitton family, however, it was not Jane this time but her older sister Mary that sparked his romantic interest. Just why Mary should have loomed large in his thoughts at this particular time, is a matter for speculation. Perhaps, it was simply a case of nostalgia for old times and old acquaintances or possibly it was occasioned by word from home that Mary's mother, Rebecca Mitton, had died just a few months previously. Whatever triggered the recollection, it prompted memories of how Mary had shown him more affection than her younger, more vivacious, sister, but at that time, fixated on Jenny, he largely ignored her protestations. As he expressed it:

> *Oh how they fly, the hastin' years!*
>   *It seems scarce half a dozen,*
> *Though twenty 'tis since both my ears*
>   *Wi' bonnie words were buzzin',*
> *An' yet, not half so deeply then*
>   *Was somebody love-smitten*
> *As now he is - so take this pen,*
>   *And write to Mary Mitton.*[79]

Whether he ever wrote, or had a reply from her, is not recorded, but Mary never came to America, settling instead in Dublin where she married George Henry Gabriel in Eustace Street Meeting House in June, 1907. There were no children of this union and she died in 1933.

It is quite evident that at this time, Teggart was going through some kind of emotional, mid-life crisis. Lonely and dispirited, he was acutely aware that the sands of time were running out and that each passing day diminished his chances of ever finding someone to share his life. Some idea of the depth of his depression can be evinced from a few lines he composed in the spring of that year. Reflecting on the brevity and uncertainly of life, he mused that he might never have another opportunity to walk the mountain slopes, to rejoice once more in the glories of nature, to see again his homeland and friends or to find personal happiness as *'love's porch'* had been passed *'for the last time'*.[80]

By the summer, the black mood had largely dissipated. Whilst out walking one evening in Forest Park, he chanced to meet the attractive Christina Pietersz,[81] youngest daughter of a Dutch immigrant family who had arrived in the United States some six years previously.

---

[79] *'Mary Mitton', Springfield Republican,* January 1904.
[80] *'For the Last Time', Springfield Republican,* March 1904.
[81] Her brothers, John, Herman and Bertus were talented artists and at one stage all three were employed in Springfield by Milton Bradley, lithographers and manufacturers of jigsaws, board games and kindergarden materials. The company, which is still in existence, employs over 2,000 people and is the biggest games manufacturer in the world. Paintings by Bertus, the most famous of the three brothers, can be found in, the Whistler House Museum of Art, Lowell, MA, Springfield Museum of Art, George Walter Smith Museum, Springfield and High Museum of Art, Atlanta, GA.

Forest Park, Springfield, 1907.

Born in May, 1873, she worked as a clerk in Forbes and Wallace. It was a case of love at first sight for Moses. Indeed, he could hardly believe his good fortune in finding someone who also shared his passion for rambling and was quite happy to accompany him on walks in Forest Park and along the banks of the Connecticut River. Though he was now 51, he was delighted to have found love again, even if the prospect was scarcely believable. In a poem addressed to her and written in the early autumn of that year, the note of bemusement was evident:

> *A lass on one her bonny looks bestowing*
> *Is, in the desert of my life, like finding*
> *On sunburnt rocks and bare, bonnily blowing*
> *Harebell and gerardia! my soul reminding*
> *That love still smiles although the summer's going.*

That he was completely bowled over by Christina there can be no doubt:

> *Oh, once more in woodlands green to meet her!*
> *Oh, once more her olive cheek, slight tanned, to glance at,*
> *And glancing have, love-born, love visions sweeter*
> *Than ever bard of old bade heart romance at!*
> *To see the vision, and though sore heart-troubled,*
> *To be soul-kindled, as if one had seen a*
> *Green-robbed joy! to have life's few pleasures doubled.*
> *This were to meet once more and see Christina—*
> *This were with startled breath and being wildly to discover*
> *That one may have grey hairs and still love like a lover.*[82]

---

[82] *'Christina', Springfield Republican,* September 1904.

In the course of the following three years, the besotted poet importuned Christina to marry him on a number of occasions but she, twenty years his junior, was understandably reluctant to commit herself to marriage. For Moses, the courtship was unbearably prolonged, complaining on one occasion of *'the long time of wooing over which my spirit grieves'*. As time passed, he became increasingly worried that the disparity in their ages was going to be the undoing of the whole affair: *'But my lady will not listen - she has seen the red leaf flung,/She has seen the leaves lie scattered when the summer wind was gone.'* [83]

However, his persistence and patience were eventually rewarded and his *'dark-eyed nymph'* finally accepted his proposal. They were married on 3 September, 1907, the ceremony being conducted by the minister of Springfield's South Congregational Church, the Rev Dr Philip Moxon, at his residence in Dartmouth Terrace.

Dartmouth Terrace, Springfield, c.1910.

Interestingly, the details recorded on the marriage certificate were again incorrect. As, on the previous occasion, the marriage was given as his 'first' and his age was stated as 48 when it should have been 54!

---

83 *'The Wind and the Leaves', Springfield Republican,* July 1905.

COMMONWEALTH OF MASSACHUSETTS

City of Springfield, August 3 2005

I, Mary C Powers, hereby certify that it appears by the Record of Marriages in said Springfield, that a marriage was solemnized, between Moses Teggart and Christina Pietersz on the 3rd day of September in the year 1907.

The Record is in the following words and figures, to wit:

GROOM.		BRIDE.	
Name,	Moses Teggart	Name,	Christina Pietersz
Color,	W	Color,	W
Age,	48	Age,	33
No. of Marriage,	First	No. of Marriage,	First
Residence,	182 Maple St Springfield	Residence,	14 Stebbins St Springfield
Occupation,	Bookkeeper	Occupation,	Clerk
Birthplace,	Ireland	Birthplace,	Holland
Father's Name,	Moses Teggart	Father's Name,	Peter Pietersz
Mother's Name,	Charlotte McNally	Mother's Name,	Bertha Beckholdt

Place and Date of Marriage, Springfield - Sept 3 1907
By whom Married, Philip S Moxom - Minister of the Gospel - Springfield

I, Mary C Powers above named, despose and say, that I hold the office of Asst City Clerk of the City of Springfield, in the County of Hampden and Commonwealth of Massachusetts; that the Record of Births, Marriages, and Deaths in said City are in my custody, and that the above is a true copy from the Records of Marriages, in said City, as certified by me.

Witness my hand and the Seal of said City of Springfield on the day and year first above written.

Copy of Marriage Certificate, Moses Teggart to Christina Pietersz, 1907.

The *Springfield Republican* reported the happy event thus:

> *The ceremony was performed in the presence of a few friends, including Herman Pietersz, brother of the bride and his wife, Mrs Antoinette Pietersz . . . After the ceremony light refreshments were served. On their return from a brief wedding trip Mr and Mrs Teggart will be at home at 88 Central Street. The bride is the sister of Bertus Pietersz, the well-known artist, and Mr Teggart is the charming singer of Irish bogland and lowland Scotch lyrics, in the school of Burns.*[84]

---

[84] 4 September 1907.

The Return of the Native

Just over a year later Moses decided to return to Ireland to visit his father, who was in his eighty-third year and in failing health. He sailed from Boston in late October, arriving at Glasgow on 3 November, before continuing his onward journey to the Birches, where he arrived two days later. He found the situation there rather worse than he anticipated, as his step-mother took ill shortly after his arrival and died a few weeks later from *'coronary dropsy'*. She was buried on 22 December in the old parish graveyard at Loughgall.

Grave of Mary Stapelton-Teggart, Loughgall Old Cemetery.

As his father was too ill to look after himself, both he and Moses moved from Ballinary to nearby Clonmacate, where they stayed with his aunt, Margaret Teggart.[85]

Margaret Teggart's cottage, Clonmacate where Moses Teggart wrote his last poems, now the home of Francis Teggart, pictured above, a first cousin, once removed, of the poet.

[85] Born Margaret Cassells in 1850, she married Hamilton Teggart, 18 January 1873, and died 17 June 1918. Hamilton predeceased her, dying on 15 April 1908.

As he had been away for over twenty years, he noticed many changes to the countryside. As a result of the Land Purchase Act (1903), the vast majority of the former tenant farmers now owned their land, paying substantially less rent to the government than they had once paid to the local landlords. As Moses observed:

> *They pay it gladly and cheerfully, for the land is now their own, and, as a consequence, their little places look lovely, their homes and houses are kept neat and clean, and the people themselves are, and look, bright and happy.*[86]

Much of the new prosperity was due to improved agricultural practices, and the financial and personal investments that farmers were now prepared to make in their land. Strawberries and raspberries were widely cultivated, in addition to turnips, cabbages, wheat and oats. With the growth of Portadown and Lurgan demand for turf was strong and, as the poet noted:

> *Everyday, Sunday excepted, the carts, mostly painted red and blue, are quite a feature of the roads leading to the towns . . . peat is also ground up by machine, baled and wired up . . . then shipped on lighters*[87] *down the river Bann to Belfast and from there to Liverpool, London and other cities where it takes the place of rough straw and is used by liverymen for litter, and rare and capital litter it makes.*[88]

The 'litter', referred to above, was manufactured by the Derrylard Peat Factory which was established in the mid 1890s. A contemporary columnist in the *Portadown News* described the peat moss as, '*soft as a feather bed and as absorbent as a sponge*'.

While he was acutely aware of the changes in the people and the economy, he remained as much under the spell of the boglands as ever:

> *Yesterday evening, behind the heads of some tall, dark green firs, one slim and lovely poplar standing up in their midst, set the golden sun, and a rarer, rosier afterglow could scarcely be imagined. Hushed were the birds in the boglands; and when the stars came out, led by a large, yellow and lustrous moon, the whole countryside seemed to lie enchanted and slumberous in the golden mist. Red glowed the lights in the windows of the little bogland homes; and a peace and quiet, unknown in great cities, wrapped all the landscape, even the nearer waters of Lough Neagh, as in a holy calm.*[89]

Such an evocative description bears testimony to his prowess as a writer of elegant prose and it is to be regretted that someone with such a talent produced so little in this medium.

---

[86] 'In the Boglands of Co Armagh', *Springfield Republican*, 6 February 1909.
[87] Large, flat-bottomed barges used for transporting heavy cargoes.
[88] 'In the Boglands of Co Armagh', *Springfield Republican*, 6 February 1909.
[89] Ibid.

Even though it was mid-winter, he took great delight in seeing once again the plants, flowers and birds which had given him so much pleasure during his boyhood days and which later featured so prominently in many of his poems:

> *Flowers are in abundance everywhere. Daisies, dandelions and ragweeds by the roadsides; clumps of golden whin . . . the ripe black pods of the green-haired bloom . . . the scarlet hips of the wildrose and sweetbrier, side by side with the red haws on the whitehorn, give an added charm to the rustic lanes and to the ever enduring hawthorn hedges. Birds are numberless. From dawn till dark the robin redbreasts sing . . . linnets, green and grey, alight on and bend the twigs of the silver birches; hedgesparrows come out from the thorn bushes and twitter their dulcet little songs in the sunshine; jenny wrens jink here and there . . . the lovely little bluecap makes merry among the orchard boughs; tomtits are a continual delight; skylarks fly skirling in little flocks under dark grey clouds; starlings come with the whirr of a mighty host; . . . pied wagtails skip and chirp in the dug-out potato plots; chaffinches fly 'pink-winking' from tree to tree; 'saygulls' may be seen flying during a storm, to or from Lough Neagh; and alas there are two birds, once very plentiful, which I have not yet seen - the yellow yorlin and the meadow pipit, the latter the dear little mosscheeper of childhood.*[90]

Lough Neagh, thirty miles long and fifteen wide, is the largest fresh water lake in the British Isles and the fifth biggest in Europe. Situated about six miles from Portadown and less than three from Ballinary, its sheer size makes it the most distinctive and dominant natural feature in the area. Moses had always been fascinated by its mystical presence and its changing moods, sometimes tranquil, sometimes tempest tossed.

One morning, in early December, he set out from the Birches to visit the lough shore at Maghery. On the way he stopped off at Milltown where he bemoaned the fact that the once thriving village *'had sunk into ruin and decay'* and the former large distillery was now but *'a collection of useless walls and abandoned buildings'*.

One but can imagine his feelings as he passed Milltown Church, which, as a boy, he attended regularly, and the adjacent school house where he had once taught.

On arrival at Maghery he recollected that it was in this district, many years ago, that he first observed barefooted girls, *'tripping along the moss ramparts, a basket of fresh pullen borne saucily on the head; hands on hunches and the whole body swaying in perfect rhythm.'*[91] No doubt this sight was the genesis of one of his most popular poems, *'The Milltown Maid'*:

---

[90] *Ibid.*
[91] *'The Legendary Lough Neagh'*, *Springfield Republican*, 3 January 1909.

When the summer morning rising red
  Breaks o'er the bog so brown,
With a basket of pullens on her head
  She jog trots into town.
Her bare feet down the dusty road
  Do not take time to wade,
A catch of fresh fish is the load
  Laid on the Milltown Maid.[92]

On his return journey he paused for a few moments on the summit of Derryagh Hill to take a last lingering glimpse of the lough shore by moonlight:

Like a great bird, Coney Island lies dark and slumberous on the grey calm; Derrywarroch pile stands up too firmly fixed to nod: so still is the night one can almost hear the splash of the wave on Milltown shore; and far in the distance, Slieve Gallion lifts his dark and bulky back to a sky of amber. The lough itself looks like a level floor, palish grey, stretching on and on and around, till lake and sky seem lost in each other.[93]

Perhaps, all too aware that he might never see the lough and his beloved boglands again, he was overcome with emotion. He was reminded of a verse from *'Let Erin Remember'* by Thomas Moore that accurately reflected his mood:

Remains of O'Neill's fortified dwelling, Derrywarroch, near Lough Neagh.

[92] *Boston Pilot,* November 1906.
[93] 'The Legendary Lough Neagh', *Springfield Republican,* 3 January 1909.

So shall memory often, in dreams sublime,
Catch a glimpse of the days that are over,
And sighing look back through the waves of time,
To the long faded glories they cover.[94]

His last excursion, in late January, took him, by jaunting car, from The Birches to the neighbouring villages of Annaghmore, Loughgall and onward to the city of Armagh. After visiting both the Roman Catholic and Church of Ireland cathedrals, he returned home in the evening via Portadown. It was a town he knew well, having gone there scores of times in his younger days, when he and his father had brought turf or linen to market.

On his way home, about a couple of miles from Ballinary, he noted the cattle standing at the gaps, waiting to be driven home to their snug byres and barns *'and occasionally there was the coaxing call of some little girl to the 'chay lady'*[95] *standing at the gate in some lone field.'* [96] After a short detour to Tartaraghan Parish Church and its churchyard, where his maternal ancestors lay buried, his jaunting car was soon *'rattling along the smooth moss ramparts of home.'* [97]

The winter of 1908-09, being particularly cold and wet[98] had a deleterious effect on his health. As he informed his friend Charles Whiting, he thought it advisable that he should soon return to the still cold but drier climate of Springfield. Accordingly, he left the Birches on 11 February en route to Glasgow where he embarked on the S.S. Carthaginian bound for Boston. He had left Clonmacate with mixed emotions: his father's health had improved somewhat but he also realised that it was unlikely that he would ever see him alive again. He sailed from Greenock on the 13 February. Six days later, on a windy Friday morning, Moses suffered a severe cerebral haemorrhage from which he never recovered. The captain of the Carthaginian, Richard Bamber, stopped the vessel at noon, and after a short religious service conducted by the surgeon, Dr J V O'Haggan, his body was consigned to the deep in the midst of a raging gale.

There can be little doubt that if he had realised his death was so imminent, he would never have left his beloved homeland. In 1889, shortly after his arrival in the USA, he wrote one of his most memorable bogland poems, *'The House at the Head of the Town'*. In it he recollected his childhood days in Ballinary and contrasted them with his present situation. He concluded that the attractions of urban America were nothing compared to the glories of his own townland. Contemplating his death, he made it clear where he wished to be buried:

---

[94] *Ibid.*
[95] Pet name for the family cow. This may come from the Irish 'téigh' meaning 'go'.
[96] *'Spring Coming in Ireland', Springfield Republican,* 14 February 1909.
[97] *Ibid.*
[98] Meteorological records for Co Armagh reveal that both December and January were particularly inclement months. The temperature seldom rose more than a few degrees above freezing and the rainfall was higher than average.

> *And I long for the day the night to bring,*
> *When at peace I shall lay me down,*
> *Where daisies spring and the songbirds sing*
> *Near the house at the head of the town.*[99]

Unfortunately, it was not to be. In some ways, however, his burial in mid-Atlantic was quite fitting. He had a genuine fondness for Springfield and had made many friends there. Indeed, his obituary in the *Portadown News*, drawing heavily on an unnamed American source, claimed that *'he grew to love Springfield more than any spot on earth - even than his native soil'*.[100] Whilst recognizing his sincere affection for the city's many parks and forest glades and his many friends there, the statement could not be further from the truth. Moses Teggart loved the boglands, and its people with a powerful, all-consuming passion. On more than one occasion he had made it clear that there was *'no heart and no home'* for him in America. In the last poem he ever published, *'A Farewell'*, composed at Clonmacate just eight days before his death, he seemed to have had a premonition that his days were numbered. Though brief, it serves as a fitting epitaph, for it contains many of the poetic themes for which he was justly celebrated: his appreciation of nature, his affection for birds, and above all else, his deep, abiding love for his own people. No one can read its final stanza without a lump in the throat and a tear in the eye. If there ever was any doubt about his devotion to the Birches community then surely here is the answer:

> *Farewell ye kindly people all*
> *In bogland and in town,*
> *Your friendship I esteem, and shall*
> *Till I this head lay down*
> *In that last sleep o'er which the dawn*
> *Of heaven some morn shall rise,*
> *When I, fond hope! though sometime gone*
> *Shall join you in the skies.*[101]

His passing was universally mourned, both in his native county and in many areas of New England. The *Springfield Republican*, to which he had been a frequent contributor, was lavish in its praise:

> *Mr Teggart was one of the rarest of men - a genius of song, one of the class of Robert Burns . . . much of his song and ballad work in the Scottish dialect will stand comparison with the exquisite sentiment . . . and especially the singing quality of the Ayrshire poet.*[102]

The newspaper also had particular praise, and rightly so, for those poems which were rooted in the townlands of North Armagh:

---

[99] *Springfield Republican*, November 1889.
[100] 3 April 1909.
[101] *Portadown News*, February 1909.
[102] 2 March 1909.

> *In his verse about the boglands he struck a new and original vein - no poet before had seen the beauty and charm of this, at first sight, unattractive region . . . No sweeter love songs have been written than Teggart's.*[103]

The *Springfield Daily News* also paid tribute to the quality of his Irish poems whilst, at the same time, heaping praise on the poet himself:

> *To know Moses Teggart was to know a man with a wealth of humour, a fund of information and an ability to see the beautiful in life. There is a host of people in Springfield who will count his death a direct personal loss.*[104]

Yet another Springfield newspaper *The Union*, commented on the popularity of his poems including *'his workings of Greek themes and his touching Scotch lyrics'*. [105] Like the previous two journals, it too had particular praise for the originality of his bogland verse.

His death was also noted in several other American newspapers, far removed from Massachusetts. The *Marian Daily Star* in Ohio extolled the quality of *'his remarkable poems in Scottish and North of Ireland dialects, and in the choicest English as well, which have made him familiar in New England'*[106] and the Mississippi *Biloxi Herald* remarked on the passing of a true poet *'whose work deserved the appreciation of a wider public'*.[107]

His passing caused much sorrow amongst the literary coterie who regularly contributed to the columns of the *Springfield Republican,* and one of them, the poetess, Mabel Antoinette Paine, was sufficiently moved by the unusual and dramatic circumstances surrounding his death to pen the following tribute:

> *Stricken, sighing,*
> *Lone and dying,*
> *None to comfort,*
> *None to mourn.*
>
> *But the surges*
> *Sang his dirges;*
> *Winds tempestuous*
> *Hymned his song*

---

[103] *Ibid.*
[104] 2 March 1909.
[105] 2 March 1909.
[106] 9 March 1909.
[107] 10 March 1909. *The New York Times* also carried an obituary on 4 March 1909.

Heart of fire,
With a lyre
Tuned to echoes
Infinite!

Waves sobbed clearer,
Heaven came nearer,
When God claimed him
For His own![108]

Five years after her husband's death, Christina Teggart married again. This time the groom was August (Gus) Schneeloch,[109] a postman of Hall Street, Springfield. On the 23 January, 1915 she gave birth to a son, Richard August, in Wesson Memorial Hospital.

Wesson Memorial Hospital, Springfield, 1910.

Unfortunately, she died in childbirth and three days later she was interred in the city's Oak Grove Cemetery. The funeral service was conducted by the Rev Philip Moxon, the same minister who had married her to Moses eight years previously.

108	*'The Passing of a Poet', Portadown News*, 3 April 1909.
109	Born 5 June 1869; died 28 September 1920 as a result of a traffic accident.

Schneeloch Grave, Oak Grove Cemetery, Springfield, the final resting place of Christina Teggart.

Moses Teggart died shortly after his fifty-sixth birthday. Not a great age by modern norms of life expectancy, but much longer than the forty-six years then predicted for males born in the 1850s. Indeed, out of the eight other members of his family, only William Francis (born 1851), Hamilton (born 1859) and Mary (born 1855) survived him - all the rest were dead by April, 1907 when Moses Teggart (Senior) made his will, leaving his pocket watch and chain to Moses and the small farm to Hamilton, then currently employed by Customs and Excise in Delny, Ross, Scotland. As events turned out, Moses never lived to inherit the watch as his father did not die until 1913.

Though Moses was married three times, long term happiness eluded him. During the twenty years he spent in Massachusetts he was especially prone to periodic bouts of depression and though he was seldom unemployed, his bookkeeper's salary was never more than adequate. His last position at Forbes and Wallace was perhaps his most remunerative, allowing him to rent a room in Maple Street - one of the most elegant and sought-after locations in suburban Springfield.

Maple Street, Springfield, Moses Teggart lived in No 182, opposite street lamp. (Courtesy Connecticut Valley Museum)

Generally, there was no money for luxuries and on many occasions he was glad of the extra few dollars he received for his poems that were published in the *Springfield Republican* or the *Boston Pilot*.

Like the Birches man he was, he was never really at ease with indoor life. He revelled in rambles over the unspoilt acres of Forest Park and Mount Tom or the strolls along the meandering banks of the Connecticut River where every twist and turn opened up new vistas to gratify the wayfarer's eye. He also enjoyed the cultural opportunities afforded by Springfield to meet and mix with the ever-growing number of artists, writers and musicians[110] who had taken up residence there. However, despite all the advantages that Springfield had to offer, not the least of which was the literary recognition he had gained there, his thoughts were never far away from his spiritual home in Armagh and the sights and sounds of Milltown Parish.

Almost a hundred years of blur and blot have now elapsed since his death and the townlands of North Armagh have changed almost beyond recognition. Much of the all pervasive bogland that gave the area its unique character has been reclaimed for arable farming and many of the indigenous birds that once delighted the poet's eye

---

[110] He is known to have composed a number of song lyrics for performance at various soirées in the city, see *Springfield Republican*, 21 January 1894 and 7 May 1908. He also wrote a number of hymns, including *'When Children Lift Their Voices'*, 1896; *'Tidings of Great Joy'*, 1906 and *'God is in the Sky'*, 1908.

are now so few in number that those like the yellowhammer, the quail and the meadow pipit have become endangered species and are rarely seen. The red and blue turf carts that erstwhile trundled into Portadown are but a distant memory to even the oldest of local inhabitants and the ubiquitous, lime-washed, thatched cottages that formerly dotted the countryside have become a great rarity. The modern dwellings of Milltown Parish no longer resonate to the whirr of the spinning wheel and the clack of the loom; no bare-footed Milltown maids now grace the green moss rampers; and the rural postman's shrill whistle disturbs not the silence of the fields. And yet, despite all these changes, there remains an indefinable, mystical quality about the district, an almost tangible sense of ancient times when the black, primeval bogs brooded over a landscape little altered in more than ten thousand years. It is the most atmospheric of places and no doubt the young Moses Teggart sensed it too when he dallied on his way to school to listen to the skylark raising his song to the heavens or gazed in childish wonderment at the frog spawn in the roadside 'sheugh'. He would also have noted the wee mosscheeper sunning himself upon an old turf stack, the gossamer cobwebs on the thorn hedge, and the aroma of the blue turf smoke *'up-curling in the breathless air'*.[111]

Although fate ordained that he was not laid to rest, as he so ardently hoped, beside his parents in Milltown Churchyard, his love and affection for the Birches area lives on in his numerous poems that vividly recapture the quintessential spirit of his native countryside almost one hundred and fifty years ago. His concept of *'home'*, surely the most evocative word in the English language, was not limited to his own house and family, but also embraced the whole environment of the boglands. It was, as he once explained, the song of the yorlin, the miry rampers, the smell of bracken and heather, the mossy lanes, the morning blaze of a turf fire, the fragrance of light brown loam, the laughter of barefoot children, the turfcutters with their barrows, spades and graips, even the drizzling rain and dripping trees were *'also part of home'*.[112] He was inordinately proud of his roots, and as he once averred, *"'Twas the grandest thing in all the world,/To be a Birches Boy.'*[113]

In turn, North Armagh should be proud of its prodigal son who wandered half a world away in search of fame, if not fortune. It is now time for his literary talent to be recognised more widely in his own country, and especially by his own people in North Armagh.

---

111 *'Turf Smoke'*, October 1925.
112 *'Home'*, *Boston Pilot*, September 1905.
113 *'A Birches Boy'*, *Portadown News*, June 1900.

A SHORT INTRODUCTION TO THE POETRY OF MOSES TEGGART

In many respects, Moses Teggart was heir to that remarkable tradition of peasant verse which was such a feature of the literary scene in the Ulster counties of Antrim and Down during the period 1780-1850. Like so many of these country poets he was an ardent admirer of *'the Ayrshire ploughman'*, Robert Burns. As one critic expressed it:

> 'It was the fame of . . . Burns which established the archetypal figure in the general imagination . . . and it was the idea of the peasant poet as an acceptable role, which certainly inspired many country folk to try their hands at the making of verses since there seemed to be a reservoir of goodwill for the intention and support for the effort among the educated classes.'[1]

Though the veneration of Burns in the above counties can be largely explained by the huge number of Scottish emigrants who settled there from the seventeenth century onwards, his popularity was not confined to these areas. As Nelson McCausland of the Ulster-Scots Heritage Council once observed, *'It was said there was a time when there were but two books in Ulster homes, the Bible and Burns.'*[2] For his part, Teggart had long regarded the Ayrshire poet as an inspirational figure. Whilst living in Scotland in the late 1870s, he made several trips from his home in Kirkintilloch, near Glasgow, to visit Burns' country, including the poet's home farm at Mossgiel and birthplace in Alloway. In a poem, published in 1895, but almost certainly written ten or more years earlier, he acknowledged Burns' genius and the importance of the cottage as a place of pilgrimage for all admirers, but reserved his greatest approbation for the natural landscape which had been such an inspiration to the bard:

> *A laigh bit biggin by the road —*
> *The level road that leads frae Ayr,*
> *Of genius ance the trig abode,*
> *Is noo a treasure kept wi' care . . .*
>
> *Lang may the lave admire his hame!*
> *Gie me the scenes o'er which he smiled —*
> *In these days as in his the same —*
> *The poet still is Nature's child.*[3]

The Ulster writer and poet, John Hewitt, observed that the so-called 'rhyming

---

1   *Rhyming Weavers,* John Hewitt, Belfast 2004, pp.1-2.
2   *Robert Burns - The Ulster Connection,* p.1.
3   'At the Birthplace of Burns', *Springfield Republican,* February 1895.

weavers'[4] of Antrim and Down composed verses on similar subjects to the Scottish master: citing in evidence, *'The Irish Cottier's Death and Burial'* by James Orr of Ballycarry, directly inspired by Burns', *'The Cotter's Saturday Night'*; and Gransha's Francis Boyle's, *'The Author's Address to his Old Gelding'*, modelled on Burns' *'The Auld Farmer's Salutation to his Auld Mare'*. Teggart, whilst avoiding such obvious comparisons, wrote a number of poems addressed to young ladies in the local community. His 'belles'; Mary Black, Lillian Martin, Daisy Tennyson and Mary Mitton are paralleled by Burns' Scottish 'lasses'; Jenny Clow, Nellie Kilpatrick, Mary Campbell and Jean Armour. Likewise, Teggart's lyrics celebrating the virtues of the attractive and largely anonymous colleens who inhabited the various townlands of Milltown parish, are very similar to those Burns wrote about the unnamed lasses of Ballochmyle, Albany, Ecclefechan and Inverness.

However, it would be unwise, as well as just plain wrong, to over-emphasise the similarities between Teggart and Burns. Whilst Burns wrote in Lowland Scots vernacular, (Lallans), the Armagh bard's poetic idiom was firmly rooted in the everyday language of the country folk who inhabited the shores of South Lough Neagh, and though this dialect was well-flavoured with words and phrases of Scottish origin, it was more English than Scots - with a dash of Irish Gaelic thrown in for good measure. It was the language which Providence had brought to his door and which he was to use so effectively to depict the people and landscape of his native boglands. It was only in those poems with Scottish themes that Teggart consciously imitated the language of Burns, and though some of these stand comparison with those from the master's pen, it is his Milltown poems which show him at his individual best - fresh, original and with an innocent, lyrical charm that is unsurpassed by any other Ulster poet of his generation.

Another poet whose work was much admired by Teggart was William Wordsworth. He saw in him a kindred spirit, someone who had a passionate love of the natural world; someone who had never any wish to escape from the commonplaces of life - *'the natural world of our familiar days'* and, above all, someone who saw Nature as a living soul that revealed itself in the movement of the stars, the song of the birds, the decay of a wildflower, the beauty of woodland clover, the gurgling of a mountain stream and, just as importantly, the yearning of the human heart. Though Wordsworth died three years before Teggart was born, he saw him as a role-model. He was never to express it in so many words but he may well have felt that if Wordsworth could write great poetry about the rocky, barren fells of the Lake District, then there was no reason why he could not do likewise for an equally unpromising landscape - the boglands of North Armagh. Whether, in fact, his aspirations were ever as ambitious as this is a moot question but there can be no doubt that he always harboured high hopes of ultimate literary recognition and acclaim. He was certainly very familiar with Wordsworth's verse, often prefacing a number of his own poems with short quotations from the older poet.[5] Indeed, his regard for the Bard of Windermere amounted, at times, almost to hero-worship, as

---

[4] A generic term here used to include, not only such weaver poets as Hugh Porter of Moneyslane, near Rathfriland and Joseph Carson of Kilpike, Banbridge but also country schoolmasters like Henry McDonald Flecher of Moneyreagh and Hugh McWilliams of Loughgeel in North Antrim.

[5] For example, *'Under the Elms'*, December 1897, *'A Piece of Pasture Land'*, May 1899 and *'Love for Things of the Bogland'*, April 1904.

is evidenced by the opening lines of the sonnet he dedicated to Wordsworth's memory:

> *O sage! O seer! O soul most ministrant!*
> *Thou who art still a living voice among*
> *The mountains! thou whose still all tuneful tongue*
> *Wild Duddon, Tweed and Windermere doth haunt.*[6]

The third poet to influence Teggart was lawyer and newspaper editor, William Cullen Bryant.[7] Born in Cummington, Massachusetts in 1794, he became known as 'the American Wordsworth' for his poems on the grandeur and majesty of nature - the plants, flowers, trees and birds that were such a notable feature of the New England landscape. In particular, he had a special affection for the wild, remote, solitary places where the natural world, untouched by man, burgeoned in all its magnificent glory. The style and content of his poems would undoubtedly have struck a sympathetic chord with the young Teggart who had been an enthusiastic reader of Bryant's verse long before he emigrated to America. Indeed, in 1888, the year prior to his arrival in Philadelphia, he admitted that he had always wanted to visit, in Bryant's phrase, *'the land of the goldenrod and the sumach'*.[8] Many of the American writer's poems, such as *'The Planting of the Apple Tree'*, *'To the Fringed Gentian'*, and *'The Yellow Violet'* would certainly have appealed to Teggart's love of the natural world. The latter, in particular, was very similar in theme and form to many of his own bogland lyrics:

> *When beechen buds begin to swell,*
> *And woods the blue-bird's warble know,*
> *The yellow violet's modest bell*
> *Peeps from last year's leaves below.*
>
> *And when again the genial hour*
> *Awakes the painted tribes of light,*
> *I'll not o'erlook the modest flower*
> *That made the woods of April bright.*[9]

It was surely more than coincidental that Bryant's blank verse translations of Homer's *'Iliad'* and *'Odyssey'*, published in 1870 and 1872 respectively, were paralleled by Teggart's paraphrases from the same source. Moreover, it is interesting to note that the American's sonnets, *'Midsummer'* and *'October'*, were closely mirrored by Teggart's *'June'* and *'Autumn'*. Perhaps, above all, Teggart was attracted to Bryant's pantheistic belief that the natural world, created and inhabited by God, had a profound influence on the human spirit - chastening, soothing, encouraging and ennobling. To avail of this source of comfort and inspiration all

---

6 'Wordsworth', *Springfield Republican*, March 1906.
7 A child prodigy, he penned his first poem when he was only ten years old, published his first book at thirteen, and whilst still a teenager, he learnt enough Greek in two months to allow him to read the whole of the New Testament in that language.
8 Barrows, *op. cit.*, p.141.
9 *The Poems of William Bryant*, Oxford 1914, pp. 13-14.

the onlooker had to do was listen, or, as he put it in probably his greatest poem, *'Thanatopsis'*:

> *Go forth under the open sky, and list*
> > *To Nature's teachings . . .*
> *To him who in the love of Nature holds*
> > *Communion with her visible forms, she speaks*
> *A various language.*[10]

It was an exhortation with which Teggart was happy to comply.

He would also have readily accepted Bryant's belief that forest groves were *'God's first temples'* and that even the most delicate woodland flower is *'an emanation of the indwelling Life'* present in all nature, or, as he once expressed it himself, *'all green life, is part of Him whose name is Love'*.[11]

Whilst his rural lyrics written in the North Armagh vernacular will surely remain his greatest legacy, Teggart felt pressurised to write sonnets, dramatic monologues and even paraphrases of epic legends from classical mythology. It was generally accepted by the literary world of that time that no poet could possibly hope to be taken seriously unless he could demonstrate his mastery of a variety of poetic forms. Though his decision to experiment with the sonnet form may have been taken somewhat reluctantly, the resultant compositions were often impressive. Even the most carping of critics would surely admit the excellence of many of these superbly crafted poems, including *'Listening to the Lark at Sunrise'*, *'To James Duncan'* and *'Autumn'*. The latter, reminiscent of Keats' famous ode on the same theme, deserves to be more widely appreciated:

> *She of the yellow hair and sandaled feet,*
> > *She of the laughing looks and cheeks brown-tanned,*
> > *Blithe passing goes now through the pleasant land*
> *Rich in the ripening corn and garnered wheat.*
> *Blessing on blessing, sweeter sweet on sweet,*
> > *When she on some green hillock takes her stand,*
> > *Sees she up-piled and stored on either hand,*
> *While her the labourers with glad looks greet.*
> *Aster and goldenrod, in dim woods these,*
> > *And on the mountains, oak and maple shine;*
> *Joyed by her presence flash the inland seas,*
> > *And run the rivers, as if brimmed with wine;*
> *Laugh the red apples on rejoicing trees,*
> > *And hails her all the land as queen divine.*[12]

Whilst the above is arguably the best of his sonnets, it is rivalled closely by at least two others, *'June'* and *'To Spring'*. In the former, replete with evocative images of a balmy summer's day, Teggart contrasts a parched and manicured lawn, where

---

[10] *Ibid.*, p.11.
[11] *'Brothers'*, *Springfield Republican*, May 1905.
[12] Barrows, *op. cit.*, p.159.

baked ridges expose *'Bare root and stubble to the burning noon'*, with the shaded abode of the *'white and cool'* water nymph who sits dangling her feet in a sequestered pool. *'To Spring'*, on the other hand, conjures up a more sombre mood as the poet toys with the fanciful notion that even after his burial, the spirit of the season will somehow make him aware of its yearly arrival. In such an event, he would rest contentedly:

> *And though no longer with the sons of men*
>   *Number'd, yet may have reason none to weep,*
> *But be as one who smileth softly when*
>   *He in his happy dreams hath soundest sleep.*[13]

It is to be regretted that Teggart wrote only a handful of 'dramatic monologues', for it was a verse form in which he particularly excelled. Developed during the Victorian era, the dramatic monologue was a type of poem in which the main character, usually male, revealed in speech, his thoughts, feelings or actions to an ever-present but silent listener. In *'The Bogland Farmer to his Wife'*, for instance, the farmer directly addresses his wife Emily and urges her to accompany him on a walk along the moss path:

> *On the street the children are spininin' their tops,*
>   *While the light is still in the sky,*
> *Let us walk by the ramper and look at the craps,*
>   *And see if the rickles are dhry.*

On the way out of the house he notices that the garden is rather untidy and could do with a good sprucing up:

> *That garden, dear Emily - some day when you've time*
>   *I wish you would weed it an' show*
> *The naybors who pass - that it isn't the clime*
>   *But neglect makes the chicken-weed grow*[14].

Being a dramatic monologue, Emily's response to the reprimand is not recorded, which is just as well, perhaps!

Another poem, *'The Turf Cutter'*, also shows Teggart's mastery of this genre. As in the previous example, his handling of dialect is superb. The turf cutter addresses his tardy, young helper in forthright terms:

> *Don't stand there with your mouth agape!*
>   *Find something else to do!*
> *Come, get the turf spade an' the graip,*
>   *An' the turf-barra, too.*

It is only after the denouement in the final stanza that we realise that his much put-upon assistant is his own son:

---

[13] *Ibid.*, p.157.
[14] *Springfield Republican*, August 1898.

> *Wheest! isn't yon your mother's 'hoagh'?*
> *The mugs are on the shelf!*
> *Run on, my boy, an I'll bring Coagh —*
> *The craythur, home, myself.*[15]

Though few in number, the monologues are amongst the best of Teggart's canon. Set in a landscape he knew so well and populated with country folk who speak and act as they should, they exhibit a convincing realism that captures the very essence of rural life in North Armagh over a century ago.

Influenced by his admiration for Bryant and Tennyson in particular, and acutely aware that the literary establishment in both Britain and America expected 'serious' poets to produce long, verse translations of epic Greek tales, Teggart composed some half a dozen poems in this genre. Perhaps the best was his polished and refined narration of the story of *'Aurora and Tithonus'*, in which Aurora, goddess of the Dawn, falls in love with Tithonus, son of Laomedon, King of Troy. She abducts him and then persuades Jupiter to grant him immortality. Unfortunately, she neglects to ensure that he has also eternal youth, so he gradually becomes older and older until he no longer has any resemblance to the vigorous youth of yesteryear. Eventually, disenchanted with her erstwhile lover, she turns him into a grasshopper. The opening lines of the poem are indicative of Teggart's assured handling of unrhymed verse, even though it was an unfamiliar medium which he never employed in any other context:

> *When thou wert young, and when I loved thee well,*
> *When thy warm cheek and mine, fresh from the fount,*
> *Together pressed did make the morning!*
>   *When our smiles*
> *And love-illumined eyes did warm the glad blue day,*
> *When those, in far sky spaces calm and cool,*
> *Wert lying in my lap, nor shading half-shut eyes*
> *Would ask me list that earth-born bird - the lark,*
> *Of muted love loud carolling.*[16]

Teggart's other classically inspired poems included the much admired *'The Vision of Penelope'* and *'Helen's Gift to Telemachus'*. The latter, which was an especial favourite of Charles Barrows, was included in his aforementioned anthology of Springfield verse. While these poems inevitably lack appeal for a modern readership no longer educated along classical lines, they serve to illustrate the versatility and competence which prompted one of Teggart's obituarists to comment:

> *The essential poetic gift of the man was shown in his treatment of classical themes, which possessed the finish and grace of the scholar.*[17]

---

[15] *Portadown News*, June 1901.
[16] *Springfield Republican*, November 1906.
[17] *Springfield Republican*, 2 March 1909.

It is generally assumed that Teggart composed his poems with a particular audience in mind, but the picture is by no means clear. His earliest work, written in Scotland during the fifteen years he spent there as a civil servant, was clearly influenced by Burns. However, there is no indication that his verse was ever published in Scottish newspapers, as would have been the most likely scenario, or in any literary periodical. Some, like the excellent *'At the Birthplace of Burns'*, *'Keepin' Tryst'* and *'The Bonnie Rose O'Airlie'*, were clearly inspired by events in the mid 1870s, but never saw the light of day until being published, much later, in the *Springfield Republican*. Though an American readership might have been expected to have some difficulty with the 'lallans' in which they were written, the popularity and appeal of Burns in New England ensured some degree of familiarity with the dialect. To muddy the waters even further, there is some evidence to suggest that a few of the Scottish lyrics, *'Campsie Glen'*, *'To the New Year'* and *'The Wimplin' Luggie'* were probably written in Massachusetts. Whatever the truth of the matter, over thirty of the Caledonian poems were eventually published in the columns of the *Boston Pilot* and the *Springfield Republican*. Written for the most part in traditional iambic tetrameters,[18] the poems are similar in theme and form to those he wrote about the landscape and people of his native county. Like Burns, he found many of the Scottish lassies particularly attractive, especially those in the Kirkintilloch area where he worked and resided for a number of years. Amongst those who caught his roving eye were Elizabeth Mirren, *'she of the red hair an' saft blue eye'*, and Jenny Gow, *'the red-lipped maiden'* of the Campsie Hills.

Two other Scottish lyrics worthy of note are *'Anither Year'*, one of the very few in which Teggart used the Standard Habbie[19] verse form, so popular with generations of Scottish poets, and *'Where the Bonnie Kelvin Winds'*. In the former, he reflects on the passing year and concludes that, for good or ill, it is now gone and a new one has dawned:

> *However, wild the nicht, and wan,*
> *We ken the dark precedes the dawn;*
> *That, too, was guid which noo is gone,*
> *An' this is clear —*
> *For weel or woe we've entered on*
> *Anither year.*[20]

'Where the Bonnie Kelvin Winds', written in Standard English, is typical of the poet, showing his love for birds and unspoilt nature:

---

[18] Each line would have four beats or 'feet' (tetrameter). The word iambic comes from the Latin for 'lame'. So just as a lame man might walk putting forward first the lame foot and then the strong foot, the rhythm of the line would sound like the soft stress of the lame foot followed by the heavy stress of the strong foot. In iambic tetrameter then, the line would sound like soft stress, strong stress repeated four times.

[19] In this form, the first three lines rhyme with each other, (wan, dawn, gone), the fourth line starts a new rhyme, the fifth line repeats the rhyme sound of the first three lines and the last line rhymes with the fourth (AAA BAB).

[20] *Springfield Republican*, January 1897.

Half laughingly the whirlpool whips
    The ledge that light doth know,
Where hurriedly the ousel dips,
    Black-edged his breast of snow;
And where she may alloy love's thirst,
    Her nest the peewit finds,
In meadows wide; through which, at first,
    The bonnie Kelvin winds.[21]

Though they lack something of the originality of the Ayrshire ploughman, many of his Scottish poems, have an engaging simplicity and spontaneity that makes them particularly appealing.

Those poems that Teggart composed on American themes and intended, primarily, for a New England audience, were somewhat different to his Scottish and Irish lyrics. To begin with, he wrote comparatively little about the people of Springfield area. Apart from two *'in memoriam'* pieces dedicated to his friends, Aella Green and John B Stebbins, another addressed to his last wife, Christina and a rather sombre monody for a largely faceless Lenora, he seemed strangely reluctant to describe or comment on local characters. Perhaps he found the young ladies of Springfield less noteworthy than the Scottish 'lassies' or Irish 'belles'.

His Springfield poems also lack the *joie de vivre* which characterised much of his other verse. Perhaps it was partly due to his age - he was almost forty when he settled in the city and the confident optimism of youth had largely dissipated. It is not surprising, therefore, that with the onset of middle age, the tenor of his work took on a more philosophical, even pessimistic, tone. His inability to find another soul-mate after the death of Margaret in 1891 also contributed to his general unhappiness. The titles of many of his poems are indicative of his mood during those early Springfield years: *'Cast Down'*, *'Forebodings'*, *'Remembrance'*, *'The Moon and the Soul'* and *'The Music of Sorrow'*. Prefaced, significantly, by Bryant's, line - *'The melancholy days are come'*,[22] *'Cast Down'* written in Forest Park in 1895 is typical of his mood at this time:

The doleful days are come, indeed,
    The days that drag so dreary;
The ribbon rustles on the reed
    The willow's worn and weary.[23]

---

[21] *Springfield Republican*, August 1905.
[22] 'The melancholy days are come, the saddest of the year,/Of wailing wind and naked woods and meadows brown and sear', 'The Death of Flowers', *op. cit.*, p.80.
[23] *Springfield Republican*, November 1895.

In *'Forebodings'*, published around the same time, the melancholy note is equally apparent:

> *Are these loved voices that I hear*
> *In dreams at dawn of day,*
> *Celestial sounds; or, what I fear —*
> *Sweet preludes to decay?*
> *O heart, my heart!*
> *Oh what is that they say?*
> *That we, as visions seen, depart*
> *As dreams, we pass away.*[24]

Yet again, in the same autumn, in a poem addressed to an anonymous female, the heavy heart and world weariness is unmistakable:

> *Oh! blest are they who still can borrow*
> *Balm for the weary mind;*
> *And happy those who know tomorrow*
> *Will sure their chains unbind;*
> *But this sad heart to life-long sorrow*
> *Thou hast consigned.*[25]

The year 1895 was not unique and there were several other periods during his Springfield years when the black mood would re-emerge. Around 1907, for example, the sad note is heard again. This time, even though he appeared to be conscious of his depression, he seems to have accepted that it was an intrinsic character trait:

> *The cheerful note let others love,*
> *I envy not their glee,*
> *But, mindful of the mateless dove,*
> *The sad, sweet note for me.*[26]

There were times when he resolved to assume a more cheerful disposition and show the world his sunny side, but these periods of buoyant optimism inevitably gave way to feelings of dejection and despair. For poets, indeed for artists in general, to suffer bouts of depression is almost *de rigeur*, so, in this context, Teggart differed little from so many others of his ilk, and whatever the personal unhappiness it may have brought him, these discordant notes penned during periods of despondency, were not in anyway inferior to his other 'brighter' verse, and often have an emotional impact that is rarely found elsewhere in his work.

Teggart's American nature poems, though obviously differing in content, manifest a similar approach to those which featured the landscapes of East Dunbartonshire or North Armagh. As ever, with his observant eye he was able to seek out the beauty

---

[24] *Springfield Republican*, September 1895.
[25] *'Remembrance'*, *Springfield Republican*, October 1895.
[26] *'The Music of Sorrow'*, *Springfield Republican*, April 1907.

in nature, be it bird, flower, tree or plant and graphically describe them with an accuracy and vividness that leaves an indelible impression on the reader's mind. Once read, who can forget the scarlet tanager *'among dark boughs and branches dim'*; the red pines on Mount Tom, *'storm-battered, great-souled, grand'*; the crimson columbines, *'sweet gypsies of the mountain path'*; the blue jay on the banks of the Quaboag river that *'flashes under the cerulean sky'*; *'the sudden swirl of snowbirds in a downward flight'*; the August firefly whose flashes *'gems the darkness'*; *'the sunny piece of pasture land'* on Springfield's Ames Hill or the noble elms and giant oaks that *'make dance for joy the poet's eye'*.

All these vibrant images are typical of Teggart's ability to encapsulate, with a few strokes of the pen, the essential beauty of the living world around him. Though he could find something to delight his eye, even in the city, he was only truly happy when roaming the acres of Forest Park or the slopes of Mount Tom or Mount Holyoke, away from *'the reeking city's deep and deaf'ning roar'* to *'walk where Nature converse holds with man.'* [27]

Some of Teggart's American poems reflect his genuine concern for the welfare of birds and animals. On one occasion, whilst walking in Forest Park, he chanced upon a group of caged skylarks, in the municipal aviary. The scene caused him so much distress that he was moved to write:

> *Poor hapless things! pent up while you—*
>   *Mad for the month of May,*
> *Should soaring be in yonder blue*
>   *So glorious today.*
>
> *And gazing at you, ill-starred birds,*
>   *So beautiful and shy,*
> *My sorrow grew too deep for words,*
>   *At heart in tears was I.*[28]

He struck a similar note in another poem, *'Our Dumb Animals'*, published in the columns of the prestigious *New York Times*. This time his solicitude embraced domestic pets and animals who, as he argued, in contravention of contemporary opinion, deserved humanitarian treatment irrespective of *'whether they have souls or not,'* for they all can feel the pain when ill-treated, or as he put it:

> *They shrink before the cruel blow,*
> *They moan, they groan, they hirpling go,*
> *They cannot speak, they only know.*
>
> *In barn and byre, in stall and sty,*
> *There's still some soft beseeching eye*
> *Appeals to our humanity.*[29]

---

[27] 'The Welcome of the Fields', *Springfield Republican*, April 1903.
[28] 'Caged Skylarks in Forest Park', *Springfield Republican*, May 1902.
[29] *Portadown News*, August 1901.

Written in the summer of 1901, the poet's message was almost avant-garde in a world which, at that time, paid scant attention to the well-being of animals.

Though the Scottish and American poems have much to recommend them, it is undoubtedly those written in his own native dialect for which he will be best remembered, and on which posterity will base his reputation. It is in these poems which describe the sights and sounds of the boglands and the everyday activities of its inhabitants, that we find the essential Teggart at his very best. As D J O'Donoghue, the Dublin editor and literary critic commented: *'I propose to write an article on Teggart's poems, which I think deserve to rank beside those of Moira O'Neill*[30] *and John Stevenson.*[31] *The dialect seems admirably true.'*[32]

He was especially impressed with Teggart's description of bogland birds, citing as an example, the quail or *'wet-my-lip'* which he considered superior to the swallows depicted in Edward Dowden's[33] poem, *'In the Cathedral Close'*.[34] High praise indeed, considering the latter's exalted reputation at the time. In truth, O'Donoghue could have chosen any number of superb examples from the rich variety on offer, for nearly every aspect of the bogland environment is portrayed with such dexterity and authenticity that the reader is magically transported through the mists of time to a world pulsing with life and vitality. The wee mosscheeper making *'sweet the throbbing air'*, *'the rumble of the wheels'* of the red and blue turf carts returning from Portadown, the red sunset that lights up the bogland valley *'with candles of the Lord'*, the bluecap *'making merry among the orchard boughs'*, the curling blue turf smoke *'o'er the low thatched cabin'*, the tolling of the Milltown bell *'the hours of sorrow markin'*', the sonsy belles *'delightin' more than one townland'*, the blue-eyed flower bud *'mild with the grace of maidenhood'*, the sound of the distant surf *'tumbling on Lough Neagh shore'*, the humble dandelion *'blooming at the ramper's edge'*, the honeyed clover *'sweet with its wealth of wild perfume'*, the blush of dawn seen *'through leafless tops of dreaming trees'*, the old footstick across the bogland drain over which *'the barefoot lass skips on her way to school'*, the sylvan parish of Tartaraghan *'watered by the silver Bann'* - all these evocative images, and many more, were sketched by a masterhand.

Teggart's Irish poems embodied many of the themes that had latterly occupied the minds of the earlier rhyming weavers: rural superstitions, seasonal agricultural tasks, local characters, pretty girls and the love pangs of youth - all of them described in an idiomatic and vivid language that engages and holds the reader's attention. Like all rural communities in mid-nineteenth century Ulster, many of the country folk of North Armagh readily accepted the existence of a hidden

---

[30] Aka Nesta Higginson (1864-1955). She published two volumes of poems: *Songs of the Glens of Antrim* (1909) and *More Songs of the Glens of Antrim* (1921). Mother of Molly Keane, the celebrated Kildare novelist.

[31] Irish poet (1850-1932). Probably best known for *Pat M'Carty, Farmer of Antrim: his rhymes, with a setting*, London 1905.

[32] *Irish Book Lover II*, August 1910, pp.92-3.

[33] Cork born critic, biographer and poet (1843-1913). Professor of English Literature at Trinity College, Dublin and sometime lecturer at Oxford and Cambridge.

[34] *Irish Book Lover V*, August 1913, p.203.

preternatural world populated by spectral figures. It was widely believed that apparitions or *'big, black boogles'*, as Teggart termed them, lay in wait for the unwary *'at every hawthorn gap'* and that banshees, those harbingers of imminent death, could be heard groaning and wailing as they spirited their victims *'down to dismal purgatory'*. It was also firmly rooted in the collective psyche that the thorn bush was possessed of magical powers that could turn aspirations into reality. Hence, it was quite common to see *'a rag upon a thorn'*, put there by some individual hoping to ward off ill-fortune or receive some sought-after outcome. There was also a similar faith in the supernatural capability of the so-called *'spey wife'* to foretell the future before *'. . . limping off with a spit and a cough/When you your white shilling have paid.'*[35]

In one of his most engaging poems, *'The Peasant Folk's Hallowe'en'*, Teggart described the various activities of the young people on Hallowe'en night when superstitions abounded. In an attempt to divine her prospective marriage partner, a teenage girl would place hazel nuts, each one symbolising a particular suitor, very close to the fire and when they exploded across the kitchen floor, the one that travelled furthest represented her future husband. Other youthful activities associated with the occasion included bobbing for apples, eating boxty and harassing nosy, unpopular neighbours:

> *Although outside it teems an' pours—*
> *The boys, about sixteen,*
> *Are busy runnin', rappin' doors*
> *With turf - at Hallowe'en.*
>
> *While speech and laughter both are stilled,*
> *For all his spyin' keen,*
> *Pilgarlic,*[36] *finds his cabin filled*
> *Wi' smoke at Hallowe'en.*[37]

Despite the fact that the Birches folk had to work extremely hard for their living, life was not altogether joyless, and this mood was reflected in a number of Teggart's poems that relate to the seasonal activities of the agricultural year. Even ploughing, which was a slow and laborious task, was greeted with marked enthusiasm as the small farmers seized the opportunity to welcome the Spring with all its promise of new life and growth:

> *They're ploughin' at the Birches,*
> *The barrow's in the hill,*
> *An' the land they cannot purchase*
> *Is the land they're doomed to till . . .*

---

[35] *'The Spey Wife'*, Springfield Republican, August 1902.
[36] A sneaky, disagreeable fellow.
[37] Springfield Republican, October 1898.

> *On the brown twigs turnin' sappy*
> *   Raindrops sparkle night an' morn,*
> *And the bog folk all are happy*
> *   When the bud is on the thorn*[38].

Similarly, when it came to the time for harvesting the flax crop, there was much good humour in evidence as the labourers went about their task with energy and purpose:

> *That jokes pass' round, ye well may ken;*
> *   And spite of aching backs,*
> *That peals of laughter reach us when*
> *   A dozen women, helped by men,*
> *Are busy pullin' flax.*[39]

Even though the Birches undoubtedly had its fair share of eccentric and charismatic characters, Teggart chose to write about the ordinary, salt-of-the-earth individuals whose modest demeanour, integrity and industry he particularly admired. Amongst these was Ben the thatcher, one of those most fortunate of people who found work a pleasurable activity. Rising early in the morning, he whistled merrily as he painstakingly ensured that *'no loose wisps'* or *'tight bulges'* spoilt the final appearance of his handiwork. He had much in common with another Ballinary resident, old Ned, who spent his days laboriously breaking up stones for road mending, taking only the occasional rest to smoke his pipe or eat his lunch. *'Stout of heart'* he pegged away in all weathers, and though he largely missed out on *'joyous life and all its pleasures'* he was content with his lot. Much older than either of the above, was Granny Roe. Born in the last decade of the eighteenth century, she was already an old woman when the poet was just a schoolboy. Despite the considerable age difference, he recollected her with much affection, noting her dexterity at the spinning wheel and warmly approving of her legendary kindness and charity:

> *Gowpens of meal, full oft, full oft,*
> *   Poured from her kindly han',*
> *Some homeless mother's face made soft*
> *   Or cheered the beggarman.*[40]

It is evident that Teggart had the greatest respect for all these individuals and the peasant society in which they moved. After all, they were his own people and though circumstances ordained that a large part of his life was to be spent in distant climes, he never for a moment forgot the humble country folk of his native parish. As he once made clear in some verses, published in the winter of 1902, he had no wish to write about *'belted lords'* or *'dames of high degree'*, preferring instead to celebrate '. . . *the lords of loam and clay'* and the dignity of manual labour:

---

[38] *'When the Bud is on the Thorn'*, *Portadown News*, May 1900.
[39] *'Pulling Flax'*, *Springfield Republican*, October 1902.
[40] *'Granny Roe'*, *Boston Pilot*, September 1906.

All honour to the horny hands
    That dig and delve and toil,
And make to laugh the niggard lands,
    And plant with seed the soil,
No palsied poet, shunned by Pan
    Is he - the nobler made,
Who sings with all the might of man,
    The Shovel and the Spade.[41]

Apart from his well-documented affairs with Jane and Mary Mitton, there is clear evidence that Teggart found many other local girls particularly attractive, including blue-eyed Teresa from Derrykarn, rosy-lipped Betty of Derrylee, Daisy Tennyson, the pride of Columbkill and dark-haired Mary of Drumcree. The lyrics which featured these local beauties, together with those which extolled the qualities of the anonymous 'belles' of Ballinary, Clonmacate, Derrykeevin and Derryagh, are surely destined to be amongst the most popular examples of his verse. A couple of stanzas from the *'The Belle of Derryagh'* are illustrative of the lively, confident tone that is typical of the genre:

These boys from up the country,
    They boast about their girls
Wi' cheeks as red as rosies,
    An' teeth as white as pearls;
An' then they tell how fine it is
    To sue for favours - Bagh!
They never coaxed at milkin' time
    The Belle of Derryagh.

The ould men laugh an' listen,
    An' then wi' them agree;
The young blades sit an' snigger
    Then slyly wink at me.
These boys from up the country
    Have been enchanted - Bagh!
They never lapped their arms aroun'
    The Belle of Derryagh.[42]

Mention should also be made of one final poem in this category - *'Lizzie Wall'*. On this occasion, the inspiration of his muse, was not a local girl but a former colleague at St Nicholas' National School in Cork. One of the most bewitching and captivating of colleens, her looks were more than enough *'to hold a saint in thrall'*. The jaunty rhythm is totally in keeping with the tone of the poem and reflects the poet's youthful exuberance at that time:

---

[41] *'The Shovel and the Spade'*, *Springfield Republican,* February 1902.
[42] *Portadown News*, August 1901.

Oft in the gloaming, when we went roaming,
  The round moon rising o'er the hills to see,
We'd our walk abandon when the bells of Shandon
  Pealed out sudden o'er the rippling Lee.
Oh, as if still near them, I think I hear them,
  I seem to listen to each rise and fall,
Of their silver chiming, till I'm once more climbing
  The dusky hillside with Lizzie Wall.[43]

Teggart also wrote some love poems of a much more tender and personal nature. They have all the hallmarks of having been inspired by painful, personal experience. Chief amongst these were a number of *'Bogland Love Songs'* devoted to the mysterious Mary of Ballinary. Though he never reveals her full identity, there is no doubt that she was a childhood sweetheart, almost certainly a school friend and a close neighbour. Whoever this bogland girl may have been, she certainly captured the poet's heart. With blue eyes, red cheeks and dark black hair, she was a vision of rustic beauty that left an indelible impression on the adolescent poet. As he readily admitted, it was love at first sight:

Heavens! When I met her first,
  Such a rush of joy came o'er me,
All the wide world seemed to burst
  Into sudden blooms, before me.

Even the sound of her voice in the lane had an electrifying effect upon him:

Rapt upon her speech I hung,
  Till, as if our souls were mated,
To the music of her tongue,
  Every pulse in me vibrated.[44]

Unfortunately, his youthful infatuation was to end in disappointment as Mary eventually married another suitor, leaving him *'shattered among men'*. Puppy love it may have been but these sensuous and touching lyrics have an individuality that distinguishes them from the rest of his verse. Even in middle age he reacted to the news of Mary's death with words that eloquently betrayed the depth of his grief:

Cold the mould is now about thee,
  Lone thou in the grave dost lie,
All the sunlit world, without thee,
  Empty is, and hopeless I.[45]

Irrespective of the specific theme, his acutely observed depiction of bogland life in North Armagh over a century ago, is unparalleled by any other writer.

---

[43] *Springfield Republican*, April 1901.
[44] *'The Voice of Mary'*, *Portadown News*, July 1901.
[45] *'A Monody for Mary'*, *Portadown News*, July 1902.

Though Teggart was not an innovator as regards poetic technique, his range of stanza forms, metrical patterns and rhyme schemes was varied and comprehensive. Thou he experimented with ten or even twelve line stanzas, he usually adopted four or eight line verses for the majority of his poems, choosing the former for *'Columbkill'* and *'The Bullfinch'* and the latter for *'The Sally Tree'* and *'The Belle of Clonmacate'*.   For the most part, these uncomplicated forms had equally straightforward rhythmic patterns, with three or four accented syllables in each line, and monosyllabic end rhymes.   The following extract from *'The Belle of Columbkill'* is typical of his style:

> *Oh, black as any crow her hair;*
> > *An' as the vi'lets blue*
> *The eyes whose silken lashes snare*
> > *The heart that comes to woo,*
> *An' red as moonicks in the moss*
> > *When they their ripeness show,*
> *The lips the zephyrs steal across,*
> > *Then honey laden go.*[46]

The simple, unsophisticated technique so evident above, was ideally suited to Teggart's customary subject matter - the everyday lives of ordinary bogland people and the spartan landscape they inhabited. It is also worth noting that the poet's imagery was equally conventional - her hair *'black as any crow'* and her eyes *'as the vi'lets blue'*. Though these similes border on clichés, even when they were written a hundred odd years ago, their very 'unremarkability' is very much in keeping with the poet's desire to portray the belle as the epitome of unadorned, natural beauty.

Occasionally, Teggart would essay more unusual and complex stanza forms with six or uniquely, nine lines. The former was almost totally reserved for his Scottish verse which, influenced by Burns, embraced the traditional Standard Habbie format. This verse form featured appropriately in a handful of his Caledonian poems, including *'Anither Year'*, *'The Bard Greets Himsel''* and *'To the New Year'*. The rhythmic structure of these poems is very similar to that so commonly found in his Irish verse -iambic trimeters and tetrameters.   Though he seldom departed from such conventional forms and metrical patterns, he was certainly aware of the effects that could be achieved by subtle variations. In one of his most stirring of Scottish poems, *'The Rose O'Rochsilloch'*, the underlying anapaestic rhythm, the internal rhyme and the alliterative phrases combine to create the rousing, upbeat tone appropriate to the poet's theme:

> *Ye may talk o' your Jeans, your Tibs an' your Teens,*
> > *O' your lilies that bloom on the lea;*
> *But, all said and done, an' excellin' her none,*
> > *The Rose O'Rochsilloch for me!*[47]

---

[46] *Portadown News*, November 1900.
[47] *Springfield Republican*, July 1908.

It must be said that there were times - thankfully very few - when Teggart's technical ability seemed to desert him: On these occasions, rhymes appear forced, metre becomes defective and syntax is uncharacteristically awkward. All of these imperfections are apparent in the following stanza from one of his American lyrics, describing fish in a forest pool:

> *And swimming here, mouths up stream, wee minnows.*
> *By gentle current gently swayed,*
> *And darting oft, as flies white chaff when winnows*
> *The wind from the water displayed*
> *Well their spry gambols, as swift as in o's*
> *And at out o's they gaily played:*
> *Hither darting thither, darting and then*
> *Fish - still all, their wee mouths up stream again.*[48]

The lapses are particularly regrettable as he was quite capable, as he showed on many occasions, of producing the most carefully crafted verse. In one of his poems, Bryant advised budding poets to:

> *Seize the great thought, ere yet its power be past,*
> *And bind, in words, that fleet emotion fast.*[49]

It was a definition of poetry that Teggart seemed happy to endorse. Once he had written a poem, which he often did at great speed, he seldom revisited it again and only on rare occasions did he redraft earlier compositions. When he did, he was quite capable of ironing out technical flaws and enhancing the original versions. It is surely significant that when he was asked by Charles Barrows to contribute to his Springfield anthology, the poems he submitted not only displayed his ability to handle a range of poetic forms but also highlighted his technical mastery of the poet's craft. Amongst those included by Barrows were four of Teggart's best bogland lyrics: *'When the Carts come Home'*, *'The Old Cow Loanin''*, *'Autumn at Derryagh'* and *'The Belle of Ballinary'*.

Though a number of his Scottish poems - *'Jenny Gow'*, *'Aboon Ben Lomond'* and *'Keepin' Tryst'*, for example, and several of his American lyrics - *'Crowned with Glory'*, *'At Dewy Dusk in August'* and *'Remembrance'*, are well-deserving of the reader's attention, it is those verses inspired by his native boglands that will inevitably attract most praise. To the casual observer, the boglands was an unattractive region - windswept, bleak and barren, a hostile environment in which men toiled and sweated in their efforts to extract a living from ground that afforded them little encouragement. Though he readily admitted that such a terrain provided little *'to meet the wants of man'*, Teggart was able to see what others could not, that this apparently uninviting and impoverished landscape was, in reality, a place of great beauty. From what most people would consider unpromising material, he produced verse of great charm and originality, often lively, sometimes pensive, but

---

[48] *'A Woodland Cascade'*, *Springfield Republican*, January 1904.
[49] *'The Poet'*, op. cit., p.295.

always imbued with a genuine affection for the subject matter, be it the commonest fishergirl or lowly turf cutter, the daisies on a roadside verge, his grandfather's laburnum, watercress in a running drain, or the humblest of weeds in a field of oats. Such an ability to find beauty in the commonplace should not surprise us, for Teggart had a perceptive eye that took in every nuance of the natural world, especially that of his native environment to which he was attached with a strong, emotional bond that only death could sever.

His poetry was, and is, a celebration and an affirmation of life in all its myriad moods and forms, and that, despite all the vicissitudes that beset his own existence. He was, like his contemporary, Gerard Manley Hopkins, very aware of the grandeur of God's creation and it was his special gift to seek out the beauty that lived *'deep down things'*,[50] in even the unlikeliest of places or individuals and bring it to the readers' attention in such a way that they too share in the poet's insight. At his best, in a phrase borrowed from Seamus Heaney, Teggart *'made vocal the regional and the particular . . . in an authentic, lyrical utterance at the meeting-point between social realism and conventional romanticism'*.[51]

Like Burns, Teggart's work has a universal appeal that will strike a sympathetic cord with poetry lovers everywhere, and indeed even with those people who in the ordinary course of events do not care much for poetry at all, for there is nothing too perplexing or obscure in his verse. It is readily accessible to all and it is hoped that the reader will find much to admire and enjoy in this volume, but ultimately, as for every poet, the poems must be allowed to speak for themselves.

---

[50] Gardner, W.H., *God's Grandeur, Poems and Prose of Gerard Manley Hopkins,* London, 1953, p.27.
[51] *'In the Country of Convention', Preoccupations,* 1980.

SCOTTISH POEMS

THE SANDS OF TROON

Though bonnie are the banks o' Ayr
        And braw the braes o' Doon,
Our shore of beauty has its share—
        The silver sands o' Troon!

The bonnie sands, the silver sands
        That aft hae filled me shoon,
Still trickle through my empty hands—
        The silver sands o' Troon!

How aft a laddie I hae run
        And played and jumped in June,
And tossed with my twa feet in fun
        The silver sands o' Troon!

How aft my lassie there I've met
        Beneath the shining moon,
And traced a heart to please my pet
        Upon the sands o' Troon!

And though upon a foreign shore
        My morn has come to noon,
I daily long to tread once more
        The silver sands o' Troon!

The day of life is short alas!
        And night comes on too soon,
But ne'er from memory's page shall pass
        The silver sands o' Troon!

And when the sands of life run low,
        'Twill be a blessed boon
If God allows my soul to go
        Home o'er the sands of Troon!

AT THE BIRTHPLACE OF BURNS

"There was a lad was born in Kyle"
(Robert Burns)

A laigh bit biggin by the road—
    The level road that leads frae Ayr,
Of genius ance the trig abode,
    Is noo a treasure kept wi' care.

And white as driven snaw the walls,
    The stanes and porches white as snaw;
And where the gowden sunlicht falls
    Wee gowans by the gable wa'.

Stanch-built, to warstle wi' the storm,
    Compact it stands and sturdy still;
The ruif o' thack is thick and warm,
    And sonsy every window sill.

That threshold owre i've never stept,
    Nor ken I if the rooms are fair;
A bashfu' tremor always kept
    Me from in haste intrudin' there.

If the inside o't ye wad see,
    Step ben, my freen, and view it a';
It may to you a memory be,
    A pleasant ane when far awa.

While Love stood by wi' open arms,
    Here first was oped the bonnie ee
Whilk saw in Nature a' the charms
    That ithers aft pretend to see.

Here wi' some jingle on his lip,
    Some sang that down the ages chimes,
While faintly blinked the fadin' dip,
    Amid the reek he wrote his rhymes.

Saft! Let us roun' the ingle keek!
    See! There is Robbie i' his chair!
The ploughboy's rose is on his cheek
    And some one's left her kisses there.

Oh' in the love-lit days o' youth,
    How bricht the prospect maun hae been!
Heaven - Highland Mary's heart o' truth,
    And bliss - a blink of bonnie Jean.

Lang may the lave admire his hame!
        Gie me the scenes o'er which he smiled;
In these days as in his the same,
        The poet still is Nature's child.

Noo - Turn and view the hills sae brown,
        The heather hills - and - Bide a wee!
Just hear the Doon go bearing down
        His siller tribute to the sea!

This side the Brig is Alloway Kirk,
        Roofless it stands to sun and rain;
Fu' brave were he at midnicht mirk
        Wha'd willing loiter there alane.

Through distant groves the dimpled Ayr
        Goes singing to the tasseled tree,
That mirrored in it sees how fair
        The grey-green birk o' Burns should be.

Luved ane! Where'er thy footsteps prest,
        Where'er thy dark eyes roving sped,
Some daisy blushing bares her breast,
        Some bluebell hangs her dewy head.

What thing has life on field or farm,
        What tree or flower but doth possess
And seem to yield a double charm
        Sin' Burns touched a' wi' tenderness?

To some the hoose may seem forlorn
        As harried nest upo' the lea;
The lark has flown that flushed the morn,
        The face o' morn wi' melodie.

But a' the fields and groves around,
        Refreshed wi' ilka spring's return,
Rejoice as when first Robin found
        The barefoot lassie by the burn.

Come, leave behind the hushed abode,
        The muse nae langer bideth there;
Nor witch, nar warlock haunts the road,
        The level road that leads to Ayr.

Wha'd shun the Tam O'Shanter Inn?
        The tourist frae it seldom turns
Without this thocht - That deep within
        Auld Scotia's heart lives Robert Burns!

CAMPSIE GLEN[1]

Wha wadna leave the reek o' toun,
      The mouldy haunts o' men,
To danner where the linn leaps doun
      And glides through Campsie Glen?

Amang the rocks it nimbly runs,
      Runs lightly but and ben,
Or, spreading oot itself, it suns
      Like glass, in Campsie Glen.

That pretty flower which lovers prize —
      (Her name ye a' maun ken,)
Blinks owre the dubs, and bluer eyes
      Ne'er gladdened Campsie Glen.

The blooming sprigs o' blaeberrie,
      Spray-wet, are sparkling when
The sunlight fa's sae saucily
      Aglin on Campsie Glen.

The linit loups owre a dreepin' rock
      Whose ferns, - fu' nine or ten,
And frall' upon that mossy frock,
      Glory in Campsie Glen.

Frae stane to stane, (her haun' in mine)
      Aft hae I jumped wi' Jen!
Losh! How her hazel een did shine
      Wi' glee in Camspie Glen!

The sun that rises red and wet,
      Or fades aye at the fen,
Ere nicht maun aye come oot to get
      A glimpse o' Campsie Glen.

In days gane by when hearts beat high,
      (Maist hearts were high-strung then!)
Fu' oft the spy, but ne'er the sky,
      Glowred sair on Campsie Glen.

Aboon the fa', up on each wa'
      Paints Flora wi' her pen!
O many a bluebell loves to blaw
      Sun-glossed in Campsie Glen.

---

[1] Situated near Lennoxtown in East Dunbartonshire - now a designated conservation area.

Kissed rowanberries blush aboon
        The brownie's bracken den,
And mellowing wi' the harvest moon
        Glow red in Campsie Glen.

Plumped weel wi' heather buds and bells,
        The muirfowl, cock and hen,
Forsake the fells to roam the dells
        And glades o' Campsie Glen.

Fu' blithe in May the blackbird sings,
        Rolls rebel notes the wren,
Och! ither touns have dust o' kings—
        Glasgow has Campsie Glen!

And lang ere I am auld and grey,
        Ere childhood comes agen,
Some bonnie day I hope to hae
        A glimpse o' Campsie Glen.

In Campsie Glen, 1905.

THE BONNIE ROSE O'AIRLIE

When I was but a wee bit thing
    An' sabbed fu' aft an' sairly,
To hush the wean my nurse wad sing
    'The Bonnie House o' Airlie'.[2]

An' when I speeled to boyhood's brae,
    Amang the woods o' Fairlie,
Robed in my plaid I learned to play
    'The Bonnie House o' Airlie'.

Roved now beyond the rollin' brine,
    I hear it twanged but rarely,
An' when I dae - this heart o' mine
    Goes sabbin' back to Airlie.

For there in time, I spied a bud,
    An never dewdrap pearly
Shone on a blossom o' my bluid
    Sweet as the Rose o'Airlie.

Her clan was mine in the lang syne,
    And though looked on as barely
O' the same hoose - my heart ran wine,
    Won by the Rose o' Airlie.

They frowned on me as on a frere,
    A fickle-hearted ferlie;
They thocht I lo'ed her yellow gear
    And not the Rose o' Airlie.

Then spak' I out wi' princely pride.
    "Come hanselled weel or sparely,
I want the leddy for my bride,
    An' no' the House o' Airlie."

I cared na for her time-dark towers,
    I spak' up fair and squarely,
"The warld is rich in gowden flowers—
    There's but ae Rose o' Airlie."

Oh, when my ain bit humble wa'
    Wi' buds was covered fairly,
In blush and bloom I only saw
    The bonnie Rose o' Airlie.

---

[2] Seat of the Ogilvy family, Earls of Airlie, in Angus. The poem's title is taken from a popular Scottish ballad, *'The Bonnie House of Airlie'*, mentioned in Robert Louis Stevenson's novel, *'Kidnapped'*.

An' feared I was, fu' mony a time,
        Lest some bedizened carlie,
Some border lad her bower wad climb
        And clasp the Rose o' Airlie.

But perverse fate - the worser will
        That warps what we'd do yarely,
Lost me the prize I sigh for still,
        The bonnie Rose o' Airlie.

And so, in lands beyond the sea,
        I mourn baith late and early
The bonnie bud I'll never pree,
        The radiant Rose o' Airlie.

Nae wonner sigh an' sab I should,
        An' greet fu' sad an' sairly,
Anither lo'ed an' picked an' pu'd
        My bonnie Rose o' Airlie.

The tune that dried the bairnie's tear
        Doth noo unman me fairly;
My heart still sorrows when I hear
        'The Bonnie House o' Airlie'.

MIRREN[3]

Weel, by St Mirren! - your hair is red;
    But your eyes are saft an' blue;
An' your lips are twa strawberries, fed
    On sunlicht an' on dew;
An' - never!- what was that you said?
    Your name is Mirren, too!
        Weel, ma heid is whirrin',
        But here's tae ye, Mirren,
    An' your een sae saft an' blue.

You're a tall an' strappin', sonsie lass;
    Your coaties kiss your knee;
Ye rise wi' the lark, an' oot tae grass
    Tak' the kye, richt saucily!—
An' there's ne'er a laddie does ye pass
    But he gets a blink o' your ee.
        Weel, ma heid is whirrin',
        But here's tae ye, Mirren,
    An' your saft an' sweet blue ee.

I hae seen ye when the March winds cauld
    Bleak owre the hillside blew;
I hae seen ye the wee lammie fauld
    In your plaid, - an' hug it, too;
I hae seen ye when the cuckoo called,
    An' the lambs were buntin' you.
        Weel, ma heid is whirrin',
        But here's tae ye, Mirren,
    An' your een sae saft an' blue.

I hae seen ye wi' the shepherd lad
    Below the hawthorn tree,
An' the faithful' collies barkit glad
    Sic a bonnie sight tae see!
It may gien ye joy the mirth ye had,
    But it wasna sae wi' me.
        Weel, ma heid is whirrin',
        But here's tae ye, Mirren,
    An' your saft an' sweet blue ee.

Ye wark in the fields, ye wark in the byre,
    Ye are warkin' when ye woo;
The cocks in the midden craw an' admire
    When ye shake ower them your shoe;
An' yet, wi' me there is nae maid shyer,

---

[3] Elizabeth Mirren, born 1854; married 1876 Andrew McKim in Old Kilpatrick, Dunbatonshire, about 15 miles from Kirkintilloch.

Nae lass mair blate than you.
        Weel, ma heid is whirrin,
        But here's tae ye, Mirren,
An' your een sae saft an' blue.

I heard ye when ye sang sae sweet
        'I'd lay me down an' dee';
An' lovers in it seemed to meet
        An' tremble 'neath the tree—
An' the grass shed tears around your feet,
        Ye sang sae tenderly!
        Weel, my heid is whirrin',
        But here's tae ye, Mirren,
An' your saft an' sweet blue ee.

HER LOVER'S LASS

She isna bonny a bit,
        Not as the warld ca's bonny;
Yet her saft brown een wi' love are lit,
        An' her lips are wat wi' honey.

There are nae roses upo' her cheeks,
        Nae red blooms warth the kissin,'
An' yet, when this beautiful spirit speaks,
        The Lord himsel' micht listen.

Also, I ken if a kiss were laid
        On either cheek's white clover,
It wad spread an' spread - without her aid,
        Her face an' her neck a' over.

Yet, she's no bonny a bit,
        Tae those wha'll ne'er discover
How her face an'her een as wi' flame are lit
        When she clings to the lips o' her lover.

THE BONNY SCOTCH BLUEBELL

When March win's blaw the caps o' snaw
    Frae aff the Campsie fells,
On Luggie's banks an' borders blaw
    The bonny Scotch bluebells,
    The glossy dark bluebells,
The flowers that sweeten mony a song—
    The bonny Scotch bluebells.

When to the tender heart o' Spring,
    Love's song the mavis tells;
Low winds inhale their sweets an' swing
    The bonny Scotch bluebells,
    The glossy dark bluebells,
The flowers that bloom in mony a song—
    The bonny Scotch bluebells.

When mounds o' new-mown hay perfume
    The daisy-dappled dells,
Alang the banks o' Kelvin bloom
    The bonny Scotch bluebells,
    The glossy dark bluebells,
The flowers that bloom in many a song—
    The bonny Scotch bluebells.

When a' the air, frae sea to sea.
    Is fraught wi' fragrant smells,
The weans an' wee ones pu' wi' glee
    The bonny Scotch bluebells,
    The glossy dark bluebells,
The flowers that bloom in mony a song—
    The bonny Scotch bluebells.

When spreads o'er a' the autumn hush—
    When lone the redbreast dwells,
Softly he chants frae field and bush
    The dirge o' the bluebells,
    The glossy dark bluebells,
The flowers that bloom in mony a song—
    The bonny Scotch bluebells.

When cauld win's blaw, when winter snaw
    Lies deep in a' the dells,
Then in our memories 'tis they blaw—
    The bonny Scotch bluebells,
    The glossy dark bluebells,
The flowers embalmed in mony a song—
    The bonny Scotch bluebells.

JENNY'S HAZEL EEN

Hae years an' years passed owre me since,
    Or was it but yestreen
In Fairlie Glen[4] I gat a glimpse
    O' Jenny's hazel een?

The dews were eyes to every leaf
    That downward seemed to lean
To catch a glimpse - however brief,
    O' Jenny's hazel een.

The blackbird fluted low and sweet
    Amang the hawthorn's green;
He, too, seemed mair than glad to greet
    Dear Jenny's hazel een.

Though half asleep, wee gowans blushed
    The blades o' grass between;
Then slept fu' sound - to dreaming hushed
    By Jenny's hazel een.

One star from its blue throne above
    Looked down upon the scene—
The very planets were in love
    Wi' Jenny's hazel een.

Nae wonner maist things should them loe—
    For never hae I seen
A sicht sae sweet at fa' o' dew
    As Jenny's hazel een.

The licht in them at set o' sun,
    Sae bonnie was - I ween
It was her happy soul that shone
    Through Jenny's hazel een.

Since then there's been of joy a dearth,
    For still comes me between
An' a' the fairest things on earth,
    Dear Jenny's hazel een.

If doesna seem a lang time since,
    It was but life's yestreen
In Fairlie Glen I gat a glimpse
    O' Jenny's hazel een.

---

[4] Small wooded valley with a number of spectacular waterfalls, situated close to the small village of Fairlie in North Ayrshire.

KEEPIN' TRYST

The gowden day has closed his gates,
    An' noo where nane may see,
The lass o' Luggie water waits
    An' watches lone for me.

Yet strath an' burn hae I to cross,
    An' mony a wa' to stride,
An' waur than a' - the Lenzie moss[5]
    Is unco dark an' wide.

A day where the grey lintee cheeps,
    An' the blue plovers fly,
I hae been busy sneddin' neeps,
    An' wet and cauld am I.

But thinkin' o' the lass distraught,
    Her brow bent down a wee
Lest she at keepin' tryst be caught—
    Gie's lightnin's wings to me.

Richt mad I hae no roarin' fa'
    Or foamin' flood to swim,
A ba' I bound o'er dyke an' wa',
    A coot the moss I skim.

Still thinkin' the bit lassie on.
    An' loupin' owre the whins,
Wi' cap in haun' fu' soon I staun'
    Where Luggie water rins.

Wi' safe excuses nane to say,
    Nor havers richt or wrang,
I just blirt oot, "O lassie, hae
    I kept ye waitin' lang?"

An' then I hae her in my arms,
    An' soon her heirt an' mine
Luve-shielded frae the warld's alarms—
    Are makin' music fine.

And when, after a breathin' space,
    Her bonnie lips I pree,
The welcome shinin' in her face
    Is news eneuch for me.

---

5   One hundred and four acres of birch woodland and raised bog, eight miles north east of Glasgow.

An' yet she says her mammy scolds
    An' flytes her a' day long;
An' that her dour auld daddie holds
    Lad's love an idle song.

She whispers (an' her breath is spiced
    Wi' sweetness o' the rose)
To steal an' meet me at the tryst
    Is a' the joy she knows.

I tell her: "Teenie! i' the kirk
    That stands on Chryston hill,[6]
Before the bud is on the birk,
    Our weddin' hae we will."

Then sayin' "Guid-Nicht" at the byre,
    I bound the burn across,
Just as the moon - her face on fire
    Lights up the Lenzie moss.

Nicht havin' opened wide her gates,
    The stars come oot wi' glee,
An' noo 'tis my auld mither waits
    At Tintock Tap for me.

---

[6] Rolling moorland hill in North Lanarkshire.

ABOON BEN LOMOND

The Auld year's death when Winter dirges,
      When hung in black the widowed night
Glides awa' - an' the New emerges
      Fresh from the shinin' halls o' light,
When stars fade i' the stormy cary,
      When Love immortal lights the skies—
Oh! who shall say dear Highland Mary
      Asleep in Greenock kirkyard lies?

For, if some fond an' favoured mortals
      On leaving earth are spirit-born,
Then twa meet noo beside those portals
      Where melts in light the star of morn.
Far, far aboon Ben Lomond airy,
      The swirling snaw-rack far above,
This New-Year morn Burns meets wi' Mary,
      An' close beside the two walks Love.

The Doon an' Ayr dark currents shunning,
      Though hills lay cauld them aince between,
Around foam-hidden boulders running
      Meet where the ocean woods are green.
An' - clad in tartan an' glengary,
      The love-licht sparklin' in his ee,
Young Rabbie meets wi' Highland Mary
      Where gowans lauch alang the lea.

Bare-limbed the birk stands by the river,
      An' leafless noo the hawthorn hangs,
Nor shelters the wee birds that shiver
      Where sweet they thrilled their summer sangs.
But where the seasons, though they vary,
      Have less of shower than gowden shine,
The ploughboy sings where Highland Mary
      Maks life, indeed, a life divine.

The auld year's death when Winter dirges,
      When caped wi' snaw the pine trees stand,
When ocean sobs an' foams an' surges
      Around the ramparts of the land.
When stars but hide them i' the cary,
      When Love immortal lights the skies,
The bard an' blue-eyed Highland Mary
      Haud their New-year in Paradise.

ANITHER YEAR

A guid New-year, to a' who read
Or scramble through my Doric screed,
Weel writ, if but ae line in't lead
      Them ance to pause,
An' think hoo fast the seasons speed
      Doun time's dark jaws.

In youth, sae lang a towmond seemed—
So far awa, howe'er we dreamed
O' some set time, we a'most deemed
      'Twould ne'er come roun';
An' noo, howe'er we've planned and schemed,
      It comes owre soon.

Wi' us, sae fast the simmers flie
That we hae scarcely rubbed our e'e,
Or gat it opened richt to see
      One guid New-year,
Or hoo it warks, till in a wee
      Anither's here.

Oh, why sud youth sae lang to climb
To manhood, to prosaic prime,
To hights that only seem sublime
      Being unattained;
When bairntime's ane sweet flow o' rhyme
      Fresh an' unfeigned?

An' why sud manhood find sae brief
The year, that, ance a spotless leaf,
Is now owrewrit wi' groan an' grief,
      An' wat wi' tears;
When each day closed was a relief
      Frae that day's fears?

An' why sae far we'd hae it seem—
The morn, when frae this eerie dream
Of being borne on time's swift stream
      We maun awaken;
When aft by death we'd guid it deem
      To be owretaken?

However wild the nicht, and wan,
We ken the dark precedes the dawn;
That, too, was guid which noo is gone,
      An' this is clear—
For weel or woe we've entered on
      Anither year.

AILSA CRAIG

Craig of Ailsa, belted, bounded
      By the surging Irish sea;
Stark and stern and surf-surrounded,
      What are storms and tides to thee?

Safety rock of gull and gannet—
      In chaotic years lang syne,
Didst thou from some wand'ring planet
      Plunge hot-hissing in the brine?

Or, art thou a landmark only,
      Signal knowing not nor call;
An island-rock forlorn and lonely
      Where no human footsteps fall?

Firmly fixed and deeply planted,
      Still untoppled by the tides,
Oh, what moonlit waves have chanted
      Requiems round thy rocky sides!

In the deep sea firmly founded,
      Fathoms high above the brine,
Oh, what storms have pealed and pounded
      On that iron head of thine!

When sky-tempests o'er thee drifted,
      Oh the lesson sketched for me—
One stern summit lone uplifted
      High above a stormy sea.

When the seabird worn and weary
      Sought thee as the dove the ark—
All the deep below her dreary,
      All the sky above her dark.

Oh, how oft I wished my spirit—
      Worn as any wand'ring bird,
Might some sea-born isle inherit,
      Never storm or tempest-stirr'd.

"Paddy's Milestone"! Rock of Ailsa
      When the gannet, goose and gull
Fly as flies the capercailsie
      Far beyond the Sound of Mull.

Then it is when the herd laddie
        From a sunny hight and fair
See thee as the first rock Paddy
        Hails upon the coast of Ayr.

One, a dreaming, droning chappie,
        Into lands of musing led,
Sees thee when the seabirds happy
        Sun themselves upon thy head.

And although from hurried steamer,
        Men as in a vision vague
(Seeing not what haunts the dreamer)
        Get a view of Ailsa Craig.

One poor wand'rer o'er this planet,
        Sees, where'er his footsteps roam,
The island-rock where gull and gannet
        Find a haven and a home.

BURN'S GREAT-GRANDDAUGHTER
To Miss Jean Armour Burns Brown[7], Dumfries, Scotland

Jean Armour Burns, weel favoured lass,
    Your great-grand-daddie, in his day,
Could ne'er a smilin' kimmer pass
    But he had something sweet to say.

Behind his plough how aft he sang
    The merits o' the lovesome Jean
Wha thocht the shortest daytime lang
    Till rhymin' Robin came at e'en!

An' frae his hame in heaven now,
    I hae nae doubt but he can see,
Below the broad an' deep-arched brow,
    The starlight in your bonnie ee.

I, on your picture looking long,
    An' deeply touched, can see, by turns,
The dark eyes lit wi' tuneful song,
    The brow, the very look of Burns.

How aften when the shoots are green,
    An' buds the wayside bushes bear,
My fancy flies to mony a scene
    'Tween Nith an' Doon, and Doon an' Ayr!

Oh! how he in his matchless screeds
    Made Nature's children a' so dear,
The wildflowers an' the very weeds
    An' thistles blossom for him, here!

Weel may ye, Jean, be unco proud
    Of ane who as the years go by,
Still higher soars - a bard endowed
    Wi' special favour from on high.

If in your soul e'er thrills a thought
    That like a flash had quickened him
Who late and early wrote and wrought,
    That no dark byway might be dim.

Oh, treasure it as something sent
    From that unseen and unkenned sphere,
To teach your fond heart how he meant
    To show the world his meaning here.

---

[7] Born 1864; died 1937. Daughter of Thomas Brown and Jane Emma Burns and reputed to have had a marked resemblance to the Scottish poet.

There, Jean, be sure he's singing still,
    An' a' the nags he ever fed,
Are grazing on a greener hill
    Than any knowe o'erlooking Jed.

When I pass o'er the darker Doon,
    An' reach the smilin' fields an' fair,
I know I'll meet, be't night or noon,
    The couthie Bard of Coila, there.

An' when on white wings you arrive,
    My certes! But ye'll haud your breath,
An' stare, to see us a' alive,
    Victorious over time an' death.

This is my creed, Jean Armour Burns;
    I dinna ken what yours may be:
But love like mine forever turns
    From morrows to eternity.

An' noo while gowans in the grass
    The whitest sheets an' coaties shame,
I see the dark eyes, bonnie lass,
    That weel might lead a laddie hame.

I see the blue o' Scotia's skies,
    I see the winding banks o' Ayr,
I hear the Nith that sobs an' sighs
    For him who aften wandered there.

I see Peace wi' her pinions furled,
    Sae modest stand in one kirkyard,
The downcast eyes of half the world
    Mistake the vision for the Bard.

Ah kindly Jean, wha is it kens
    What shades wi' shining eyes appear
When poets, in earth's buts and bens
    Wake - knowing the new Dawn is near?

And, as to life, life always clings,
    I dream the dream that must come true;
The chiel who this rough ballad sings,
    Shall some day, somewhere, meet wi' you.

Miss Jean Armour Burns Brown (right) Great Granddaughter of Robert Burns, outside his house in Dumfries, c.1905. (Courtesy of Dumfries Museum)

ROWANBERRIES IN CAMPSIE GLEN

It's little - being city bred—
    Maist Glasgow bodies ken
About the berries, glossy red,
    To-day, in Campsie Glen,
It's little, - choked wi' smoor an reek—
    The pale-faced kimmers know
About the birds that peer an' peek
    Where rowanberries grow.
Yet, through the Clachan, near an' far,
    The youngest thrushes ken
How big the rowan bunches are,
    How ripe! in Campsie Glen.

Where pretty siskins sip an' pree,
    Where teal their tappins cool,
All graceful bends the rowan trees
    Above a glassy pool.
And while on that crowned head of hers
    The berries gleam an' glow,
If but a leaf upon her stirs,
    Its image stirs below.
Around her rise dark trees an' tall,
    One beech stands her beside,
And she - head bowed, among them all
    Is blushing like a bride.

Yet little - being lucre led—
    Maist Glasgow bodies ken
About the trees, or berries red,
    To-day in Campsie Glen,
An' less it is, aye choked wi reek,
    The croupy kimmers know
About how lovely - cheek to cheek —
    The rowanberries grow.
Or, when a shower quick outshook,
    Invites the shine, again,
How glossy-skinned the rowans look,
    How red! in Campsie Glen.

THE LUGGIE[8]

Oor hooses may be thacked wi' strae,
      Oor weavin' shaps be shoogie,
Baith front and back oor stane stairs black,
      But still we hae the Luggie,
The bonnie crystal Luggie.
      The burn that trots through alder lots
Wi' skim an' skip an' shoogie,
      O the bonnie Luggie,
The whimplin', windin' Luggie!
      May life's star set when we forget
The lovely, laughin' Luggie!

Sharp thorns an' whins may jag oor shins,
      The sheughs be wet an' shoogie,
But still we gang, or richt or wrang,
      Troot-fushin' i' the Luggie.
The bonnie sparklin' Luggie,
      The burn that sings an' sideways flings
Its foam sae white an' shoogie,
      O the bonnie Luggie,
The liltin', laughin' Luggie!
      May glade an' glen ramfoozle men
When we forget the Luggie!

River Luggie, near Kirkintilloch.

8   Tributary of River Kelvin near Kirkintilloch.

THE BARD GREETS HIMSEL' ON NEW YEAR'S EVE

Since few they be who care to greet
The puny bard of turf and peat;
The bogland poet's crouse conceit
        Is - need he tell?
Now, when the auld an' new year meet,
        To greet himsel'.

Hail! rhymer of red moss an' ling,
Of snipes that bleat, an' larks that sing,
Of weed an' bloom and like thing
        The bogs above!
Long may ye spread a warm soft wing
        O'er a' ye love.

In boyhood's days as unadvised
Ye gaed about wi' heirt disguised,
These things ye maun hae greatly prized,
        Deep loved - or how
Could ye, afar, uncatechized
        Sing o' them now?

Into your youthful' heirt - how deep
The blushing bogland's long wide sweep
Of mingled beauties, heap on heap,
        Must have sunk when
Earth wakened from her happy sleep,
        To gladden men.

When linnets drenched in every lane
Sought shelter frae the blast, in vain,
When blinding storms of sleet an' rain
        Swept hillsides bare,
Must oft hae lived in you again
        The Bard o'Ayr.

Like him ye loved the bonny lark,
The daisy blushin' in her sark,
The kiss that warmed the wintry dark
        O' barn or byre;
All things, indeed, that fanned the spark
        O' sacred fire.

Ye had the rosy bells o' ling
O'er which to rave an lilt an' sing,
The yorlin - yellower in the spring
        Than daffodil;
The tit-lark, too, that wet her wing
        In every rill.

Ye had your Mary an' your Jean—
Your loves wi' blue an' hazel een,
Kind heirts, an' mony a trusty freen
    Through stour an' strife,
To help ye owre - wi' conscience clean,
    The dubs o' life.

An' though these noo are far awa'
The sounds ye heard, the sichts ye saw,
The guid an' bad, the great an' sma',
    Wi' boyhood's eyes—
"However Fortune kick the ba',"
    Are still your prize.

Let ithers mak' their new-time noise,
Hawk owre the warld their wares an' toys,
They canna rab ye o' your joys
    When numbers sweet
As meltin' rhymes o' girls an' boys,
    In music meet.

Memory to you is all in all!
She shows ye showers afar that fall—
No matter when you on her call,
    She answers true;
Around her head she throws her shawl
    An' comes to you.

Though puir an' lonely ye may gang,
The sneaking wolf wi' hungry fang
Flies when ye tirl some rustic sang
    O' heath-clad rill,
On bird that pipes the bogs amang
    When winds are still.

Nature has gifts for you in store!
She's never false. Beloved before,
She wants to win ye more an' more
    Till that which stirs
Your being now shall burst life's door
    An' knock at hers.

An' heirts there may be, morn an' een,
Kind mortals ye hae never seen,
Wad be richt glad to ca' ye freen,
    An' share wi' you
Fond thochts, song-wakened, longings keen,
    An' throbbings new.

Aye one thing mind, Bard o' the Bann—
The bogs where first your bare feet ran,
The mosses round Tartaraghan,
                The gleam an' glow
Of sun-lit fields - braw as ye can,
                To ithers show.

An' let them hear how loud an' clear,
How far above this rolling sphere,
The gates of glittering pearl how near
                The skylark sings!
Yea, enters heaven, without a fear
                On wee brown wings.

An' now, O bogland poet, now
While the New Year, wi' open brow
Awaits your welcome, me allow
                This truth to tell—
Much in this life depends on how
                Ye greet yoursel'.

BY THE BANKS OF THE RIVER WEY[9]

Green the meadows, oh, so green!
      Where the Wey comes washing down,
Soft red sandy banks between,
      To the tide at Weymouth town.
Rich green meadows are they all,
      Level meads in which upspring
Light-stemmed buttercups and tall,
      Robed for summer blossoming.

Reedy marges are there, too,
      Little isles of silt and sand,
Tiny coves and inlets, blue
      With love's gold-eyed blossoms, and
Sudden swirls that bend the flag,
      Swirls that deeply, darkly brown,
Lap no mossy banks, nor lag
      On their way to Weymouth town.

Ripples are there, too, that lave
      Plants, that all too shy for speech,
List, at dusk, the crested wave
      Thundering on the Chesil beach;
Plants that startled hear the gun
      Rouse the guard-ship grim that rides
Where the redly rising sun
      Turns to flame the tossing tides.

Summer dusks, beside the Wey,
      How peacefully divine they are!
Silent waters glimmering grey,
      Flitting moth and folding star.
Hushed the gay sandpiper, now,
      Rest the sea gulls from their flight,
Greenfinch none stirs on the bough
      While up gets the queen of night.

Soft upon the moonlit stream
      Float the cygnet and the swan,
Lost in sleep, their lightest dream
      Scarcely broken by the dawn.
Soon across green orchards come,
      And o'er fields with bird songs rife,
The not untuneful human hum
      Of early-stirring village life.

---

[9] This poem and the following one, *'Lulworth Cove'* were written in 1885 when Teggart was briefly stationed in Weymouth, Dorset.

Sallow, alders, hawthorns boor,
    Nut and crab and bullace tree,[10]
At Upwey, blossom near or o'er
    The spring that hastes a beck to be—
Blossom o'er the beck that hastes
    Onward soon, without a frown,
As the reed-fringed Wey that tastes
    The tide ere reaching Weymouth town.

Lapwing, land-rail, water-hen
    Birds, without or with a crown,
Fill with life each field and fen,
    By the Wey, near Weymouth town.
And the soft green meadows, they
    Sound asleep from dusk to dawn,
Aglow with buttercups, by day,
    Glad the eyes to look upon.

---

[10] Small, wild damson tree.

LULWORTH COVE

Oh, this peaceful English shore!
Oh, the calm that evermore,
Shut in by the sheltering hills,
This green nook of England fills!
Oh, the waves whose rippling speech
Gladdens all the shell-strewn beach!
Oh, the old-time treasure-trove
Fathom-deep in Lulworth cove!

Lulworth castle-soft through it,
Ghosts in ghostly buckram flit,
Or when twilight, hushed and dim,
Filled is by the redbreast's hymn,
Peering through dark loopholes, they
Dream of many a bygone day,
When lusty buccaneering throve,
Loot-enriching Lulworth cove.

Backed by close-clipped verdured downs,
Where the weed autumnal browns;
Fronted by the sapphire sea,
The cove it basketh sunnily
Tempests pass but not molest,
Breezes do but fan its breast;
All the dreams by fancy wove,
Anchored are in Lulworth cove.

In the starlight night and still,
Rounding rugged Portland bill,
Battleships - their mighty, sides
Swished by pale phosphoric tides,
Steer straight out to sea, nor fear
Danger far or stormcloud near;
Wreckage none is roughly drove
Into slumbering Lulworth cove.

On the downs the woolly flock
Dreads nor gale nor earthquake's shock;
Seldom vexed it is the rill
That bubbling from a nearby hill,
Winds through ferny glade and bower
Where loved songbirds, hour by hour,
Idly rest or lightsome rove,
Life all glad in Lulworth cove.

Still the 'White Horse' on the slope
Seemeth eager-eyed as hope;

Silence only 'tis that fills,
To overflow, the green-rimmed hills;
Save when sea-born winds at play
Frolic in the outer bay,
Echoes back then one fir grove
The cradle song of Lulworth cove.

Dusk discloses not the tan
Of the Lulworth fisherman:
Scarce the evening star reveals
Crab-traps his and lobster creels;
Where to rocks wet seaweed clings,
All night long his lanthorn swings;
When his bark is landward hove,
Breaks the dawn o'er Lulworth cove.

Channel steamers come and go
Lulworth only doth them know
As it knows of ships that brave
Blustering wind and stormy wave,
White-winged skiffs that gliding pass
Over waters smooth as glass,
Struck by thunderbolt of Jove,
Move to pity Lulworth cove.

Vision only to be seen
From sunny knoll or hillside green;
Elysium but to be espied
By those who in staunch vessels ride;
Oh this peaceful English shore!
Oh the croon that evermore
Tells of sea-wrought treasure-trove,
Brought to light in Lulworth cove.

Lulworth Cove, Dorset, c.1910.

THE WIMPLIN' LUGGIE

It's but a wee bit burn, the Luggie,
      A wee bit singin' burn,
An' yet how aften, sair an' weary,
      My thochts to it return!
My thochts to it return, an' wander
      Wi' it thro' strath an' lea.
Rejoice wi' it an' then fu' cheerie
      Back return to me.

Atween the lush an' tender grasses
      Rins it a' day lang,
Rins till nicht, hushed into silence,
      Listens to its sang:
Listens to its sang, still fearing
      Morn will come too soon,
Come wi' noise o' rugged labour,
      Deaf to Luggie's tune.

Here it downward draws the alders
      To show the bright bluebells,
To the foxgloves, blushin' bonnie,
      Mony a tale it tells.
Mony a tale it tells till startled
      By the Kelvin's call,
Then it speeds alang, delighting
      The ring-ouzels all.

It's but a wee bit burn, the Luggie,
      A wee bit singin' burn,
Yet, to it aft, when worn an' weary,
      I in dreams return.
I in dreams return fu' gladly.
      For in memory,
The music o' its wimplin' waters
      Soothes an' comforts me.

LOCH-NA-GAR[11]

Hills, beyond hills ablaze with heather,
    Hills with pine trees crowned,
And, heeding not the sunlit weather,
    Tarns that sleep profound.

Calm, as in seas where cones of coral
    Rise, beyond thinking fair,
The pointed towers of white Balmoral
    Pierce the clear thin air.

No noisy burn is heard deliver
    Its force where boulders throng,
But, winding slow, the Dee, bright river,
    Signs a pleasant song.

And 'mong those hills whose heads in heaven
    Seem God's face to see—
Nor black with storm, nor red with levin,
    But rugged as can be—

Cairn Taggart, stern to the beholder,
    But peaceful all within,
Dreams, seeing still hope's star grow colder,
    Of days that might have been:

Ben Cruachan, the mighty, listens
    The march of time afar;
While, clad in cloud, nor gleams nor glistens
    Silent Loch-na-gar.

Loch na gar

---

[11] Mountain situated five miles south of Balmoral. At 1279 metres high, the mountain is classified in Scotland as 'a munro' - a name given to any peak over 3000 feet.

WHERE THE BONNIE KELVIN[12] WINDS

It's little ken they where black smoke,
      And grit and grime and gree,
Coal dust and coom and chimneys choke
      The life of bush and tree
How fresh and fair the green buds burst
      On shoots, unnumbered kinds,
In haugh and shaw, through which, at first,
      The bonnie Kelvin winds.

Contented lift the Campsie hills
      Their crests to skies of blue:
Rough corries down, a thousand rills,
      Slide ferny thickets through;
On shower and shine and nectar nurst,
      The birk her hair unbinds,
In rocky glens, through which, at first,
      The bonnie Kelvin winds.

Her blushing self she scarcely notes —
      The foxglove, bowed to see
How soft the snow-white cloudlet floats
      In pools that mirrors be;
That frown on dewdrops no flower durst,
      The rose the bud reminds,
In bushy dells, through which, at first,
      The bonnie Kelvin winds.

Glad seen and heard by sunlit day —
      Where scarce a ripple swells —
Soft rung by zephyrs, swing and sway
      Bunches of sweet bluebells;
The daisy cowers, her lips up-purs't,
      Lest her a sharp shower blinds,
In open straths, through which, at first,
      The bonnie Kelvin winds.

Half-laughingly the whirlpool whips
      The ledge that light doth know,
Where hurriedly the ousel dips,
      Black-edged, his breast of snow;
And where she may allay love's thirst,
      Her nest the peewit finds,
In meadows wide, through which, at first,
      The bonnie Kelvin winds.

---

[12] The River Kelvin rises in the Kilsyth Hills and flows southwest for twenty one miles before joining the Clyde, two miles west of Glasgow. It forms the boundary between North Lanarkshire and East Dunbartonshire.

Across the burn brown alders lean,
      Outspreads the hawthorn wide,
Idyllic all the sylvan scene,
      And clear the singing tide;
Droops no green plant on poison nurst,
      No cord the heifer binds,
In grassy fields, through which, at first,
      The bonnie Kelvin winds.

Ah, little ken they, where black smoke,
      And grit and gree and grime,
Coal dust and coom and chimneys choke
      The life that fain would climb
How fresh and fair the green buds burst,
      On boughs, unnumbered kinds,
In song-filled glens, through which, at first,
      The bonnie Kelvin winds.

River Kelvin, near Kirkintilloch, 1902.

AT NEW-YEAR'S TIME

Braw, braw it is, at New-year's time,
A song to sing, or e'en a hyme,
An' mak' it clink in braid Scots rhyme;
        But, brawer still
It is - wha canna see a stime,
Their mental een, this mornin's prime,
        Wi' licht to fill.

For, fowk there are, who, having een,
But seldom note the grass is green,
Or, sweet the licht, this world between
        An, heaven above;
Nor see they, starlicht glintin' keen,
In stolen keeks o' some blate Jean,
        Sweet looks o' love.

Also there are, at the New year,
Wha only see the sudden tear
That wets the pallid cheek o' fear;
        An' aiblins miss
The bonnie licht that, shinin' clear,
Leads upward thro' Love's atmosphere
        To realms o' bliss.

Nor mark they, in their fellow-man,
A poet, one, wha kin to Pan,
Pipes ditties braw, the best he can,
        To help uplift
Those wha, forsaking Nature's plan,
To lichts that blink an' blots that ban,
        Swift onward drift.

Gie me the hamely Scottish croon
That brawly helps, baith late an' soon,
To lift a brither wight aboon
        The pits o' shame
That flie alas ilk temptin' toun
Whaur poisoned stoups too aften droon
        An honoured name.

Burns! Aft when nichts were mirk an' wet,
An' love-ward thy first-foot was set,
A man thou wert, nor could'st forget
        How simple joys
Were better far than eerie fret
O' getting' gear where fools are met,
        An' clamor cloys.

Thy plaidle micht it fa' on me,
The whole wide warld I wad it see
United as ane family,
      An' ane in heart,
Bairns, lauchin' in their guileless glee,
An' man still proud to bear the gree
      An' noble part.

Nor with life's riddles wad I prove
Sweet lasses wi' their looks o' love;
Nor mithers, each a brooding dove,
      Wad I deny
Dumb keeks at bits o' treasure-trove,
Fond found by them when a' above
      Was saft blue sky.

But maist wi' licht I'd fill the een
That canna see how thin the screen
That sometimes veils the thochtfu' freen
      Wha's love sublime
Crosses the seas, that may be seen
How fares it there wi' Jock and Jean
      At New year's time.

JENNY GOW[13]

Here where the wimplin' Kelvin winds
    So noiselessly along,
It music only makes for minds
    In love wi' silent song.
Wi' perfect faith it seems to pause
    Below the hazel bough,
An' hark, as if it waitin' was
    For red-lipped Jenny Gow.

Oh, fair, indeed, is Hayston Hall,
    An high the Campsie hills,
Rush-dotted the sheep pastures all,
    An' pure the sparklin' rills.
An' here it is the laughing stream
    Runs sober to allow
The bonny buds to drowse an' dream
    Of blue-eyed Jenny Gow.

A bab o' flowers frae Kelvin banks
    Is better lo'ed than gear,
By one whose light an' shapely shanks
    Are often rested here.
An' so - in Nature's happy style,
    (Head bent an' dewy now)
The bluebell courts the dimpled smile
    Of darling Jenny Gow.

Though Jenny's heart fu' often fills
    For sorrow passin' by,
The eagle of her native hills
    Has not a finer eye.
An' all that wealth of dark brown hair
    Above an open brow—
O heaven! Was e'er a nymph so fair
    As charming Jenny Gow.

When having sung his blithest song,
    The bonny bird descends
To where the shining blade an' long,
    Above his wifie bends.
Where shine an' shower o'er her pass,
    The lark would not know how
To run so lightly through the grass,
    As gamesome Jenny Gow.

---

[13] Born 1852; married 1873 Robert Campbell, Kirkintilloch, Dunbartonshire.

Below the lodge, below the lawn.
      Where blushing gowans ope,
The snow-white lambs are bleating on
      The green an' sunny slope.
Where solid banks keep back the strath
      Deep furrowed by the plough,
The peewee runs along the path
      To meet wi' Jenny Gow.

IN THE STRATHAVON

Awa in far Strathavon,
      Among the neuks an' hills,
But few the noises - savin'
      Saft trinklin's o' the rills.
The burst o' some glad burnie,
      That still in jocund spring,
Gaes loupin' on its journey,
      Foam-flecked an' glittering.

Where never smoke-cloud blackens,
      Nor smoors their frounds o' green,
Stout ferns, an' stouter brackens,
      All summer long are seen.
There 'tis the green teal's wheelin',
      On misty mornin's calm,
Is heard above the bleatin'
      Of woolly sheep an' lamb.

An' where is ample leeway,
      And the wild life allures,
Silk-tappned pipes the pee-wee
      On lonely dark brown moors.
Wet shaws an' mosses miry,
      An' black dubs - not a few,
On wee red shanks an' wiry
      The pipit paidles through.

Are mossholes green wi' rushes,
      Dykes brown wi' briers that cling,
Rocks overhung wi' bushes,
      An' hillocks red wi' ling.
Are bogs where heath an' heather
      All through the autumn bloom,
An' banks that in mist weather
      Yield beauty an' perfume.

In spring, an ardent lover,
      'Neath skies of watery blue,
The long-nebb'd golden plover,
      Himself a wife doth woo.
An' where dark waters ripple
      An' blueberries are ripe,
Rill-drops his only tipple,
      Preens himself, the snipe.

Awa in far Strathavon,
      Oh for a month, to be

An' hear no noises savin'
> The wheep o' the pee-wee.
The sound o' rills that trinklin',
> Through mossy channels run;
An' see o'er all pert twinklin',
> The pale September sun.

THE ROSE O'ROCHSILLOCH

Ye may talk o' your Jeans, your Tibs an' your Teens,
      O' your lilies that bloom on the lea;
But, all said an' done, an' excellin' her-none,
      The Rose o' Rochsilloch for me!

True! The smoor an' the smoke o' coalpits an' coke,
      Her red cheeks may darken a wee;
But then when I kiss, I exclaim, in my bliss—
      The Rose o' Rochsilloch for me!

Through lashes gold-brown, when she keeks up or down,
      The glint o' her bricht hazel ee,
So bewitches my heirt, to my freens I assert—
      The Rose o' Rochsilloch for me!

Where since were green shrubs now are dark pits an' dubs,
      An' her faither a miner is he;
Yet nevertheless I am fain to confess—
      The Rose o' Rochsilloch for me!

Oh, her bonnie brown hair, o' my heirt it's the snare!
      It binds me, nor wad I be free
O' the charm o' her smile; an' I say every while—
      The Rose o' Rochsilloch for me!

An' what if the smoor frae the pits o' the muir,
      An e'en at the tounhead looks dree;
The sun or not shine, I've this happy thocht mine—
      The Rose o' Rochsilloch for me!

She's trig an' she's neat, an' her lips - oh, they're sweet
      As bells o' ling-heath on the lea;
They gar me to sweer by a' that's most dear—
      The Rose o'Rochsilloch for me!

So lads, ye may preach o' a braw lass in each
      Bit clachan frae Doon to the Dee:
But kennin' or no, where your white lilies grow—
      The Rose o' Rochsilloch for me!

AMERICAN POEMS

THE GO-AHEAD YANKEE

His standard may not be regal,
        Only white and crimson bars,
But look at the lordly eagle
        With his talons among the stars.

Of course he 'licks all creation',
        As I often hear him say,
And his is the greatest nation
        The sun shines on today.

No obstacles him encumber
        So great is his daring soul,
He'd make a fire of Canadian lumber
        That would melt the frozen pole.

'Twould not be a thing gigantic
        To make the gulfstream flow
Southwards through the Atlantic
        To warm the Antarctic snow.

Of the sea and the sky the skipper
        On starfish he should sup,
In his hand take the mighty 'Dipper'
        And scoop the Pacific up.

But with good 'squaremeal' terrestrial
        He heeds not the critics lash,
Though the pig-tail of the 'celestial'
        Somehow has got into the hash.

Should Britannia take a colic
        His medicine will not fail,
Though at times for his fun and frolic
        He twists the old Lion's tail.

O Jonathan long and lanky
        May your dollar be always bright,
Though the 'Dipper' of the yellow yankee
        Should be lost in the well of night.

CROWNED WITH GLORY[1]

He's gone whom all were glad to see!
        And yet, why should our souls be vext?
He's only gone across the sea
        From this green island to the next.

With God's light still his face upon,
        With love still shining on his way—
Out of the night into the dawn,
        Out of the darkness into day.

Though seems to sink the silver star
        And droop below the ocean's rim,
It shines in eastern skies afar
        When all the rest are faint and dim.

It shines until the morning sun
        Obscures the light of Lyra's seven;
And when we think its light is done,
        'Tis shining on serene in Heaven.

He's gone whom all were glad to see!
        Yet nevermore shall we be vext
Leaving this world - some day we'll see
        Him crowned with glory in the next.

---

[1] Dedicated to his friend, John B Stebbins, who died January 1899.

DAWN

Ere daylight through my window streams,
    Before the morning gathers grey,
'Tis hard to rise from pleasant dreams
    And get in harness for the day.

But when I reach the stair-way door
    And on the dark piazza stand,
I'm glad the sleepy night is o'er
    And that the daylight is at hand.

For o'er the stream that waking stirs,
    Beyond the shoulder of the hill
That's fringed with darkly feathered firs
    I see a light increasing still.

Warm shades of yellow, pink and rose
    And green a lighter green upon,
With blue and pearly grey, compose
    The lovely colours of the dawn.

O sweet, as blameless woman's blush
    That spreads and mounts so high and higher,
Until her face doth crimson flush,
    And the dark eye is all on fire.

Have been the dawns that I have seen,
    The dawns that I arise to see,
Beyond the mountain, darkly green,
    That watches over the rivers three.[2]

O morn, you more than recompense,
    Yea, me a hundred-fold repay,
That I should early rise and hence
    Have dawn before me all the day.

---

[2] The Swift, Quaboag and Ware Rivers all meet at the aptly named village of Three Rivers, Palmer MA, where the poem was written.

THE OLD MOON AND THE NEW

I wandered by a winding stream,
    The day had been surpassing fair,
And evening like a lovely dream
    Was melting into amber air.

The daylight died in daffodil,
    The pine trees murmured into rest;
One star shone high above the hill
    That hid the crocus-coloured West.

The moon revealed a narrow rim,
    A little arc of diamond light;
The section of the circle dim
    Was dark as any moonless night.

The new and old together made
    A picture of my human heart,
The greater portion in the shade,
    The lesser but the brighter part.

And did it bring me here to know
    That night and day the silver arc
Would still increase, until the glow
    Would cover all that now was dark?

It did not! For I also knew
    The borrowed light, a day might dim,
Would surely wane, till in the blue
    A silver thread would be the rim.

Nay, that the very thread would fade
    And darkness be again supreme,
That old and new were wisely made
    To show "things are not what they seem."

And rather than my life become
    A fickle light to wax and wane,
What's dark within me shall be dumb,
    The rest a rainbow rim remain!

If moral came to me at all,
    It came in this, that I should hide
The caverns where no sunbeams fall,
    And show the world my sunny side.

ARROW-WOUNDS

Of forest tree I've lately read
      Which felled and sawn apart,
The woodman found an arrow-head
      Hid in the giant's heart.

The outer surface naught revealed
      Of flint-wound or of flame,
The growth of centuries concealed
      And hid from sight the same.

And in this heart that seemeth sound
      And free from cankering care,
If rent apart there would be found
      A thousand arrows there.

And whose the hand that drew the bow,
      The eye whose deadly aim
Sent forth those arrows, well you know,
      Those arrows tipped with flame.

It may be that the red man's bow
      Was bent in rivalry,
Or aiming at the treacherous foe
      He chanced to strike the tree.

And so perchance it was to try
      That woman's craft of thine,
Those arrows from thy dark-brown eye
      Were aimed at heart of mine.

Or like that other shooting there
      Who chanced to pierce the tree,
Perhaps the arrow-wounds I bear
      Were never meant for me.

And though the years may heal it o'er
      And time assuage the pain,
Till death within my heart's red core
      Those arrows shall remain.

The flint, the steel I still shall feel,
      My rival has thee won,
And so the dark eyes cannot heal
      The mischief they have done.

FATE

"Oh! Come, my friend, do come with me
And we the moon asleep shall see!
Just step with me into the car
And we shall wake the morning star!"

"I will not go in your balloon
Nor be a real man in the moon;
But I'll remain on earth below
And leave you airy heights to know."

The bubble floated fair and high,
A star of wonder in the sky,
And in the morning landed down
All safe beside a quiet town.

And he who would not ride or roam,
But, fearing danger, stayed at home,
An earthquake swallowed him, and all
Who feared the bubble and its fall.

THE WOODS IN WINTER

Walking in the woods in winter
    Is a pleasant thing,
Though the rill 'neath icy splinter
    Flows so cold it cannot sing,
Brightly shines the sun today,
Let us through the forest stray.

Here the landscape rising hilly
    Faces fair the shining sun,
And the brook, unbridled filly,
    Brown with foamy sides doth run,
To the river trotteth down,
The Quaboag flowing by the town.

Cold the trees, but not a tremble
    Can be seen in branch or bough,
Hardy Spartans they resemble,
    Where are all their emeralds now?
The birch reveals a bare white limb,
The elm beside her one as dim.

The fir's green robe is covered over
    With patches of the last night's snow,
Here the hawk was wont to hover,
    Roosted here the cawing crow,
When the dreamy autumn days
Veiled the hill with purple haze.

Naked are the woods in winter,
    There is not a single leaf
On which frost, too cunning printer,
    Can set down his note of grief,
But his traceries on the trees
My gladdened eye delighted sees.

And yet distinctly I remember
    By the brook we saw a fern,
A leaf of green in dark December
    Makes us for the summer yearn;
But still this winter walk to me
Revealeth beauty fair to see.

The blue jay, giant jewel, flashes
    Under the cerulean sky,
And the stream likes wild steed dashes
    Rock and tree-root boldly by,
While pink buds on tender trees
Into uncut rubies freeze!

Like a catkin on the willow,
  On the spray there hangs a nest,
Where the red-bird found a pillow
  And her young a rosy breast,
'Tis not empty, but the snow
Would melt within it could it know.

Nature's liberal, who can stint her
  Hand if she but choose to fling?
Walking in the woods in winter
  Is a pleasant thing
If we bring the eye to see
The charms that there revealed be.

Summer woods are all the fashion,
  (They are fairer in the fall)
But in winter they're my passion
  And I love them best of all;
Wrap, O Pine! Thy head in snow,
While I happy homeward go.

THE MOON AND THE SOUL

In the crescent cradle of the new
        I saw the old moon lying,
Her curtains of transparent blue
        The night winds were untying,
And there she lay with nought to do
        But find a joy in dying.

Oh, easy death, to lie in state
        All in a silver crescent,
While winsome stars upon thee wait
        And planets smile so pleasant,
To watch before the golden gate
        The past become the present.

To lie unmoved by moan or mirth
        While you the goal are winning,
To feel that death is only birth,
        That life is but beginning,
And still have sense of this old earth
        Without a thought of sinning.

To see the old put on the new,
        To feel not pain but pleasure—
To lie at ease the long night through,
        All day to doze at leisure,
Must be elysium unto you
        And bliss beyond all measure.

How different is the fate of man
        Who, here on earth sojourning,
Spins round the sun a little span,
        And then with grief and mourning
Goes out in darkness - bitter ban—
        From which there's no returning.

Yet not a star in all the skies
        However old and hoary,
Can tell whene'er the mortal dies,
        The opening of the story
That shall begin whene'er our eyes
        Shall see the King of Glory.

THE SKY

When the clouds at eve like sheep are folded,
      And the winds are hushed over lake and lea,
I look on the dome that the Lord hath moulded,
      And think of the beauty that is to be.

And 'tis midnight now and the sky is naked,
      While the King himself wide watch doth keep
O'er a million stars and the moon that waked
      And smiled ere she sank into sounder sleep.

Oh the sky by day's like a lovely lady
      Arrayed in silver and pearl and blue,
No jewel shows until evening shady
      Brings out on her skirt a gem or two.

But now unrobed like a dusky princess,
      With all but her jewels thrown aside,
In heaven she walks nor shames nor winces
      Though the world should gaze at her open-eyed.

Choose if you will which of these two phases
      The highest lifts the immortal soul;
Or is't hope beyond that attracts and raises
      The God-made man to his final goal?

The day's decorum like sense of duty
      The soul of the many may satisfy,
But give me the princess whose dusky beauty
      Lights up the dome of the midnight sky.

FOREBODINGS

Are these foreboding of the fall,
    These airs that coldly play
Around me when the wee birds call
    Sharp-toned at close of day?
        O heart, my heart!
        Oh what is that they say?
        That e'en the perfect must depart,
        That all shall pass away.

Are these not symbols of the sere,
    These grasses turning grey,
These ferns that fade, as if with fear,
    These clover-blooms in clay?
        O heart, my heart!
        Oh, what is that they say?
        That things the fairest first depart,
        They wane and pass away.

Are these strange currents in my blood,
    That autumn's moon obey,
Not bodings of the sterner flood
    That for no man will stay?
        O heart, my heart!
        Oh what is that they say?
        That all delightful things depart,
        Or, wave-like, melt away.

Are these loved voices that I hear
    In dreams at dawn of day,
Celestial sounds; or, what I fear—
    Sweet preludes to decay?
        O heart, my heart!
        Oh what is that they say?
        That we, as visions seen, depart;
        As dreams, we pass away.

REMEMBRANCE

No more, alas, the earth may robe her
    In raiment green, till spring returns;
The sun retires and rises sober,
    Nasturtiums fade in urns;
But this fond heart, in life's October,
    For thee still burns.

Oh! blest are they who still can borrow
    Balm for the weary mind;
And happy those who know tomorrow
    Will sure their chains unbind;
But this sad heart to life-long sorrow
    Thou hast consigned.

Oh those there are who'd smile at treason,
    If treason eased their pains;
And there are those who for a season
    Give to the rich their gains;
But this poor heart, in spite of reason,
    Still thine remains.

As rise the waves of round old ocean
    To that they cannot see;
As matter moved by endless motion
    Obeys the laws that be;
So, constant I'm in my devotion,
    Dear love, to thee.

The cold grey skies of bleak December
    Forget the summer blue;
The ashes dream not of the ember
    That thrilled them through and through;
But he whom you no more remember,
    Remembers you.

CAST DOWN

The melancholy days are come
*   (Bryant)*

The doleful days are come, indeed!
        The days that drag so dreary;
The ribbon rustles on the reed,
        The willow's worn and weary
Of winds that wall along the brink
        And warp the wannish river—
An endless chain - each wave a link
        It seems loath to deliver.

The doleful days are come, indeed!
        The brier with rust is braided,
And though 'tis now her light we need—
        The goldenrod is faded.
No more the blue-eyed aster wins
        Us with her star-like beauty,
The very hemlock now begins
        To fall asleep on duty.

The doleful days are come indeed!
        Hushed are the tuneful voices;
And in the woods where wild things feed
        The jay alone rejoices.
Dank fungus grows upon the graves
        Of flowers that low are sleeping;
Red cedars stolid stand - like braves
        Eternal sentry keeping.

The doleful days are come, indeed!
        The days of dire disaster;
Maimed human blossoms blanch and bleed,
        Earth seems without a master.
The war-clouds that like hands arise
        May burst in lurid levin—
May, ere in death we close our eyes,
        Blot out the blue of heaven.

JENNY WREN[3]

When thick at morn on twig and thorn
        The pearly raindrops shine;
Rejoicing then, wee Jennie Wren
        Sings fearlessly and fine.

No note of woe doth Jennie know,
        No solemn psalm she sings,
Thrown from her throat, each rolling note
        Reverberates and rings!

So loud and long is Jenny's song,
        It marvels more than me,
When none are wooed, just why she should
        Sing so defiantly.

Oh, many a time when frosty rime
        Fringed bough and twig and spray,
I've heard her sing as if she'd fling
        Her scorn upon the day!

When through the fog upon the scrogg
        The sunshine fell like flame,
From the litten bush, in one loud gush
        Her song of triumph came!

Oh, Jenny Wren, though ne'er again
        You'll quicken song in me,
Still may the morn on twig and thorn
        Hang pearls for thine and thee.

---

[3] This poem has a marked similarity to Thomas Hardy's *'The Darkling Thrush'* though Teggart's lyric was, in fact, published six years earlier.

THE SCARLET TANAGER[4]

Refreshing fell the summer rain
        On grass and herb and flower,
On broad green leaves without a stain,
        It fell, a cooling shower.

The dark green needles of the fir
        Were tipped with diamonds fine;
The silver birch, too glad to stir,
        Drank in the healing wine.

Where lush green vines, so fair to see,
        Their festoons loop and hang,
Upon a dark and solemn tree
        A bird delighted sang.

His song me to the doorway drew,
        Nor did I go in vain;
He frolicked there as if he, too,
        Enjoyed the summer rain.

All mute I stood admiring him,
        And who would not admire,
Among dark boughs and branches dim,
        A body all of fire!

While nothing but the raindrops stirred,
        And nought but echo rang,
Upon a night-dark pine the bird
        In scarlet piped and sang.

Scarlet Tanager (Courtesy Dan Sudia)

---

[4] A North American bird with brilliant scarlet plumage and shiny black wings and tail.

UNDER THE ELMS
Her beauty made me glad
              (Wordsworth)

Her beauty was of such a kind
It brought me sudden joy!
It so wrought on my genial mind,
I felt glad as a boy.

And then as such, with happy heart,
I looked again at her;
Who, with her ripe lips just apart,
Stood there, too sweet to stir.

With soft dark eyes that seemed to melt
All shyly glanced she,
With rising blush, as if she felt
'Twas a delight to be.

Nor was I loath to think some law,
Some force beyond our ken,
Some power was kind enough to draw
Our hearts together then.

Dark-brown the coils of braided hair;
And those dark eyes did show
In that white face - bright face and fair!
Like sunlit pools in snow.

In love with her, a beam of light
Fell on her sylph-like form;
It kissed her neck so round and white,
So snowy white and warm.

It gleamed in gold upon her gown—
A white gown and a fair;
It flashed and flamed along her brow
And braids of dusky hair.

It lightly touched the pearly tip
Of one pink ear - and then
It fluttered o'er the ruby lip
That flashed it back again.

It must have been the joy she brought
Gave her such bliss the while;
It must have been some happy thought
That blossomed in a smile.

The beauty flowing from within,
The beauty which she wore,
Moved me as I have seldom been
Moved by aught else before.

And many a summer sun shall set,
And silvery moon arise,
And year go round, ere I forget
That face, and those dark eyes.

THE ENGLISH STARLING[5]

Why should the starling be unsung?
        Like burnished steel his wings,
His iridescent neck among
        The loveliest of things.

In that far-seeing eye of his
        Warm lights the iris fill,
And sharp as any dagger is
        His long and yellow bill.

Fleet as blue plovers on the wing,
        In flocks the starlings fly,
When winter giving way to spring,
        Leaves them to cloud the sky.

Low-flying over grazing grounds,
        The million's rush and roar
Heard by the lonely herdboy sounds
        Like surges on the shore.

On ash trees, when they do alight,
        Nor bough or branch is seen,
The naked trees are black as night
        With birds alert and keen.

Breaks up the flock in little bands
        When mating time is nigh,
And these seek fields and pasture lands
        And hillsides warm and high.

Liquid and low the starling's song,
        And in confinement you
May teach him airs, however long,
        To whistle sweet and true.

His family is his chief delight,
        If all is true he tells
When on the housetop day and night
        He with his consort dwells.

My heart - how it with pleasure stirred
        In boyhood's happy time,
When first I saw the bonny bird.
        That whistles in my rhyme!

---

[5] Written in Forest Park, Springfield MA, March 1898.

THE JAGUAR IN FOREST PARK

Where monkeys vent their spite and rage
        In language still unwritten,
The jaguar in his iron cage
        Is playful as a kitten.

His eyes as bright as frosty stars,
        His fur deep black and yellow,
I found him fawning at the bars,
        A very pleasant fellow.

My kindly thought he must have seized,
        For soon as I had spoken,
His purring ways that he was pleased
        Gave every sign and token.

Scarce to admire had I begun,
        Till, as if play was ended,
Couchant he lay, and let his dun
        And black hide glisten splendid.

Then turning easily as a ball—
        Soft as an upturned jelly,
Supine he lay, displaying all
        His white black-spotted belly.

And still his bright eye was on me—
        With longing none to seize me,
But from his glance that I might see
        How all was done to please me.

And yet, somehow, I thought of scenes—
        Where man - the rough intruder,
Than any cat o'er limb that leans,
        Still thinks himself the shrewder.

Of flower-lit forests far away.
        Of woods than kingdoms wider,
Of glades where tigers prowl, or play,
        And Nature their provider—

Of lashing tail and treacherous claws,
        Of fierce-curved fangs and cruel,
The blazing eyes, the savage jaws,
        The dark and bloody duel—

When lo! The jaguar at a bound
        Sprang from his wooden pallet

With such a thud - the solid sound
      It smote me like a mallet.

And then with his dried fish, or bone,
      He played so like a kitten,
I said "My boy, when I'm alone,
      There'll be some verses written."

THE LITTLE SPRIG OF GREEN

Once more the day has come around
    To patriots everywhere,
When that which grows upon the ground
    Is waved aloft in air—
The shamrock, the shamrock,
    The little sprig of green,
That every true-born Irishman
    Wears in his ould caubeen.

Oh! Blessings on Saint Patrick,
    Who, in the Emerald Isle,
Was pleased to plant the root, avick.
    The gem on which we smile—
The shamrock, the shamrock,
    The little sprig of green,
To-day worn in the guileless breast
    Of every true colleen.

Fairer far than dewy fog,
    More dear than any rose,
On every grassy bank and bog
    In Erin green it grows—
The shamrock, the shamrock,
    The little sprig of green,
Oh wet it with your pearly tears,
    And kiss it, my colleen.

May God bless poor ould Ireland,
    May all her sons to-day
Be ready with the helping hand
    To lift above the clay—
The shamrock, the shamrock,
    The little sprig of green,
That once a year the patriot here
    Still wears in his caubeen.

FLORA
A LADY TREE[6]

That Flora was a lady tree,
      We knew before her blushes
Proclaimed her sense of modesty
      Among the garden bushes.

When from the skies, like drops of lead,
      The rain came down upon it,
How bashfully she hung her head
      All in her green sunbonnet!

While others, of their beauty vain,
      Spread shining leaves and shady,
This pretty dear, amid the rain,
      Looked every inch the lady.

When torrents fell her leaves between,
      Within her and without her,
O then it was her skirts of green
      Were gathered close about her.

As if some inward glory warmed
      The bells of all the bushes,
The more it blustered, blowed and stormed,
      The deeper grew her blushes.

When other trees of blooms were bare,
      And fruit fell in the garden,
This happy creature looked as fair
      As Rosamund in Arden.

When east winds pinched the pansy bed,
      And paled the blooms of clover,
Our joy with cup-shaped blossoms red
      Was crowned and covered over.

The blue sky for her looking-glass,
      And chirped to by the thrushes,
Our bonny pet is still one mass
      Of rosy blooms and blushes.

Ah! who can tell by what bright wings
      The fair one is defended?
In Nature's world are many things
      By man not comprehended.

---

[6] According to North American folklore, the red elder is also known as *'the lady tree'*.

To know why in this flowery guise
      So late she has arrayed her,
Would be to know how great and wise
      The Power is who made her.

One thing is certain: Some loved voice
      Unheard by us must woo her,
Why blush? except some spirit choice
      Is saying sweet things to her.

We know the weakness of the sex,
      Their love for frills and flounces,
But Flora when herself she decks
      Her natural joy announces.

And now - while Summer takes her leave,
      And hastens on September,
We ask this lady to receive
      Our verses - and remember:

We loved her as a lady tree,
      Long time before her blushes
Proclaimed her sense of modesty
      Among the garden bushes.

AT DEWY DUSK IN AUGUST

Far too quickly sped the morning,
      Brief and bright the sultry noon,
The August day itself adorning,
      Vanished all too soon,

Dewy dusk has come already,
      And in peaceful fields afar,
Luminous and large and steady
      Shines the evening star,

Other worlds in millions glimmer,
      Mighty suns in millions burn,
Yet this earth of ours grows dimmer
      Still at night's return.

Where unnumbered insects, humming,
      Pair and parley, pause and pass,
To the silver dew down coming,
      Listens every leaf of grass.

Where the wand'ring bullfrog plashes,
      O'er the marshy meadow plot,
A fire-fly for a moment flashes,
      Gems the darkness - and is not.

Never needing to disrobe her,
      Always patient, always blest,
Oh, how peaceful and how sober
      Mother Nature goes to rest.

Wise they are who learn to love her
      In the fleeting years of youth;
Wise are they who still discover
      In her treasures some new truth.

And while calmly she doth slumber
      Curtained under green and grey,
May my angel help me number
      Blessings granted me today.

For while round me boughs and bushes
      Dream amid their myrrh and musk,
I feel 'tis God himself who hushes
      Life asleep at dewy dusk.

MORNING SONG OF THE WOOD THRUSH

Ere the dew was the grass adorning,
      Ere the red sun burst into flame,
Out of the mist of the morning,
      The song of the wood thrush came.

On my ear soft as flute notes falling,
      Musical, mellow and clear,
Came the voice of the sweet bird, calling
      "I'm here! I am here! I am here!"

Singing tunefully as if to capture
      All in me that remained of a boy,
The round hills harkened with rapture,
      And the dark woods listened with joy.

Singing clear, as if to awaken
      The sleepers in covert and tree,
The ragged mist-curtains were shaken
      By the ring of his melody.

On the paths not a footstep falling,
      Not a sounds afar or anear,
Save the one voice piping and calling
      "I'm here! I am here! I am here!"

Ere gems were the grasses adorning,
      While never a gossamer stirred,
Ere burst into music the morning,
      How perfect the song of the bird.

Nor ceased he his marvellous singing,
      Nor fainter his piping became,
Till the sun through the mist upspringing,
      Flashed on the hills like flame.

And then - recalling his childhood,
      Like notes of a clarion clear,
Rang out from the heart of the wildwood
      "I'm here! I am here! I am here!"

HUMILITY IN SONG

Of those endowed with honeyed speech,
    Who round Parnassus throng,
How few they are - the bards who reach
    The sovereign heights of song!

How foolish they, their feeble wings
    Still wet with sunless dew,
Who feign would soar where Shelley sings—
    A skylark in the blue.

Too eager muse whose ardent wing
    Olympian heights would dare,
Down to the native sod, and sing
    The lowly blossoms there.

And rest there, when thy rhyme's complete,
    Be it or brief or long,
Content, if 'tis but half as sweet
    As is the sparrow's song.

WHERE YELLOW POPPIES BLOW

Walled in and closed completely
    From seething stormy seas,
Where blush and blossom sweetly,
    Pinks and anemones;
Where love is a rare comer,
    A land of ice and snow,
Oh, there it is, in summer
    The yellow poppies blow.

Where reindeer roam the mountains
    In search of heath and ling,
Or feed beside the fountains,
    That bubble up in spring;
Where, piping musically,
    The gay snow buntings go,
In verdant vale and valley
    The yellow poppies blow.

Where rosy lipped Aurora
    Peeps from behind the sun,
Where furthest wanders Flora,
    Where night and day are one;
Among the silent grasses,
    That green as emerald grow,
Lone scattered and in masses
    The yellow poppies blow.

Where seal with walrus vying
    Provoke the creature - man,
Where comes the auk fleet flying,
    To see the ptarmigan;
On slopes than Lapland colder,
    Till southern winds they know,
By barren rock and boulder
    The yellow poppies blow.

Where moss and lichen cover
    The ground in early spring,
Where never comes the flower,
    And where no sparrows sing;
In wilds far off and lonely,
    This side eternal snow,
And there in summer only
    The yellow poppies blow.

OUR DUMB ANIMALS

Oh, whether they have souls or not,
Let this ne'er be by us forgot:
They all can feel! soul-tuned or not.

In plough and harrow, tug and team,
The patient beasts hitched to the beam
Are ten times wiser than they seem.

Checked at the brae the thoroughbred
Turns round a dark eye rimmed with red,
And asks if he must go ahead.

Our friend, the ever faithful hound,
Will follow us the world around
Or dying at his post be found.

Our family pets - the great and small
In house and home, in hut and hall,
To us it is they look for all.

Housed-up, afield, or on the farm,
If they but think we mean them harm,
The cows how easily we alarm.

And all the rest - the sheep and goat,
The little kid, the lively shoat,
They all can feel! would we but note.

They shrink before the cruel blow,
They moan, they groan, they hirpling go,
They cannot speak, they only know.

In barn and byre, in stall and sty,
There's still some soft beseeching eye
Appeals to our humanity.

TO THE CITY OF HOMES

Foremost of all the cities fair
    Sung to by the Connecticut,
Thou, Springfield, for all time, dost wear
    The crown of beauty! Nature put
It long since on thy lovely brows.
    And while thy river onward foams.
To thee I fain would pay my vows.
    Queen city of time-honoured homes.

Dearer thou art, indeed, to me,
    (Though mine is but an Arab's tent)
Than that far city by the sea
    Where half my schoolboy days were spent.
And if to me thou art so dear
    What must thou be to those who wait
And watch thee growing year by year
    In beauty, as in good estate?

Thy noise and bustle hum and stir,
    Thy tide of commerce swelling free.
But strength of purpose bring to her
    Whose eyes once kindly looked on me.
For though she's tender as the dove,
    Yet in her rounded woman's breast
The fine, far-reaching voice of love
    Still whispers "Where thou art is best!"

A city thou! yet Nature's green
    So nurtured is within thy walls
Great vines festooned in courts are seen,
    And grass where'er the footstep falls.
While each well-ordered park invokes
    The blessing of the passer-by,
Thy noble elms and giant oaks
    Make dance for joy the poet's eye.

Ah, who in thy God's acre walks
    That does not hail the hemlock tree?
Or bless the oak who when he talks
    Speaks to the heart as speaks the sea?
Or who, who from the loveliest hill
    First looks thy sunlit meadows o'er,
Doth not within him feel a thrill
    Of ecstasy, unfelt before.

Thy churches and thy temples all
    Are fit abodes of love and peace:

Thy sacred shrines and lanes recall
        The glories that once gladdened Greece.
Thy pleasant homes in gardens set
        Speak to the heart of thoughtful man
How hope and joy for once have met
        Where husbands help, and women plan.

When elm and maple, high o'erhead,
        Are touched with April's tender green;
Or in the fall, when flaming red
        Like banners make light the scene:
They, where the boughs delighted meet,
        Their foliage to the light unfurled,
Make for thy longest, loveliest street
        The fairest archway in the world.

Nor is this all! for nigh at hand
        The dingle and suburban dell,
Wide lawns and slopes of pasture land
        Thy people's tastes, inherent, tell.
And in the bounds of Forest Park,
        To every pensive, sylvan scene
The dawn brings music, and the dark
        A song of waters! and between

The wild bird's call - night sounds so sweet.
        The lotus blooms and lilies there
They cannot sleep till pink lips meet,
        Pale lips in kisses pure as prayer.
When hark! It is the panther's roar,
        That calling to the coming dawn,
Shakes slender shapes on every shore,
        And starts from sleep the timid fawn.

These guarded by great forest trees,
        With woodland wild and waters blue
Give zest to love and life; and these
        Are thine, O sovereign city too.
Love's home and citadel thou art,
        A dwelling place so dear to me,
Roam where I will, this throbbing heart,
        Dear Springfield, needs must think of thee.

AELLA GREEN[7]

Where art thou gone, beloved friend?
      Yesterday thou wert here,
Still willing down thy head to bend
      When Sorrow claimed thine ear.

For thou wert such a kindly soul,
      That all who met thee knew,
Thy heart, set on no common goal,
      Was tender as 'twas true.

Much given far afield to roam,
      Admiring Nature's plan,
The wilds to thee were like a home—
      Unspoiled by errant man!

And now, alas, no more thy smile
      Shall bud or berry see;
Thy neighbours sorrowing, the while
      They think of these and thee.

The while they still recount thy worth,
      And earnest blessings given,
That all, with thee, who walked this earth
      Might also dream of heaven.

And though the winds of winter blow,
      Crisping the icy wave;
And soft as flowers the flakes of snow
      Are falling on thy grave.

The silent heart is not the end,
      Love journeys on and on;
'Where the noble have their country,' friend,
      'Tis there that thou art gone.

---

[7] Dedicated to his friend and fellow American poet who died 8 January 1902. *'Where the noble have their country'* is the title of Green's best known poem.

CAGED SKYLARKS IN FOREST PARK

Poor hapless things! pent up while you—
      Mad for the mirth of May,—
Should soaring be in yonder blue
      So glorious today.

Your cage within not e'en a sod,
      No green turf to remind
You of the teeming earth where God
      Is to his creatures kind.

Your days spent all in dingy walls,
      Your mornings never new,
Upon your heads no sunlight falls,
      Upon your wings no dew.

Seeing your startled looks the while
      You held yourselves up game,
Melted my heart, and sad the smile
      That o'er my features came.

I thought of boglands far away
      Where, as a happy boy,
I heard your kindred every day
      Carol of love and joy.

I thought of soft, sun-kindled air,
      And cooling summer rain,
And fields where skylarks everywhere
      Live not their lives in vain.

And gazing at you, ill-starred birds.
      So beautiful and shy,
My sorrow grew too deep for words,
      At heart in tears was I.

To come and play, while laughing May
      Louder and louder calls,
Poor brother skylarks, night and day
      You pine in wooden walls.

You pine and fret, and back and forth
      Rapid and restless run,
Nor sing a note, although 'twere worth
      What deathless Shelley won.

TO THE FEBRUARY WIND

O wild, cold February wind!
      O wind that o'er the snow,
For some good purpose, sure, assigned,
      So bitterly doth blow—

Worn out, where wilt thou lodge, tonight?
      Exhausted, where go sleep?
On some great, craggy, star-crowned height
      Where pines wide vigil keep?
Or shall it be where billows white,
      Heave on the boundless deep?

O wild, cold February wind—
      Across the freezing snow,
Not all inclement and unkind,
      Is it they wish to blow.

Nor of thy haste do they complain,
      Those souls who hear thee sing,
"I go that I may come again,
      All softly come and bring,
Rejoicing, in my sunlit train,
      The frolic winds of spring."

THE PEABODY[8] ELM

Bitter enough it had been, when the battered snow
      Lay on thy mighty boughs, all wintry bare,
      When no young lives thou hadst for which to care.
If some wild tempest then had laid thee low,
But when thou motherhood once more didst know,
      Whilst still thy little buds and green leaves were
      Fostered and fondled by the springtime air,
And just beginning to shoot forth and grow—
When thou thyself, in all thy branched prime,
      Grand and maternal looked to thoughtful men,
Lifting to heaven a head majestic and sublime.
      And full of glorious promise - loved Elm, then,
Long ere thou hadst reached thy fading time,
In broad daylight to slay thee was, indeed, a crime.

---

[8] Peabody is a small city eighteen miles north of Boston. In 1900 its population was just over 11,000. Named after George Peabody, a noted philanthropist and one of only two US citizens ever to be awarded the Freedom of London.

FIVE UNHAPPY SONG BIRDS

In Forest Park

Among the birds close caged up here
      With sorrowing hearts I see,
Five, that flying free were dear
But now that they're imprisoned here,
      Move to deep pity - me.

A linnet grey, a linnet green,
      And - for a woeful third
A yorlin, that in tatters seen,
Looks as doth the linnet green
      A poor heartbroken bird.

With these a hapless chaffinch too
      Inglorious must remain,
And all for skies of sunny blue
Green hedgerows and the greenwood too,
      May chirp, alas in vain.

The bullfinch - Oh, the lovely bird
      Here in a dwelling dim,
By alien sounds and sights was stirred,
The black-capped rosy-bosomed bird,
      Kind heaven pity him.

If these have got their dreams of home,
      If while I by them stand,
Forget the white seas flecked with foam,
Forget all else but these and home,
      Love and my native land.

A CITY ROWAN TREE

Before the windows of my room,
A slender rowan tree in bloom
      My soul delighteth;
And she - the mornings being fair,
Her fragrance and her joy to share,
      Me oft inviteth.

And though, by day, from her afar
I work where window sash and bar
      Might well be brighter—
Immured in labour's loveless coil
The thought of her makes light my toil,
      My duties lighter.

Her snow-white tufts of wilding bloom,
My toil-time darkened brain illume,
      And soon I'm walking,
Not up and down a narrow stair,
But in a pleasant dooryard where
      Green leaves are talking.

Oh, is she not a friend to me,
This early stirring rowan tree,
      Who, sluggards scorning
Cries, "Up my friend and with me share
The sunshine and the earlier air
      This fine May morning."

And when at evening I return
The western skies in gold may burn,
      But cool and shady
The rustic seat assigned for me
Beside the graceful rowan tree,
      My love, my lady.

Only mountain ash to you,
But oh, dear Madam, if you knew
      What memories hover,
In kindly lands beyond the sea,
Around the bonnie rowan tree
      You'd think more of her.

In winter time I pity her,
But when spring airs her heart strings stir,
      And she 'gins budding,
Oh then, like some great foolish boy,
I jest with her, while tears of joy
      My eyes are flooding.

And when in bloom as she's today,
My heart goes forth beyond the May
      E'en to September,
When fond love sees her sunlit head
Crowned with clustering berries red,
      Good to remember.

But now, just off the busy street,
So cool my darling looks and sweet,
      And so inviting,
That I lone waif in alien lands
Must go and greet her where she stands,
      The dusk delighting.

WINTER GLEAMS

THE BLUE JAY[9]

Splendid in the dark green woods,
    Splendid on the bare oak bough,
Peace-perched, for in his wilder moods,
    Looketh the blue jay now.
From snow-clad pine to snow-clad pine,
    See him make his way,
Breast, head and tail and pinions shine,
    Dazzling the white day.

Now to his hoard of nuts he flies,
    Now o'er a red squirrel's nest,
His tricks and woodland craft he tries
    Half earnest and half jest.
And listen - what a joyous note!
    The tumult call of the day,
Snowflakes may fly or fall or float,
    But still give tongue the jay.

Blue Jay (Courtesy of Naturespeak)

[9] A member of the crow family native to North America. Its plumage is lavender blue to mid-blue but it has a white face. It has a pronounced crest on its head, a crown of feathers, which may be raised or lowered according to its mood.

A GIANT'S HEMLOCK

Sifting the flying flakes of snow,
      Unpierced by winds that whistle keen,
Here where the dead lie row and row,
      This giant hemlock keeps his green—
Doth neither stoop nor loll nor lean,
      But bravely facing every sky,
Stands up, deep peace his boughs between,
      A mark for men to pattern by.

What though the dead lie round his feet,
      What though his rugged roots entwine
Where moulder skulls? - his veins are sweet.
      His leaves, sunlit, like jewels shine,
Of pale decay he shows no sign,
      His amber cones are potent still,
And warm without or spice or wine,
      He doth of winter take his fill.

Hoar frost and snow they are his friends,
      And as with him he'd have them stay,
He only sighs when winter ends,
      And these, his friends, have gone away.
A tree whose boughs no tempests sway,
      A being of no common birth,
His head upholds the cold blue day,
      His roots they comfort mother Earth.

The snow, fall it so ever light,
      He hears it fall, or dreams he hears;
And in the still and starry night,
      To eerie strains stops not his ears.
The burden of the many years,
      It maketh not his lustre dim,
And never blows the storm he fears,
      Nor any crash can vanquish him.

SNOWBIRDS[10]

A sudden swirl in a downward flight,
And the hungry snowbirds they alight
    As one on the frozen snow.
Then thither running and hither they go,
    Glance at and pass
    Dead stems of grass
Naked upstanding amid the snow,
    Poor things! Poor things!
    It's little they find,
    In their crops to grind,
And the wave of a hand across the snow
  Will send them swirling, swirling all,
  With never a cheep and never a call,
    Lovely and light
    In an upward flight—
    A bevy of wings
    Sun-flashed upon,
A flurry of birds above the snow,
A flurry of shadows the birds below,
    And shadows and birds are gone.

Snowbird (Courtesy of Bill Schmoker)

[10] Small North American finch with a grey or black head and white tail feathers which flash in flight. Seen chiefly in winter in coniferous forests.

THE CHICKADEE[11]

"Chicka-dee-dee! Chicka-dee!"
      Oh thou wee
        Winter-time wonder!
        The rimy bough above or under.
How quick those round bright eyes can see
The leastest mite that there may be!
        And when the snowflakes fall,
And the pine or the cedar or hemlock is then thy tree,
        Thine is no woeful call,
But a cheery wee chanson, dear to all—
        Not very long,
        Just a sweet little song
Sent forth from the joyous wee heart in thee,
        "Chicka-dee-dee! Chicka-dee!"
And when at night in the sheltering tree,
Lone in the dark thou dost sleeping be,
'Tis God himself who cares for thee,
        Chickadee!

Chickadee

---

11 Black-capped North American bird of the tit family, about 12-15 cms long. Its name is derived from its distinctive call.

THE WELCOME OF THE FIELDS

Home from the city! and the pleasant fields—
      Oh, the glad welcome they have for me!
Even the sandy patch that only yields
      Bluets for April's mimic nursery
Smiles with delight; and as its edge along
      I walk, close by the tangled wood,
Thrilled am I by sudden bursts of song—
      Song bursts that make to leap for joy the blood.

Last night, the horrid clanging of the cars,
      The reeking city's deep and deaf'ning roar
Came to me where behind my window bars
      I lay, like one who loved the world no more.
And lo, this morning, I'm in love with life,
      With life where Nature, the good mother smiles
On all who come back, heart-whole, from the strife,
      Waged where Mammon's breath the very air defiles.

How good! how pleasant is this morning hour!
      Mosses and ferns and glist'ning blades of grass,
Weed and green herb, and flower and blushing flower,
      Bramble and brier, too, all greet me as I pass.
The air, the balmy air, it to inhale, the while
      I lean against this hillside fence, and look
On field and meadow, stretching mile on mile,
      Feeds me, as with its music doth the brook.

Ploughed is the stony field, and the dark mould,
      Smelling of Nature's wondrous chemistry,
And rich in phosphorus, and salts untold,
      What pleasant memories it doth hold for me!
Around these selfsame rocks how oft have I
      Handling right deftly so the ringing spade,
Gained health for soul and body, and thereby
      A sound foundation for my manhood laid.

But waits me now the clover field, and it, oh, it—
      A piece of God's own handiwork unrolled,
Leaf, crowding leaf, and all with sunshine lit,
      Seems twinkling as with emeralds and with gold.
Oh, how the drops of last night's rain, like gems
      Flash back their radiance to the radiant sun!
Even the weeds, the springing weeds, with diadems
      Are crowned, and sparkling gaily every one.

Along the winding road that leads to everywhere
      I walk until I halt me, and, quite still

Gaze on the woodlands, every day more fair,
      As greener, every day, the distant hill.
Far, far away the clanging of the cars,
      Distant and far the turmoils that not cease;
And here I lean against these pasture bars,
      Drinking in, thank God, my fill of peace.

Oh, those who, for a living, in the city wear
      Out brain and body, if they only knew
How natural life is, and how joyous where
      Earth laughs below her canopy of blue—
Would they not, seeing all their scheming yields
      Scarcely enough to last the allotted span,
Be glad with me to share the welcome of the fields,
      And walk where Nature converse holds with man?

WOODLAND CLOVER IN MARCH

In woodland paths, tramped roughly over
      By those who seeing do not see,
Oh how the first wild tuft of clover,
      Fresh upspringing, delighteth me!

So green, so clean above the gravel
      In tender bunches doth it grow,
Once having seen it, where'er I travel,
      It, as a joy, with me doth go.

Soon as it hears the song birds calling,
      Up it springs and outspreads, until
The April rain on its sweet leaves falling
      Makes them greener and fresher still.

Rising at dawn, love-charmed it watches
      The light of swift oncoming day;
Flames the bright sun, and thrilled it catches
      Joy from his every emerald ray.

Then while afresh, love-hushed, it listens
      Bird song and tumbling waterfall,
Oh how it gleams! Oh how it glistens!
      Splendidly shining its green leaves all.

Not Spring herself, in her airy sandals,
      In her gayest mood, would think to press
The soft green leaves that the feet of vandals,
      Later will grind into worthlessness.

Oh soft green plant! Some hearts are rougher
      And harder than the splintered stone;
When thou art crushed, Oh how I suffer!
      Thy cruellest bruise is a bruise mine own.

Step on thee? No! Round about I'd travel,
      Burst through the brush, or do anything
To spare the green that above the gravel
      So eloquent is of quickening Spring.

Come, thou sweet plant! Come, thou white clover!
      Cling to this sheltering breast of mine.
Bless with thy green the lone woodland rover,
      Who, seeing thee, sees a thought divine.

URSA MAJOR

By whatever name thou'rt known,
        Plough, or Dipper, or Great Bear,
When stars arise, and I'm alone,
        I look for thee, and thou art there.
There up in the fields of night,
        True as ever stars were true
Seven great orbs of brilliant light
        Blazing in the quiet blue.

Does the lovely Cluster know
        (The Pleiades oft by Job's eye seen,)
How thy sun-worlds seven glow
        When the nights are cold and keen?
Dost thou know how fair and far,
        Sparkling in unspoken skies,
Its least faint lamp a giant star,
        Love's abode, the Cluster lies?

All I know (with nought between
        Us, save at times a few bright tears,)
Is that these faint eyes have seen
        Thee shining from both hemispheres.
Ah, how oft, a roving boy,
        Thou my clock wert in the night.
Yes, revolving in the joy,
        Witness bore to my delight.

Now the silver in my hair
        Weighs me down with grief and shame,
Whilst thou still art shining there,
        Young as ever; just the same
Wondrous Plough that 'fore my eyes
        Travelled without let or aid,
Wheeled and turned, nor in the skies
        Any sign of furrow made.

Aeons old when I was born,
        Taking all, like me, on trust,
Still with thee 'tis early morn,
        And will be, when I'm in dust.
Seven great orbs of brilliant light,
        Thou art still the Plough to me;
And through star-sown fields of night
        God's own hand is guiding thee.

LINES TO A LONELY PINE

Pitch-blooded pine, I pity thee,
      So lone and old thou art;
Still in my sight the alien tree,
      From friends so far apart.

With naught to shelter or to shield,
      And yet with none to crowd—
Above the bare and barren field
      Thy dreamy head is bowed.

And never does the woodman hear
      The warmer zephyrs play
Among thy needles, turning sere,
      And darker day by day.

Blighted by every blast that blows,
      A target for the storm—
Fall'n on thy head a hundred snows
      Have bent thy rugged form.

Naught thee from wintry gloom can win,
      Nor soothe thy seeming pain,
For still toward thy distant kin
      Thine arms are stretched in vain.

Oh! had it been thy happier fate
      In forest depths to stand,
Then had thine head been lifted straight
      As any in the land.

For there with all thy strength and might—
      Constrained thou wouldst have striven
Thine head to lift up to the light
      And breathe the air of heaven.

Oh, dreaming pine, my heart is shook!
      So lone thou art and drear,
Thou causest me to forward look
      With less of hope than fear.

Of love and home and friends bereft,
      Well may the outcast moan!
God pity us when we are left
      To fight the fates alone.

THE REDBREAST'S VESPER

In the grey twilight - O from whence
Cometh this song of innocence?

The bush is dark, the tall trees darken,
While here at peace I sit and hearken

To notes so pensive and so sweet
They in my heart themselves repeat,

Dim in dusky fields afar —
Seems to listen yon faint star

To these twitterings soft and low,
Twilight's peaceful overflow—

Music sweet with many a break
Made by one who's scarce awake.

Softer and lower - now it seems
The lullaby of fancy's dreams.

And now it is not - silence deep
Holds the warbler fast asleep.

Oh, may I oft, ere I go hence,
Hear this song of innocence.

IN CARLO'S COMPANY

When from the wet and wintry skies
      The darksome night falls down,
Curled at my feet old Carlo lies
      A mass of matted brown,
Without, may wail the loveless night,
      And bleak the winds may blow,
Within, upon my hearthstone white,
      The ruddy embers glow.

Oft, as the enchanted hours go by
      Unchimed by silver bell,
Old Carlo lifts a kindly eye
      To see if all is well.
And all is well - for in the fire
      The pictured past I see,
The face that I must still admire
      Shines love-lit there for me.

Without the rain and hail and sleet
      May rattle at the pane—
I only hear two lightsome feet
      That faster fall than rain—
I only see the old-world boys
      With heath and heather bright,
I only smell the crackling logs
      That clothe the room with light.

Thus, while the world without may give
      Concern to other men,
I sit before the fire and live
      My boyhood o'er again.
Thus, while the night to bedtime flies,
      And I my visions make,
Curled at my feet old Carlo lies
      And dreams till I awake.

A LOVER'S SONG TO SPRING

Thou gold-haired joy of hoping hearts,
      And art thou here again,
Smiling while winter slow departs,
      Unblest by ailing men?
Love in thy laughing light-blue eyes,
      Young flowers about thy feet,
Loved things thou bidd'st from death arise,
      Once more to find life sweet.

Thy presence to the waking woods
      Is dear as 'tis divine,
Blush on their boughs a million buds,
      Meeting that love-look thine,
And, soft new-robed in quiet grace,
      'Mong other creatures fair,
One floweret shows her blushing face,
      And one her yellow hair.

The grass and clover, taking heart,
      And gladdened by thy voice,
Sprout and spread, and, greening, start
      To silently rejoice.
The bluebird, thy first messenger,
      A threefold note he sings:
And from thy tallest chestnut, rare
      The robin's piping rings.

The brown songsparrow, without pomp,
      On fence and rail and tree,
And, 'mong the willows by the swamp,
      Makes joyous melody.
And while he flies, the blue-black crow,
      Waffing a wider wing,
In a loud voice and glad, also,
      Salutes thee, radiant Spring.

Below the brown and trodden leaves
      That 'neath the oak tree lie,
Some mystic Being warps and weaves
      Young rootlets, silently.
And lo! Where budding undergrowth
      A pleasant smell outgives,
At newly dressed, and nothing loath,
      Anew the bloodroot lives.

A thousand things, unseen by man,
      In glen and wildwood grow,

All piped to by a willing Pan
      Whose presence well they know.
The very flies thy voice have heard,
      And by the sunn'd moss-stone,
To hum of bee and song of bird,
      Reply in undertone.

Oh, ailing man, in cities pent,
      Come forth, come forth and see,
What God has in his mercy sent,
      To bless and comfort thee!
The rills rejoice, the green buds ope,
      Love brightens breast and wing,
And laughs the blue, that, like my hope,
      Salutes thee, radiant Spring!

THE WIND AND THE LEAVES

Wind, if I could tell my lady what you tell the leaves,
      If I could only move her as you move the leaf,
Then the long time of the wooing, over which my spirit grieves,
      Would be as bright and brilliant as the day of joy is brief.

Today all in a birchen bower I sat and heard you say
      The sweetest words, the softest words that I have ever heard;
And you said them to the laughing leaves in such a loving way
      That the delight between you for half and hour I shared.

And as I sat there listening to the happy leaves and you,
      Behold, my mind went back again to when I was a boy,
And I saw a maiden tremble, and love in eyes of blue,
      And a world that seemed revolving with a sudden sense of joy.

O wind, you love to whisper to the leaves when they are young,
      You toy with them at twilight and you fondle them at dawn.
But my lady will not listen - she has seen the red leaf flung,
      She has seen the leaves lie scattered when the summer wind was gone.

LENORA

A Song of Sorrow

Oh, shining river, rolling wave,
      Beamed on by autumn's sun—
Lenora's in her cold dark grave,
      And still you race and run.

Yet often she, your tide upon.
      A rose 'tween blue and blue,
And radiant as is summer dawn,
      Made still more lovely you.

And now - to endless sleep disposed—
      Whate'er their visions be,
Her lidded eyes, in darkness closed,
      No more they ope for me.

O'er lip and limb, o'er brain and brow,
      A sudden change has come;
The pallid cheeks are cold, somehow,
      The mouth as marble dumb.

The life that circling to that brain,
      Touched lip and limb and brow,
And raced back to the heart again—
      Oh, God, where is it now?

When winter's icy hand is laid,
      Oh, wave, your bosom on,
Think how it fared with this dear maid,
      Unwilling to be gone.

Remember, too, your summer tide,
      And how, when love was new,
A happy rose, in maiden pride,
      She graced your shining blue.

And think you now, while autumn greets
      All glad things pleasantly,
And life to life its joy repeats,
      How mourns the soul in me.

Nor can wise Nature make me wise,
      Nor ease my sighing breath,
The heart is dumb, the splendid eyes,
      Are closed in silent death.

Sun-litten river, chilly eve,
      And dull and chilly dawn,
They mourn, but not like me they grieve
      For loved Lenora, gone.

MEMORIES OF MOUNT TOM

"Jesus went up into a mountain"

ON THE LORD'S DAY

As up that mountain path we climbed—
    While woke to life the flowers,
Big drops of dew their falling timed
    To slow-timed footsteps ours.

Awake the morn! and all besprent
    The leaves and ferns with dew;
Glad song and call the veeries sent
    Wide oaks and maples through.

Awake our souls! and every sense
    Of kinship us within,
Glowed with a love, the more intense,
    That more was still to win.

THE HAREBELL

The mountain's side adown, or o'er
    Rough cairns - where silent doze
Great stones and rocks; or, 'mid rough store
    Of shale - well known to those
Who love her haunts; these tell the more,
    How sweet the harebell blows.

The rubble and the rocks among,
    Shy bells, a trembling few,
Become, when May her song has sung,
    The flowers, that, gemm'd with dew,
Across some cliff's glad face are strung —
    A veil of living blue.

THE RED PINES

Stone-deaf to man's desultory strife
    Storm-battered, great-souled, grand,
And looking to the Lord for life,
    Thought-rapt these red pines stand.

And, oh, the dreams, the peaceful dreams,
    They have of great days, when
Around them life surges in such streams,
    Its like comes not again.

Yet have they still a fine regard
        For those who come to hear,
Soul-musings, deep as ever bard
        Poured in a monarch's ear.

At dusk, to hither come and wait
        The stars flash out in glee,
And watch these trees, is at the gate
        Of heaven itself to be.

Communion hold they with those pines
        That, long-time, passed away,
Yet were so great in life, there shines
        God's face on these today.

Lift they their heads, but not in pride,
        While smiles the morning sky,
Pity and love them long denied,
        They not these things deny.

Teachers are they, these sturdy pines,
        That dwell upon the rocks,
Thrusting strong roots within deep mines,
        Withstanding tempest shocks.

Unto the ripe and thoughtful mind
        They breathe forth strength and rest
The rest of strength - content the wind
        Blows where it listeth best.

At dawn, to hither come and walk,
        Is, rapt of soul, to be
A spirit where great spirits talk
        Of heaven's felicity.

At noon to hither come and sit,
        Is, hushed of soul, to see
A larger heaven, by love uplit
        Through all eternity.

DISTANT HILLS

Distant hills, so blue, so blue!
        Just pleasant journeys from
This mighty peak, this wonder view,
        This Nebo, this Mount Tom.
Here well might man, some Lord's day on,
        Enraptured take his stand,

And view those hills, till, distance gone,
      Laughed back the promised land.

THE WOOD THRUSH AND HIS SONG

As on a bough at eve he sang
      A song nor gay nor sad,
Though grey cliff none with echo rang,
      Yet we at heart were glad.

For 'ware of all that listening was,
      That song we hear for aye,
Since, quiet piped, we heard it then—
      The hymn of closing day.

Oh, happy thrush! that thus could sing,
      Nor worried be with care,
Then to thy rest, to dream of spring—
      Spent here, or otherwhere!

O thrice blest bird, thy mate thee nigh,
      The while she heard thee sing,
Sweet visions had of love's own sky,
      Thy speckled breast, and - spring!

Yet not of these things 'twas we thought,
      As slow we walked along,
But of the where thy soul had caught
      The spirit-tones of song.

AT SUNSET

Look! Day now passing to its rest,
      See how the sunset shines
And glows upon that broad deep breast
      Of silent, breathing pines!

Full well these know that never day
      Goes downward to its rest,
But one upsprings, at dawn, to say
      "I, too, will make you blest!"

O, happy, happy sunset hour!
      Oh, day of days divine!
Sleep sweet, thou modest mountain flower,
      And dream, thou mountain pine!—

For though soul love the dream survives,
        Yet are there moments blest,
When sunset dreams are for true lives
        Eternities of rest.

MORE MOUNT TOM MEMORIES

A NOVEMBER HEPATICA[12]

Splendid it was through those brown woods that tower
        The wide Connecticut so far above,
        At noon to walk and with the eye of love
See there in bloom the shy November flower!
Sheltered alike from shine and from the shower
        That oft is like a chilly rain to prove,
        Buds are that feeling a new life to move
Within them, bloom! if 'tis but for an hour.

And one of these - its wrappings first descried,
        Lone on that mountain, gloriously wild!
        Cradled, as it had been a little child—
By careful hands the brown leaves brushed aside,
Its blue eyes opened, opened, oh, so wide,
        And looked at us, the bonnie dear, and smiled.

Hepaticas.

---

[12] A genus of a herbaceous perennial plant belonging to buttercup family that grows in shady wooded areas. A few botanists include it within a wider interpretation of anemone. Usually flowers from February to May with white, pink or bluish-purple petals.

THE MUSIC OF THE CROWS

Afar we heard them - far, so far,
      The wind it scarce there blows,
Yet came to us, by note and bar,
      The music of the crows.

Big oaks, oh, how they skyward looked,
      And strained them - all one ear,
And rigidly their great arms crooked,
      That far-off chime to hear!

And we, aware of how a sense
      Of silence, without sound,
If stirr'd becomes the more intense,
      Joy in far singing found.

Those mighty brown woods high above—
      Far as wild fancy dared
Her wing to try, a song of love,
      All joyous clanged, we heard.

And now at dawn, at close of day,
      Or when the winds repose,
Still hear we, miles and miles away,
      The music of the crows.

THE WIND AND BROWN OAK LEAVES

Where aster stalks snow-freighted hung,
    And grass stalks drooped in sheaves,
Sweet, oh sweet, the west wind sung
    Among the brown oak leaves.
A rustle now, then a stir more loud,
    And still in a joyous key,
Among those oaks, a sturdy crowd,
    The wind sang gloriously!

Snowflakes and sunshine! Oh the sight;
    And the little brook that ran—
Here inky dark, there flashing bright,
    A mirror for God Pan.
Snow in the hollow, snow on the height,
    And snowflakes thick that fell,
And sweet through all the gold sunlight,
    Seeming to say "'Tis well!"

And ever and ever, those leaves among,
    Pleasing the parent tree,
Flattered by snowflakes, the west wind sung
    And made sweet melody,
Nor might the snow on the withered grass
    Murmur or sad repine,
For flashed on it, as on polished glass,
    Shafts of the gold sunshine.

Rough briery roots and bramble roots,
    And roots bared to the sun,
Stiff aster stalks and snow-clad shoots,
    Gemmed and bejewelled shone.
Snow on the glistering pine tree eaves
    Snow to rough knots that clung,
And ever the wind 'mong those brown oak leaves
    Lilted and laughed and sung.

THE MUSIC OF SORROW

The cheerful note let others love,
    I envy not their glee,
But, mindful of the mateless dove,
    The sad, sweet note for me.

The notes that by their tenderness,
    The depth of love reveal,
Oh, be they mine, some heart to bless,
    And mine, to soothe and heal.

In sadness 'tis come to our aid
    The life-strains, deep and strong,
Through which, in time, are happy made,
    Loved souls that sorrow long.

The organ note of deepest tone,
    That quivering on the air,
Has in it pity, love, and moan,
    And hope, and earnest prayer.

The note that dies not, being gone,
    But charged with sympathy,
And still melodious, still lives on
    In dearest memory.

This healing note, oh be it mine,
    That, restful, it may reach
Some heart that, fated to repine,
    Loves music more than speech.

The cheerful note let others love,
    I envy not their glee,
But, mindful of the mateless dove,
    The sad, sweet note, for me.

AMES HILL[13]

A sunny piece of pasture land
      Has been my soul's delight so long,
Time after time I've hoped and planned
      Some day to circle it with song.

Where stately mansions, right and left,
      Are homes for peers or poets fit,
This green field stands still unbereft
      Of all the Lord has done for it.

Above the city's topmost tiles,
      Still from the azure sky unshut,
It looks beyond the hills, and smiles
      Upon the wide Connecticut.

The day be warm, or wild, or wet,
      I never pass it but I lean
Against the yellow bars, and let
      My soul feed on the quiet scene.

Even in winter, when the snow
      The highest windlestraw has hid,
I pause to think of life below
      The long-time frozen coverlid.

In summer time, below the boughs,
      In a green covert nature-made,
Full oft I watch the peaceful cows
      Cud-chewing in the scented shade.

With the still green and stalwart oak
      That patient at the gateway stands,
Though words between us ne'er are spoke,
      In spirit oft I've shaken hands.

Long ere the blazing summer suns
      Have burned the herbage up with heat,
Light-hearted here the robin runs—
      A lovely bird, on lightsome feet.

Here sweetly the song sparrow sings
      What time the red March dawns awake
The blushing, blue-eyed one that brings
      The bonnie birds to bush and brake.

---

[13] A well-known landmark close to the poet's residence in Maple Street, Springfield.

And when tanned autumn's magic touch
        Has turned the birken leaves to gold,
Oh, then it is I see how much
        Warm sunshine a green field can hold.

A house on it might rise up fair,
        A mansion scarce would hide the view,
But would the dewy grass be there,
        Or any herb to drink the dew?

Like treasure true uplaid above,
        This pasture me such joy doth yield,
I thank my God the owners love
        Cold siller less than shining field.

Blest are the trees that near it stand,
        And green the shrubs that round it grow,
For love it is that keeps the land
        Secure from Nature's deadly foe.

A grassy slope may it remain
        So long as eyes delighted see,
When falls the sunlit April rain,
        The herb upspringing fresh and free.

INNOCENCE

At dark or dawn, in shine or shower,
    Without offence
At skies that scorch or skies that lower—
    Modest as shame—
The bonnie little smiling flower
    That hath for name—
        Innocence!

It brightens swamps, it talks with rills,
    With stone and fence;
The spongy mead with light it fills—
    Modest as shame,
It hallows all the herbaged hills,
    Its holy name—
        Innocence!

Its happy face - oh how it charms
    Those souls intense
That roam o'er fair forsaken farms—
    Modest as shame,
It hides within the woodland's arms,
    Its lovely name—
        Innocence!

In vacant lots, by cattle trod—
    When these go hence,
In tufts it gems the tussocked sod—
    Modest as shame,
It blooms a gentle child of God,
    Its holy name—
        Innocence!

On rocky knolls, on upland slopes,
    In Spring's defence,
Its golden eye in April opes—
    Modest as shame,
It fills our souls with larger hopes,
    Its charming name—
        Innocence!

Now good the Power who it befriends,
    Nor can dispense
Without its love when springtime ends—
    Modest as shame,
Its dewy head at dusk it bends,
    Its holy name—
        Innocence!

May grander be the costly blooms,
      Come - who knows whence?
That gair and garnish rich men's rooms—
      Modest as shame,
The lowly flower whose light illumes
      Its own loved name—
            Innocence!

FIVE SONNETS

TO SPRING

Spring! If when I am dead, thy light feet pass
      Above the turf that hides my humble clay,
      E'en while thou passest, one brief moment stay
To tell me if the rain is on the grass,
Or if God's blessed sunshine (then, alas!
      Invisible to me) doth make the day
      Pleasant above my grave; or, far away,
If life requickens on the wild morass.
This would I know, so that I, even then,
      May filled be with a holy joy and deep—
And though no longer with the sons of men
      Number'd, yet may have reason none to weep,
But be as one who smileth softly when
      He in his happy dreams hath soundest sleep.

LISTENING TO THE LARK AT SUNRISE

Oh, when the wakeful lark, brave free-born bird!
      Up from his dewy couch, at sunrise springing,
Is, by the wonder and the glory, stirred
      To sudden rapture, and to upward winging,
      Circling he takes his happy flight whilst singing
The splendid paean that, in heaven heard,
      Sets there a myriad of joy-bells ringing—
Who's he that listening, the briefest word
      Would whisper? Who then would thoughtless mar
The blest enchantment? Who would not far rather
      The bird adore, that, like a singing star,
From higher heights still seems new force to gather,
      And while he hearkens to the song afar,
Silently thank, for it, the great All-Father?

TO JAMES DUNCAN[14]

O Mage of my young manhood! whose ripe mind,
      Though in moons younger, was with knowledge stored,
      And wise in counsel; thou who in soul adored
Beauty and truth; whose inborn taste, refined,
Won to thy side the young Ruskins of our kind—
      Oh thou who wert my Jonathan; thou who soared
      So far above me that thy aphorisms poured
Into glad ears, still most to thee inclined.
Friend Duncan! Dost thou not whiles backward glance
      And muse upon the great life we lived then?
Dost thou not sometimes see the countenance
      Of him who, in love, slow-wielding now this pen,
Still think'st of thee, as knight of old romance,
      A very prince among the sons of men?

JUNE

Where was it that I met with flower-crowned June?
      Not in the garden where red roses blow,
      Nor on the shaven lawn whose ridges show
Bare root and stubble to the burning noon.
The brook was singing a delightful tune,
      Broad ferns grew thick the alders green below,
      And plants so lush they scarcely seemed to know
If late the leafy season was or soon—
Here 'twas the nymph I startled! White and cool
      The lilies in her gold locks twined; and she
Her feet was dabbling in a little pool
      That else had mirrored the young poplar tree
Whose leaves above her laughed, as beautiful,
      Dimpling she smiled at poor intruding me.

---

[14] A close Scottish friend of the poet and a witness to his first marriage to Janet Main in Glasgow (1877).

AUTUMN

She of the yellow hair and sandaled feet,
    She of the laughing looks and cheeks brown-tanned,
    Blithe passing goes now through the pleasant land
Rich in the ripening corn and garnered wheat.
Blessing on blessing, sweeter sweet on sweet,
    When she on some green hillock takes her stand,
    Sees she up-piled and stored on either hand,
While her the labourers with glad looks greet.
Aster and goldenrod, in dim woods these,
    And on the mountains, oak and maple shine;
Joyed by her presence flash the inland seas,
    And run the rivers, as if brimmed with wine;
Laugh the red apples on rejoicing trees,
    And hails her all the land as queen divine.

THE DAFFODILS

A plot of garden the sunshine fills,
    And here it is the first daffodils
Send up their green spikes all a row;
    Shoot up their stems till the blossoms blow.
And then while the sparrow sings and trills,
    Nod and curtsey the daffodils.

The south wind woos them, the night wind chills,
    But morn brings joy to the daffodils,
And lovely they look as their heads incline
    Now this way, now that, in the bright sunshine.
Stirs them a breeze, a light one, and they,
    Golden and sunny, shine like the day.

O how the mind with delight it fills—
    The gleam and glow of the daffodils,
That garden plot with its blossoms then
    Makes to rejoice toil-weary men.
Gay, while the sparrow sings and trills,
    Nod and curtsey the daffodils.

FOR THE LAST TIME

A last time always, a very last,
      In every clime!
But oh, the pain! when love's porch we've passed
      For the last time.

With eyes soul-filled the wide sky we view
      At morning's prime,
Nor know, it may be, we've seen heaven's blue
      For the last time.

Up some road we stray, or, listening, roam
      Where sweet bells chime,
Nor know, it may be, we've seen our home
      For the last time.

With some true mind-mate, blithe and bland,
      We rhyme and rhyme,
Part then, nor know we've clasped his hand
      For the last time.

Where wild blooms sweeten their morning bath
      Upward we climb,
Nor know we ascend the mountain path
      For the last time.

With some grand woman, a soul of grace,
      And robed sublime,
We speak, nor know we have seen her face
      For the last time.

And those there are, who, blessed from above,
      Sip sweets at prime,
Nor know they've kissed the lips they love
      For the last time.

A last time always, a very last,
      In every clime!
But oh, the pain! when love's porch we've passed,
      For the last time.

HERO TO LEANDER

To night no brooks meander
      Foam-brimmed they seek the brine;
Oh! Leave me not Leander,
      Some danger I divine;
Rill-thoughts through meads meander,
      In one dark channel mine.
With Hero stay, Leander.
      Nor breast, tonight, the brine.

II

This eve the sun sank heaping
      Up flame clouds in the west,
O'er which pale Hesperus peeping
      Saw blood-red seas unblessed.
The year's last rose went weeping
      And worn out to her rest,
Ere Hesperus on her peeping
      Sank weary in the west.

III

Leander, loved Leander
      Oh! Leave me not alone!
My thoughts through marshes wonder
      To where dark waters moan.

IV

This morn the sun rose quaffing
      Raindrops from lawn and lea;
A thousand rills ran laughing
      And thoughtless to the sea.
Shy song-birds left the mountain
      And trilled on every tree
Whose leaves blush by the fountain—
      Mirror for them and me.
And now a demon rideth
      The winged and starless storm;
In bush the bird abideth.
      The leaves no longer warm—
Are changed and cold and chilly,
      The night wind, o'er them sighs
In ponds where e'en the lily,
      The dark-blue lily dies.

V

Cross not the strait that Io crossed,
  Tonight Leander mine;
About the tower the foam is tossed,
  The billows break in brine.
You go - I mourn my lover lost,
  Remain and Hero's thine.
Or, if you must, my tears shall drown thee
  Ere the deep has drowned;
Before you go my love shall crown thee
  Ere cold death has crowned.
This night my foam-white pillows
  Shall softer be than foam;
This night these warm twin billows
  Shall rest thee ere you roam.
These arms shall fondly fold thee,
  These lips to thine shall cling,
This heaving heart shall hold thee
  To its own sorrowing.
You shall not go, Leander,
  Nor to the steps below
Through the dark night meander,
  Or I with thee shall go.
Shall I sit here in sorrow
  Wan as these marble walls,
While the dim ghost - tomorrow—
  For loved Leander calls?
Go and ye will, Leander,
  See thy dark bride, the sea,
But I with thee shall wander,
  My ghost will follow thee.

VI

Though thou are mute, Leander,
  And sad's the soul in me;
List, while my lute, Leander,
  I lift and sing to thee;
O, hearken, loved Leander,
  Thy own soul sings in me;
Hearken, beloved Leander,
  Thy Hero sings for thee.
Tonight the floods are robbing
  Banks of their golden store;
Tonight the waves are sobbing
  On many a sunless shore.
Tonight the fiends are fouling
  The Heliconian font;

Mad winds are hoarse with howling
        Across the Hellespont.
The rill that runs and ripples
        By zephyrs sweet addressed,
Tonight would drench the nipples
        On yonder mountain's breast.
Mars scowls upon the stranger—
        The star astray above;
Without is death and danger,
        Within is life and love.
Dark night doth now command her
        Furies forth to go;
With Hero stay, Leander,
        And soothe her inward woe.

VII

Cross not the strait that streaming,
        Rushing through rocky walls,
Yon cradled moon is creaming
        With foam that floats and falls,
With foam that jeers gyrating
        To winds that laugh aloud,
To winds that are but waiting
        To make of it thy shroud,
The red rose all to-morrow
        Shall shed her leaves for thee;
Thy white rose from dark sorrow
        Divorced shall never be.
Thy hands no more shall clamber,
        Nor clasp the clinging vine;
Thy curls - soft-kissing amber—
        Shall brittle be with brine.
The strait so often forded,
        Though perilous in the past,
Its strength has only hoarded
        To suck thee down at last.
Thy cheeks no change opining
        Blanch not their ruddy bloom;
Thy lips - red coral shining—
        Denote no common doom.
Go not this night, Leander,
        My loved one, hearken me;
My soul goes forth to wander
        With thine on yonder sea.

THE VISION AND PENELOPE

When sick at heart, Penelope
Lay grieving for her boy at sea;
And mourning sore, as women mourn
For those who go, but not return,
Mourning her absent lord - the great
Ulysses, lost, or held by fate
On some far-off, forgotten shore,
Whence he might come again no more—
This, and on the wine-dark sea,
Telemachus (their one son he)
Made the poor mother's woes so deep,
Her sorrow saddened into sleep.

Then 'twas the clear-eyed goddess - she—
Pallas Athene - cunningly
A Phantom shaped, life-like and warm,
And fashioned fair in woman's form,
Even like lovely Iphthime,
Own sister to Penelope;
And this the goddess straightway sent
To that great house where sorrow pent
Might for a season banished be,
And comfort brought Penelope.
Into the chamber swift it passed
Where slumber held the sleeper fast.

There without mantle, wrap or hood,
By the lone sleeper's head it stood,
And eager-like, with heaving breast,
It thus the dreamless one addressed:
"Are you asleep, Penelope?
Dear troubled heart, it cannot be
The gods that live at ease, and shine,
Shall leave you long to weep and pine;
Your son to you will soon return;
No longer weep, no longer mourn;
The gods are good, your grief they see,
In their eyes no transgressor he."

Made answer then the sleeping form,
All mother-like, and wife-like, warm:
(At the gate of dreams, sweet slumbering, she
Was now the glad Penelope):
"My sister, do you come from far?
For sister mine I know you are;
You never came before to me,
Your home lies far beyond the sea;

You bid me cease from grief and all
The pangs that vex me and enthrall,
Me, who from grief to grief still tossed,
Lament the absent and the lost,"

Then answered her the Phantom dim,
"For your fond boy, oh mourn not him!
Nor in your mind be sore afraid;
For the great goddess doth him aid,
Even Athene, powerful she
With Zeus, the lord of land and sea.
And sister dear, I tell you true,
Seeing you grieve, she grieves for you;
And she it was, you e'en must know,
Who sent me here to tell you so."
Penelope, all heedful then,
Her seeming sister asked again:—

"If a god you are, and but obey
Some heavenly bidding; oh, then say,
Nay tell me also of that one—
My hapless husband! if the sun
Still shines upon his noble head;
Or, is he, as I think him, dead,
And in the house of Hades now
Still - sitting with a brooding brow?"
To this Vision slow replied:
"Some things there are e'en gods must hide;
Nor may I tell you good or ill
Of great Ulysses - Hush! Be still."

So saying, out the Phantom passed,
Mixed with the breezes and the vast.
A creature of Athene's skill,
She comes to men and women still;
In dreams she tells them truths, nor may
She more to them, than told, convey.
Heedful Penelope meanwhile
Awoke, and on her lip a smile;
Her very soul was warmed, and all
Her sense freed from sorrow's thrall,
So much sweet comfort and delight
Her dream had brought her in the night.

THE DOG ARGOS

From the Greek of Homer

When Odysseus home returned,
        A seeming beggar to his halls,
A dog - by evil servants spurned—
        Lay lorn within the courtyard walls.

Mangy and sick and lone he lay,
        Without e'en any strength to move,
Yet was he, on this wondrous day,
        His love, long dormant, well to prove.

For, as if joy bade him rejoice,
        And had not passed the many years,
Soon as he heard his master's voice,
        He lifted up his head and ears.

And while of him the wanderer spake,
        And while the swineherd made reply,
Poor Argos - all his brain awake,
        Answered with listening ear and eye.

And wagged his tail, as if to give
        Glad welcome to the pilgrim grim,
Who while his years were still to live
        By kindliness had made of him.

No mortal of the many there
        The beggar-seeming master knew,
Only the dog, with instinct rare.
        Had memory fond as it was true.

When to the ten years' war in Troy,
        Wise Odysseus had been gone,
Argos, with many a brave-souled boy,
        Pursued the fox, wild goat, and fawn.

In forest-depths no started thing,
        No deer, however swiftly shaped,
No goat that left the mountain spring,
        From this fleet-footed dog escaped.

But time wore on, and from the war
        When he who reared him not returned,
The dog grown old, nor spoken for,
        Was by the foot of servant spurned.

The kindly master long forgot,
      'Twas only fit the cur should lie
Lone on a refuse heap to rot,
      Or when his time came, dog-like, die.

Yet now when twenty years had passed,
      Though feeble, all outworn and sore,
His master's voice he hears at last,
      The face, long loved, he sees once more.

But even while his joy was near,
      Did darksome death upon him come,
Glazed the kind eyes, and each rough ear,
      For very happiness grew dumb.

For having seen his master's face,
      And all too weak to rise, he passed—
Poor Argos! to that happy place
      Where even dog-love lives at last.

HELEN'S GIFT TO TELEMACHUS

When his young guest-lord would be gone
    From the great Spartan's home,
In fiery splendour broke the dawn
    Above the barren foam.

Then Menelaus (well he knew
    How gifts befit a crown),
His son, and Helen's self, into
    Their treasure house went down.

A silver bowl deep-rimmed with gold,
    Likewise a double cup
Selected were, and these right bold
    The sire and son bore up—

Bore to the hall with zeal and zest,
    With gladness and good will;
While by her perfumed cedar chests,
    Queen Helen lingered still.

The gifts to the young guest were given;
    But ere he outward passed,
Fair as the shining moon in heaven
    Came Helen up at last.

Then well the beardless youth might lift
    Eyes filled with wondering thought
As she held out the lovely gift
    Her own white hands had wrought.

"I, too, dear boy" (thus she commenced
    Her speech, as matrons may),
"Will give a gift, a keepsake 'gainst
    The wished-for wedding day."

"From Helen's hands," (and ne'er in rhyme
    Was sung a gift so fair)
"This robe against the wedding time,
    For your fair wife to wear.

Meanwhile - for mothers wisely teach,
    Let yours keep this at hand,
And may you soon rejoicing reach
    Your home and native land."

Are long time gone the hollow ships,
    And gone the Argive men,

But these fond words from Helen's lips
    Are lovely now, as then.

AURORA TO TITHONUS

When thou wert young, and I loved thee well,
When thy warm cheek and mine, fresh from the fount,
Together pressed did make the morning! When our smiles
And love-illumined eyes did warm the glad blue day,
When thou, in far sky spaces calm and cool,
Wert lying in my lap, nor shading half-shut eyes,
Would ask me list the earth-born bird - the lark,
Of mated love loud carolling.
And oh! How oft for hours we harked enchanted!
While our hushed wheels and sun-lit car slow-loitering
Slid down the crimson slope, until ere dusk they dipped
In that far western wave that, blushing, hid the happy steeds
Still speeding to the scented isle where all night long we lay—
The dewy dark around, the burning stars above,
Awaiting joys to be renewed, and thinking love
Must still abide; then did I, in my joy, entreat the gods
To give thee immortality. Which being given, lo! In a day
Didst thou begin to fade.   Oh! having asked so much,
Why did I not beseech for more? Blind, blind I was
Not to request with this: that thou shouldst never
Fading know! The gods were just! They gave all that I asked.
But, had I known that thou, so soon to be by time
And mortal love consumed, shouldst wane and wither;
Shouldst wander lone and grey, or stand, as stands
The pulseless pine its brethren green among, songless
And sapless, in the flush of thy young manhood,
Even while they cheek was pressed to mine, yea, at risk
Of blinding the blue day, then had I rather craved
The gods to send thee death, immortal death!
So shouldest thou, by sages mourned, by poets sung,
In memory evermore alive, have gone down crowned
With deathless love, nor lorn of sad Aurora's smile.
Now when my steeds
Career along the east, parting with fiery breath
The sullen cloud, long time before they take the steep
And swift ascent, or pausing on the peerless hill,
With glad wild eyes and neighings wake the golden morn,
Lo! rosy from my car I lean and shed the tears
That are the dews around thy feet on that cold hillside
Where I see thee stand - life in the garb of age,
And hoary with grey hairs.

                              Then when the misty cloud
Begot of grief, comes thee and me between,
When I am far upborne to airy spaces calm and cool—
Though sunlit all, I shut my ears, I will not hear the lark
Loud carolling of mated joys - but nursing still
My sorrow, one moment see the fresh young face,
The love-lit eyes, that meeting mine, once more
Make sweet the morning! and the next and this my torture
Is until night returns my saddened eyes behold
The lorn old man - my lover still - who, on the grey
Hillside, lone trembling stands, his bleared and faded eyes
Sun-smitten, his wrinkled hands in vain uplifted.
A million winters ever bleaching more and more
The onetime snow-white throat where oft my blushing face
I cooled, where oft I found love's joy and warm delight.
                              Then, as to my ears
Come his heart-rending cry for death, loved death,
To him for evermore denied, I shudder in my gilded car:
Lie loose the reins in the neglected lap, once soft
And warm and filled with the fair head of young Tithonus,
Then, shutting dark my tear dimmed eyes, whate'er
The gods may think, no longer am I to myself
Aurora! Clothed with clouds my vexed steeds swerve,
Or, wandering lost, do bear me where they will,
This is they punishment and mine.

IRISH POEMS

THE OLD STRIPPER

We bought her in the Por'down fair
      Twelve long years ago.
She was the sleekest 'moiley' there
      And made the finest show.

We brought her home sound as a bell,
      And didn't the childer smile!
To see that udder - milky well—
      Fill cans in proper style.

On curly kail we fed her long
      On praties and on straw,
But we must sell her for a song
      Or whatever she will draw.

In May she fed on buttercups
      And dandelions too,
And all the neighbours came for sups
      Of cream, as neighbours do.

She turned out butter as the mine.
      Turns out the yellow gold,
And now when daisies blossom fine,
      Poor 'moiley' must be sold.

That head that we have petted oft,
      Must feel the butcher's blow,
And from that neck once fine and soft
      The dark red blood will flow.

But poor old cow, yours is the fate
      That waits so many kine,
It cometh soon or cometh late—
      But 'moiley', you were mine!

And though we have a 'speckled' calf.
      A yearling of thine own—
It never makes the childer laugh—
      The childer all are flown!

There, take a drink old 'moiley', there,
      Where water lilies lie,
For you I'm taking to the fair
      Because that you are 'dry'.

BRINGING HOME THE COWS

The sun was sinking in the west,
        The lark had sought the lea,
The dew fell on the roses' breast
        Both soft and silently.
The honeysuckle in the lane
        Was sweet as honeycomb,
When last I helpéd Mary Jane
        To bring the cattle home.
But sweeter was the dewy kiss
        No lassie disallows;
When she with lover shares the bliss
        When bringing home the cows.
And gives the kiss, she'll never miss
        When bringing home the cows.

She was no soft and silly maid
        To kiss and then to cry,
Her eye was bright as dewy pearl
        And full of witchery.
And well I loved with her to stray
        Below the darkened dome,
Her starry eye lit up the way
        That went the cattle home.
Nor did her lip disdain to kiss,
        Which every swain allows
Is half the joy and all the bliss
        Of bringing home the cows.
The dewy kiss I did not miss
        When bringing home the cows.

The eve was dusky in the lane
        Though light upon the lea,
The twilight suited Mary Jane,
        The twilight suited me.
And if we strayed beside the stile
        'Twas better than to roam,
For we were bringing all the while
        The lazy cattle home.
Her rosy lips received the kiss
        No lover disallows,
When he with lassie shares the bliss
        Of bringing home the cows.
And gives the kiss he'll never miss
        When bringing home the cows.

THE MONTIAGH MOSS[1]

The turf bummer rises early,
    Early rises from his 'doss',
'Pangs' his bed both neat and fairly,
    Somewhere in the Montiagh moss.

Be they brown or be they 'marly',
    Be they black or only 'fums',
They're to him as golden barley,
    From them the money comes.

His cheeks are red as ripe tomatoes,
    Or brown as his abode,
He takes his breakfast of potatoes,
    Starts his 'shilty' on the road.

Cracks his whip along the highway,
    Loops the birch or sings a song,
Stones the sparrows in the byway,
    As he rides in state along.

Jogging through any weather,
    Happy as a circus clown,
The turf and he arrive together,
    Near the tunnel of the town.

Here he sells his load of fuel,
    For a 'bob', or half a crown,
The foreman handily give him gruel,
    The latter pinks of porter brown.

Be him John or be he Jacky,
    He's a cunning crafty card,
But if he's small and smokes 'tobaccy',
    The road for him is rotten hard.

Then he joins the ragged many,
    If he has a coin to spare,
Tries to turn an honest penny,
    Tries to turn it in the air!

See his thumb along the 'tosser',
    While he throws the pennies high,
Quaking lest he be a 'loser',
    When upon the ground they lie.

---

[1] A lowland raised bog about 1.25 miles east of Lough Neagh. It consists of an intricate mosaic of turf ramparts, trenches, pools and drains interspersed with small hay fields. It is now an area of Special Scientific Interest.

If he's big and takes a 'johnny',
    O the lies he then can tell,
The master tells him to drive 'conny',
    But he gallops home like hell.

And as homeward thus he journeys,
    If he 'jockeys' with a friend,
A letter from some sharp attorneys,
    Teaches him his ways to mend.

MY SCHOOL-GIRL

Once more thy school face I behold —
    A wood flower washed in dew!
The sweet blue eyes each day that told
    The tender tale anew.

The raven hair that lightly hung
    A shadow on thy slip,
The strawberries young Love had strung
    To lure me on thy lip.

The music of thy merry voice,
    Thy laughter and thy play,
The jest o'er which we did rejoice,
    Are in my heart today.

The way to school was never long.
    Accompanied by thee,
We heard the skylark's matin' song
    Or rested by the tree.

Our quiet homes divided lay
    By only rustic stile,
Ah! we were young and every day
    We parted with a smile;

And every morn the lane was green
    And every eve was fair;
And you the bud and rose between,
    The fairest blossom there!

And now that we are worlds apart,
    How truly I discern,
The lesson then I got by heart
    I never can unlearn.

SWEET-BRIER

Out of the brier the soft green leaf
      Came when the April rain
Brought the bursting buds relief
      In many a lonely lane,
When April sunshine bright and brief
      Alternated with the rain,
When shine and shower, like love and grief,
      Kissed in the lonely lane.

Often adown that way I went
      To see the primrose pale,
And oft the sweet-brier's fragrant scent
      With gladness I'd inhale;
For oft as a boy were my footsteps bent
      To see the primrose pale;
When the winds of March were well nigh spent
      The sweet-brier I'd inhale.

After the shower how sweet the smell
      Of the violet and the rose,
But the scent of the sweet-brier who can tell
      When the young green leaves unclose,
When with sweetness the green buds swell
      On the brier and the rose,
When spring doth with the sweet-brier dwell
      And her scented leaves unclose?

In dreams I wander adown the lane
      To see the primrose blow,
And I see the sweet-brier once again
      As I did long years ago,
But woke by the wind at the window pane
      That bringeth the winter snow;
For the sweet-brier's breath I may sigh in vain,
      It will never come back, I know.

HOME THOUGHTS FROM ABROAD

Ballinary, Ballinary, it is there I am again,
      With its long green rampers, caressed by gentle rain,
And is that my childhood home, my eyes now see once more,
      With rows of dancing marigolds, a pathway to the door?

Ballinary, Ballinary, it is there I am again,
      And is that the footstick that straddles Brannon's drain?
And that's me in the sally tree, by Cupid's arrow smitten,
      When from its leafy branches, I first spied Jenny Mitton.

Ballinary, Ballinary, it is there I am again,
      Upon a Sabbath morning by the hawthorn lane,
In the distance faintly ringing the Milltown bell I hear,
      Calling all good folk to worship, the sinner and sincere.

Ballinary, Ballinary, it is there I am again,
      And there's old Bella lilting a pensive, sad refrain,
Her voice I've heard a hundred times, in summer days gone by,
      As I lay upon the stubble rig and watched the marbled sky.

Ballinary, Ballinary, it is there I am again,
      Can you still get tea from Palmer's and spuds from Billy Swain?
I hear the children's voices, coming home from Cloncore School,
      Some teasing, some squabbling and some just playing fool.

Ballinary, Ballinary, it is there I am again,
      The linnets and the yorlins, O I can see them plain,
And if these eyes should close in death upon a foreign shore,
      May my spirit cross the great divide, and bring me home once more.

THE REPLY TO MR. FRANK BURNS[2], RURAL POSTMAN, PORTADOWN, IRELAND,
Written on receiving a souvenir from him.

From Erin's Isle, o'er many a mile
    Of green sea water and of foam,
The letter came, and in the same
    A worthy souvenir of home;
And safe inside I found with pride
    What I shall prize where'er I roam.

The photograph it made me laugh
    With joy to see on single card,
Ta'en by the son (and finely done),
    The sweet musician and the bard;
The bond between you plainly seen—
    'Tis brotherhood and kind regard.

Words fail to thank thee friendly Frank,
    For the sweet shamrocks and the name,
Address and all, and what I call
    Remembrance writ in flowery flame—
The graceful bird my bosom stirred—
    A Noah's dove to me she came.

I look on these, and o'er the seas
    Swifter than bird my fancy flies—
My father grey, you in your May
    I see with boyhood's happy eyes!
Ah! Many a mile from Erin's Isle
    To-night the weary wanderer lies!

But wherefore grieve when I receive
    Such offerings from the good and just?
In foreign parts, from loving hearts,
    Such souvenirs of hope and trust!
Ah! Who shall dry lov'd Erin's eye
    When we three slumber in the dust?

But duty's breath and life - not death!
    Duty! - The same where'er we be,
It lifts us higher, and fills with fire
    Each soul that throbbing, still is free;
As to the moon, this night in June,
    Throbs all the silvery flashing sea.

---

[2] Francis Burns (1854-1921), born in Derryadd, married Ellen Martin of Park Road, Portadown, 6 April 1904. He was the President of the Portadown branch of the Postmen's Federation.

Chaste lo! Beam on land and stream,
        On lowly hut and lordly pile;
Thy silver pour around that shore
        That I have loved and lost a while,
And make the road to Frank's abode
        The brightest path in Erin's Isle.

O FRESH AND FRAGRANT ROSES

O fresh and fragrant roses,
        O radiant, joyful June!
Whene'er the rare day closes
        Up gets the yellow moon:
Whene'er the bright day breaketh
        And laughs the East along,
The sound old world awaketh
        To mirth and joy and song.

O fresh and fragrant roses,
        O flushed and flaming flowers!
What time the daylight dozes
        The dew descends in showers;
What time the round sun rises
        And shapeless shadows flee,
Some bud new-blown surprises
        Him who has eyes to see.

O fresh and fragrant roses,
        O light without alloy!
Each shining day still shows us
        Some gem that we enjoy,
When dewy night and dusky
        Reveals the kindling stars,
Balmy's the air and musky
        Beside the garden bars.

O fresh and fragrant roses!
        Breathe till the summer brings
The garlands gay she owes us,
        The thousand longed for things,
The flowers that in the wildwood
        Remind us of the hours,
The charming hours of childhood,
        And wee hands full of flowers.

O fresh and fragrant roses!
        All pearled with silver dew,

Till life and longing closes
> One face I'll see is you.
Within my heart an ember
> Burns morning, night and noon;
One face to misremember
> Would take the joy from June.

THE WATER WAGTAIL[3]

At home, the wagtail black and white,
    The water-willy grey,
Would on our level street alight
    A dozen times a day.
        Willy-wagtail, water wagtail,
            Running o'er the street;
Oft, as a child, on you I smiled,
            And heard you twitter sweet.

With now and then a lively leap,
    And now and then a lag,
You nimbly ran or stopped to cheep
    And give your tail a wag.
        Willy-wagtail, water wagtail,
            Running round the door;
Ah! It may be I'll never see
            Or mock you any more.

In spring your slender cousin came
    From o'er the northern sea;
He flashed across, a yellow flame,
    He came to visit thee.
        Willy-wagtail, water wagtail,
            Yellow willy too,
Though far away I am to-day,
            My heart's at home with you.

Were black and clean your supple claws,
    And black your little bill;
And though each eyelid inky was,
    Each eye was blacker still,
        Willy-wagtail, water wagtail,
            Soft as flakes of snow
Your flecks of white - a pretty sight—
            The blossom and the sloe.

And if I tried to follow you,
    To see if you were wild,
Then up and down, away you flew,
    To charm some other child,
        Willy-wagtail, water wagtail,
            Running round the door;
The child in me may never see
            Or chase you any more.

---

[3] Bird with slender body and a long tail that constantly moves up and down - hence its name. Also known as the pied wagtail, it inhabits areas near ponds or streams.

UPON THE SALLY TREE

In boyhood's days beyond the sea,
    When blushed the buds of spring,
How often on the sally tree
    I heard the throstle sing!
When blue-eyed violets in the vale
    Hung down their heads so coy,
The speckled thrush o'er hill and dale
    Sent forth his song of joy.
He sang as if he only cared
    'Twas good alive to be;
And never sweeter song was heard
    Than on the sally tree.

When February mornings fair
    Brought Nature close to me,
I always heard him singing there,
    Upon the sally tree.
So fine he sang, so free and frank,
    So clear and loud and long.
The primrose in the mossy bank
    Awoke to hear his song.
He shook dark winter from his wing,
    He struck a melting key,
And nowhere sweeter did he sing
    Than on the sally tree.

He sang - and baby runlets rushed
    Adown the hills in glee;
He piped, - and every bud was hushed
    Upon the sally tree,
The wished-for flowers that long had slept
    Their curtains wide did fling,
And flushed and danced and smiled and wept
    To hear the song of spring.
The rosy-fingered Morning ripe
    Came linking o'er the lea
Thinking she heard Apollo pipe
    Upon the sally tree.

A greener hue the holly bush
    Took on, it seemed to me,
Each morning when the speckled thrush
    Sang on the sally tree,
The amber beads upon the oak
    Began to shine and show;
The buds upon the blackthorn broke
    In blossom white as snow,

Grim death for me would have no sting
    And far would sorrow flee
If when I pass the thrush might sing
    Upon the sally tree.

WHEN THE SKYLARK SOARS AND SINGS

Full of merriment and mirth,
Full of laughter is the earth;
Full of blessed labour, too,
For the skies are bright and blue,
And the land with music rings
When the skylark soars and sings.

Flowers white and flowers blue
Are all dabbled o'er with dew;
And the daisy, bonny lass,
Blushes in the dewy grass;
From her velvet couch she springs
When the skylark soars and sings.

Blackthorns bursting with delight,
Bud and blossom snowy white;
Briers shooting up between
Mix and toss their tufts of green;
And the woodbine - how she clings!
When the skylark soars and sings.

Boys and men, and men and boys,
In the fields are full of noise;
Full of healthy vigour, too,
Doing nobly all they do.
They are happier far than kings
When the skylark soars and sings.

Back and forth across the rows
Up and down the harrow goes;
The two horses they enjoy
The light chirpings of the boy;
His old jacket off he flings
When the skylark soars and sings.

Cows and calves and heifers pass
Lightly o'er the springing grass;
Kids are bleating on the hill,
Goats are bleating louder still,
Straining hard at twisted strings
When the skylark soars and sings.

Barefoot boys go roaming round
Glad if one wee nest is found;
Little maidens' faces shine
With a light that is divine;
So much joy the season brings
When the skylark soars and sings.

Joy below and joy above,
All the land is full of love;
Heaven's not so far away
As some silly people say;
For the door wide open swings
When the skylark soars and sings.

CHILDHOOD

All around us in our childhood
    Lies the fields of paradise,
Dewy violets in the wildwood
    Are not sweeter than our eyes,
And the skies are not far from us,
    Earth and Heaven must surely meet,
Shutting in this land of pleasure
    For the pleasure of our feet.

With no thought of a hereafter,
    Knowing not that some must weep,
All our days are mirth and laughter,
    All our nights are lost in sleep.
Hearts as light as any feather,
    Feet that run like any bird,
Dance our happiness together,
    Sorrow never says a word.

TARTARAGHAN

A Memorial and Pastoral Poem

Breathes there a man with soul so dead,
Who never to himself hath said,
"This is my own, my native land?"
                    (Sir Walter Scott)

O, sylvan parish, wooded well
      And watered by the silver Bann,
In dreams I hear thy drowsy bell
      Low toiling o'er Tartaraghan.[4]
Thy lesser sister lifts her spire
      Where Lough Neagh's waters sob forlorn,
The last to feel the sunset's fire,
      The first to flash the light of morn.
Whilst thou, amongst thy leafy trees,
      Art partly hidden from the eye
That opening in the valley sees
      Thee dark against an opal sky,
And there, by loving mourners laid,
      In chosen chambers dark and deep,
Sire and son, matron and maid
      Rest, as if death were happy sleep.
'Neath grassy barrows moulder there
      The bones of my maternal clan,
While winds are hushed as if in prayer
      Around they shrine, Tartaraghan.

Thy former pastor's lamp and light—
      The Master shining through the man[5]—
Oft made a clouded evening bright
      Toiling for thee, Tartaraghan.
His voice gave dove's wings to the word,
      On wounded bosoms fell like balm,
Or, like Bethesda's angel, stirred
      The depths that quivered into calm.
The memory of the good and just
      Outlives the oak upon the hill;
Although the mortal man is dust
      His starry spirit quickens still;
Yea, loves as messenger to meet
      The liberated soul that flies,

---

[4] The Parish of Tartaraghan was constituted by Parliament in 1709 and consisted of 31 townlands. Following the creation of Milltown Parish in 1871 the number of townlands was reduced to 19. The present parish church was erected in 1818, replacing an earlier structure of 1712.

[5] George Robinson, Rector of Tartaraghan, 1849-82.

On pinions fair as they are fleet,
      To the white walls of paradise.
And half a lifetime now away,
      With memory's eyes I love to scan
The face that in my childhood's day
      Was loved through all Tartaraghan.

For patron saint: - No servant calls
      Thee by Saint Mary or Saint Anne,
They worship God within thy walls
      And Him alone, Tartaraghan.
What image formed of wood or stone
      Can hear His children when they cry?
'Tis to the living Lord alone
      They lift, unveiled, the loving eye.
The faith that kept their fathers pure,
      The love that kindled hearts of old,
That faith thy children keep secure,
      That love has never yet grown cold.
It burns among them when they meet;
      On wings of earnest, fervent prayer
It rises to the mercy-seat
      And finds a love responsive there.
Oh! beautiful in any time,
      E'en in this age Victorian,
The simple faith is sublime,
      The highest, too, Tartaraghan.

Thou art not first to greet the new
      Nor last to follow in the van
Of all that's lovely, good and true,
      And temperate, Tartaraghan.
If unrenowned for valiant deeds,
      Or if not as a victor crowned,
No stricken heart within thee bleeds
      But there is healing for it found.
Noble by nature are thy sons,
      Thy daughters virtuous and fair,
The father wine and folly shuns,
      The mother's whisper is a prayer.
Thy children, charming as the flowers,
      Delight and gladden every eye;
Thy light and sunshine, yea, thy showers
      Still fall from a benignant sky.
Thy cultured fields, thy silver streams,
      The flowery meads o'er which I ran,
Make thee the Eden of my dreams,
      My paradise, Tartaraghan.

The brook that babbles through thy glades
        Is haunted by some happy Pan
Whose reedy pipe is tuned when shades
        Of evening veil Tartaraghan.
The primrose, darling of the dyke,
        Stars all the mossy banks in May,
Fragrant the hawthorns, patriarch-like
        Above them growing old and grey;
The creeper crimson on the craig
        Where the rose-breasted linnets sing,
Where thrushes in no language vague
        Tell the delights of early spring.
Twilight descends on silent wings,
        Her tears on folded daisies fall,
And then the little redbreast sings
        The sweetest, softest song of all.
Oh! surely 'twas a loving Power
        That did thy pleasant features plan,
That gave me for my natal bower
        A home in thee, Tartaraghan.

Ah! How thy favoured ones must grieve
        That life on earth is but a span;
Thou art so fair, 'tis hard to leave
        Thy pleasant courts, Tartaraghan.
With what delight the rambler strays
        Thy mounds of golden gorse among,
Or sees, across thy broomy braes,
        Hedges with honeysuckle hung.
Spring hangs her sprays on every bush
        And where the tender lovers stray,
The newly-blown wild-roses blush,
        Or violets turn their eyes away.
Thy league-long meadows emerald green,
        The rippling rills that seldom cease
And sunny vales make thee a scene
        Of pensive beauty and of peace.
And over all the skylark pours
        A flood of song as only can
The bonnie bird that singing soars
        And carols o'er Tartaraghan.

No wily schemers wander there
        The hearts within to cheat and ban,
But those in suffering always share
        Thy tender love, Tartaraghan.
Dire poverty is not disdained
        Nor any home however poor,
So long as virtue keeps unstained

    The lives created to endure.
If frozen rain at Christmas falls
    It is to let thy cottars know
The porches and the lime-washed walls
    Are not so white as driven snow.
The shining showers of April rain,
    The sun that lingers on the latch,
Or blasts of Boreas, all in vain
    Beat on thy thousand roofs of thatch;
Harm not the homes whose chimneys white
    To thy Beersheba from thy Dan
Draw spiral wreaths from fires that light
    Thy open hearths, Tartaraghan.

O'er harpstrings in the courts of kings
    The roving minstrel's fingers ran
In days of old, but Nature sings
    For thee and thine, Tartaraghan.
Sweet song-birds all thy thickets throng,
    But always welcome, always new,
And sweeter far than trill or song
    The two-fold note of the cuckoo.
While labour lifts the tuneful ear
    And milkmaids list'ning cease to sing,
The choirs are hushed as if to hear
    The clearer clarion of spring.
When April's showery dawn is o'er
    The shining fields and folds rejoice,
Heaven opens wide a sun-lit door,
    And gives to every grove a voice.
O foster-nurtured, bashful bird,
    Beloved by woman, child and man.
The woodland's fragrant heart is stirred,
    When you cry in Tartaraghan.

Beyond the domes of Portadown,
    Beyond the windings of the Bann,
Beyond the spires of Lurgan town,
    Long leagues from green Tartaraghan,
Taking their azure from the skies
    And watching over land and sea.
The sun-lit Mourne mountains rise
    In grandeur and in majesty.
And when the winds of winter moan,
    Where icy gales a-roving go,
Far in the wilds of dark Tyrone
    Slieve Gallon' head is white with snow.
Thus when the toiler digs or delves,
    On looking up he has in view,

Not rugged shores or rocky shelves,
      But peaks whose summits pierce the blue,
And when his native hill he climbs,
      His roving eye may also scan
Cathedral towers whose louder chimes
      May chance to reach Tartaraghan.

Thy markets reach the mystic East
      And, it may be, in Hindustan
The robe worn by the royal priest
      Was woven in Tartaraghan.
Oh, when the flax unfolds her flower,
      Delightful 'tis at dawn to see
Eyes dewy wet that in an hour
      Will bells of azure beauty be.
While Nature in the fields without
      Weaves fibre fine for man to spin
The golden sunbeams dance about
      The winking woof and warp within.
The linen woven in those looms
      Makes dusky dames in India smile,
Is prized more than almond blooms
      By dark-eyed daughters of the Nile.
The snowy awnings keeping cool
      The courts or harem of a khan
Had their first bath in some deep pool
      Pellucid in Tartaraghan.

No ruder wind around thee flirts
      Than zephyrs wooing while they fan
The heather-bloom that round thy skirts
      Is blushing deep, Tartaraghan.
Sheltered from tempest, tide and storm,
      Refreshed by pearly dew and rain,
Thy frosts are only such as form
      Ice-ferns upon the window pane.
Rest easy in thy rushy chair,
      Drink in the air that is like wine,
Till sweeter rhymer tells how rare,
      How fair is this first love of mine.
The bee to bloomy clover clings
      That honey may melt in her mouth,
And brave old ocean's current brings
      Her favours from the sunny South.
Around her loyal souls and true
      Shine radiant through the rustic tan,
Souls stainless as the smiling blue
      That bends above Tartaraghan.

Hail, native parish! Loved as well
      As when my life in thee began,
'Twere music now to hear thy bell
      Sweet pealing o'er Tartaraghan.
And sweeter music still, to hear
      Loved voices that in dreams alone
Fall on my world-aweary ear,
      And seem like echoes of mine own.
The dear old temple's rugged walls
      Are venerable and grey with age,
Through choir and apside window falls
      The light subdued on holy page.
Thus, while the furrowed glebe and all
      Becomes a sacred shrine to me,
May tender beams of mercy fall
      On every loving heart in thee.
And while the happy earth goes round,
      While floods and flows the silver Bann,
May peace and joy and love abound
      In all thy tents, Tartaraghan.

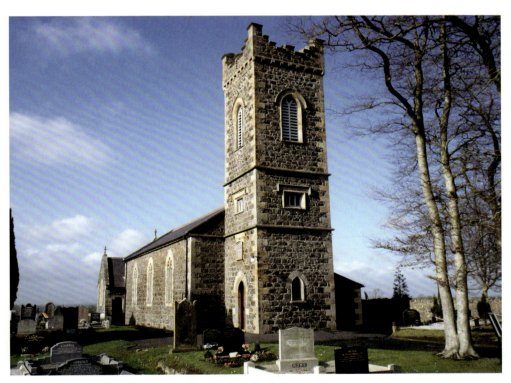

Tartaraghan Parish Church

LOVE IN SPRING

Waiting, wearying for the spring,
What if it should only bring
Bonny buds and birds that sing,
  And not the love of Mary!

Spring of yore that brought me bliss,
Now can bring me more than this,
The beaming smile, the balmy kiss,
  The glowing glance of Mary!

Milk-white flowers were only curds,
Boasting beggars all the birds,
Spring were naught without the words,
  The melting words of Mary!

Hoping, longing for the spring,
How my heart would leap and sing
If't to me as bride should bring
  Blushing, brown-eyed Mary!

BILZY[6]

While in his eyes the light of truth
    Shone brighter than a star,
He left our home a sturdy youth,
    To wander wide and far.

A smart walk to the neighbouring town,
    A gay young sergeant there,
A glass of Dunvilles' swallowed down,
    One word and then and there

Before his heart back home had gone
    Or kind looks come between,
His sonsy fist was shut upon
    The shilling of the Queen.

And now good-bye to country pranks,
    Adieu to rustic joy,
At Belfast barracks in the ranks,
    Behold our Bilzy boy.

Him soon the major's eye discerned,
    Straight as a stripling larch,
In a brief time had Bilzy learned
    To march and countermarch.

Extension drill and rifle drill,
    Swift handling of the steel
So supple made his joints, that Bill
    Could like a swallow wheel.

How bright the flag above them flew,
    How danced delighted eyes,
When Bilzy led battalions through
    The bayonet exercise.

Still brimming o'er with native wit,
    Taught how to step and stand,
Our Bilzy was a soldier fit
    To fight in any land.

Then with his comrades o'er the seas
    Was our young hero sent,
To bring the dark skins to their knees,
    To break what had been bent.

---

[6] Probably the poet's brother, William Francis Teggart.

At torrid noon, by night by day
      Below the brassy blue
They stormed, they forced, they fought their way,
      Wild India through and through.

Across the Ganges' yellow flood
      O'er hills without a name,
Ablaze through seas of blood
      Till they to Delhi came.

And there still warring for the right
      In many a bloody fray,
Through many a fierce-contested fight
      Brave Bilzy led the way.

Ah me! the fearful pranks they played,
      These soldiers of the line,
They oft in dust and ashes laid
      The loved and sacred shrine.

How oft the chieftain proud they slew,
      And giving blow for blow,
How oft they drove the bayonet through
      The fierce heart of the foe.

How often did it them befall
      To send to Allah souls,
Whose black eyes gleaming o'er the wall
      Were red as blazing coals!

How oft with blackened throats athirst
      And souls to heaven that cried,
They saw life's crimson fountain burst
      From some brave comrade's side.

How oft on sultry nights they sat
      The tamarind trees below,
How oft at fiery noon, they spat
      Their fury on the foe.

Then, then was shown in danger's hour
      When shafts were thickest hurled,
The dash, the daring of the power
      That dominates the world.

While sore at home their mothers wept
      While England anguish knew,
Victorious still these onward swept
      To conquer and subdue.

To hearts pierced by a cruel blow
        Nought as revenge is sweet,
These rested not until the foe
        Lay grovelling at their feet.

And through it all where'er engaged
        The demons to destroy,
Where'er the conflict fiercest raged
        There was our Bilzy boy.

And when at last with time to breathe
        Their gaping wounds they dressed,
While Victory did their laurels wreath
        How sweet it was to rest.

With boon companions seated oft
        Below the mango tree,
Of home of sweet blue eyes and soft
        Full many a dream had he.

And there, the stoutest heart to tame,
        Heard once - heard evermore,
Full often from the jungle came
        The hungry lion's roar.

Full oft the jackal's midnight howl
        Made creep their hardihood,
Full oft the tawny tiger's growl
        To water turned their blood.

Yet through it all Bill bore his part
        Nor ever once did fail,
Whate'er might hap, this Briton's heart
        Was never known to quail.

For twenty years in Hindustan
        Through weather foul and fair,
This Birches boy, this Ulsterman
        Did bravely do and dare.

Sick once, to far-off Simla sent
        Though lying at death's door,
Our Bilzy boy was quite content
        Fresh air to feel once more.

There when the snowy mountain peaks
        Were rosed with dawn of day,
How of the thought of blushing cheeks
        And blue eyes far away.

Heaven 'twas to him who o'er Kabul
        Had felt the simoom blow,
To taste the water sweet and cool
        With Himalayan snow.

At last, although not seeking rest
        Nor halt nor blind nor lame,
With "Bravery's" medal on his breast
        Back home our Bilzy came.

No grizzled warrior grim and grey
        But lithe, alert, and brown,
Well had he earned for life each day
        A shilling from the crown.

And when he came no more a lad
        But smiling and serene,
His greatest pride was that he had
        The throne of Delhi seen.

So brief the many seasons seemed
        So full of joy the day,
Could it have been we only dreamed
        Our Bilzy was away.

Though he since that first day in sooth
        Had wandered wide and far,
Still in his eyes the light of truth
        Shone brighter than a star.

THE PEASANT FOLKS' HALLOWE'EN

(North of Ireland)

The wind is blowin' from the hill
      Wi' squally gusts between,
The night is dark, an' showers fill
      The sheughs, this Hallowe'en.

Old granny has a handy press
      Where apples, hoarded green,
Divided out - the wee ones bless
      An' please at Hallowe'en.

A few have nuts, a very few,
      Poor withered ones, I ween,
An' these when burnin', two and two,
      Tell tales at Hallowe'en.

An' some have acorns - those once graced
      By fairy king an' queen,
Upon the low back hob are placed
      For luck at Hallowe'en.

The older boys, the spruce young buck
      An' girls about thirteen
For red-cheeked apples dip an' duck
      In tubs at Hallowe'en.

Where there are neither sweets nor cakes
      Nor mutton, fat or lean,
In a big pot the mother makes
      Boxty at Hallowe'en

Young Liza at her bobbin wheel
      Tangles a cotton skene,
Then shuts her eyes lest Ham may steal
      A kiss at Hallowe'en.

Although outside it teems an' pours —
      The boys, about sixteen,
Are busy runnin', rappin' doors
      With turf - at Hallowe'en.

While speech an' laughter both are stilled,
      For all his spyin' keen,
Pilgarlic finds his cabin filled
      Wi' smoke at Hallowe'en.

At witches grinnin' in their sarks,
      At hags of gruesome mien,
The chained-up bandog growls an' barks
      An' howls at Hallowe'en

The boogles in the gravel hole
      Behind the brambly screen,
Just wait to grab - body and soul —
      Some boy at Hallowe'en.

False-face is laughin' in his sleeve
      At sober Jock and Jean
An' at the wight who won't believe
      In freets at Hallowe'en.

But wind and wet have ta'en the route,
      Stars peep the clouds between,
The house is hushed, the lights are out,
      Down! Ghosts of Hallowe'en.

LOVE IN THE KAIL-PLAT

When in the plats at Martinmas
      The curlys fresh an' green,
Stand as if waitin' for the lass
      Who walks the rows between.
An' blades the stalks an' stuffs her bag
      Wi' crisp an' sappy leaves —
O then it is light-hearted Meg
      Loves lesson first receives.

Young Billy comin' from the moss
      Just sets his barrow down,
Spits on his hands an' jumps across
      The bog-hole wide an' brown.
Nor stops till he has in his arms
      The girl wi' wringin' sleeves,
The lass who loud in her alarms
      Love's lesson first receives.

The raindrops on the blades o' kail
      Like quiv'rin' diamonds shine,
Whirr: from the fur a frightened quail
      Makes noise enough for nine.
But Billy, mindful of the prize,
      His prisoner not relieves
Till she on cheeks an' lips an' eyes
      Love's lesson first receives.

O sonsy smacks that sting an' burn
      Heart-deep as soon as giv'n,
O two-fold passion that can turn
      A kail-plat into heaven.
Delight seems strugglin' in the bog,
      Joy skips among the leaves,
The willy-wagtails laugh when Meg
      Love's lesson first receives.

THE BOOR-TREE

An' they have cut the boor tree down
        They have! Ah dear me!
I wouldn't for a silver crown
        Have hurt the boor-tree.

The snowy blooms - I see them yet
        As sweet as they could be!
And then the berries - black as jet
        Upon the boor-tree.

How often from my granny's door
        Have I looked up to see
The swifts and swallows flyin' o'er
        The big green boor-tree.

Well now I think it was a sin!
        For oft when I was wee
The marley pullets roosted in
        The big dark boor-tree.

Admired by people far an' near
        An' sound as it could be
We knew the seasons of the year
        By the big boor-tree.

How cruel of them! How unkind!
        The stump is all I see
An' yet the longest thing I mind
        Was the big boor-tree.

Ah! when they went to cut it down
        They never thought of me!
I would have giv'n my last half crown
        To save the boor-tree.

AN EXILE

When I look 'round and see the land
        All covered up wi' snow
        I wish I was in Ireland
Where the green bushes grow.
        In Ireland, in Ireland,
        That charming little isle
Where colleens neat as they are sweet
        The boys wi' love beguile.

Oh, when I see on quakin' sands
        These buildings grim an' grey
        I wish I was in Ireland
A dozen times a day.
        In Ireland, in Ireland,
        The home of heath and ling,
Where cabins sleep an' fairies peep
        Into each holy spring.

An' when I hear on every hand
        These foreign tongues untied,
        I wish I was in Ireland
The bonnie Bann beside.
        In Ireland, in Ireland,
        An' livin' near Lough Neagh,
Wi' Nora's tongue on music hung
        To charm me night and day.

Oh, when I tramp these pavements plann'd
        To weary me wi' pain,
        I wish I was in Ireland
In Derryaugh again.
        In Ireland, in Ireland,
        That long neglected isle,
That through her tears a thousands years
        Has never ceased to smile.

THE BOYS AN' THE BIRD-CREEL

In winter when the nipping frost
        Makes toes and fingers numb,
When larks an' linnets, storm toss'd,
        To the oat stubbles come—
Then 'tis at night, by the turf fire,
        A likely lad an' fair,
Wi' toughened fingers hard to tire
        Throws dull an' loop an' snare.

In the far corner, where the glakes
        Shine in the ruddy glow,
Another boy a bird creel makes,
        Bent trigger, fork an' bow.
An' these - the wattle creel an' snare—
        Soon as the morning comes,
Are both set out in places bare
        Of everything but crumbs.

Woe to the linnet golden green,
        Or rosy-breasted grey,
Or yorlin pressed by hunger keen,
        That lightly hops that way.
When comes the cry - the joy of joys—
        "Quick, quick, the creel has fell!"
The wild delight of those two boys
        No words of mine can tell.

Sometimes the trap is slyly set
        Where briers loose an' long
Are haunted by some charming pet
        Once cherished for its song.
From the thick hawthorn where she dwells,
        Or from the holly-bush,
A roasted spud - so fine it smells—
        Will often draw the thrush.

An' when a bigger prize the boys
        In snare or bird creel take,
The timber tingles wi' the noise
        The happy laddies make.
No haystack round the building dulls
        The young buck's ringin' shout,
When he puts in his hand an' pulls
        A skirlin' blackbird out.

Too oft, alas, they snare the lark,
        The minstrel of the sky,

And it, poor thing, in prison dark
  Full soon will drop and die.
Ah! little think the two brave boys
  The warm turf fire beside,
The trapper never yet had joys
  But some poor creature died.

SPRING IN BALLINARY

In that far-off happy valley,
    Where wi' song the hedges ring,
How pleasant out at morn to sally,
    And, it might be, meet wi' Spring!

Fair of form and fine of feature,
    What true poet hasn't seen
The bonny, laughing, blushing creature
    Putting on her robe of green?

Let nor hawk nor hound alarm her,
    As, lone wand'ring by the rill
She listens to the songs that charm her,
    While her dimples deepen still.

Chilly snowdrops might remind her
    Of the winter past and gone,
Warmer flowerets let us find her,
    Buds to feast her eyes upon.

Where the sallow and the scion
    And the hawthorn form a hedge,
Isn't that a dandelion
    Blooming at the ramper edge?

On the budding garden bushes,
    Are those emeralds that shine?
Is that gleam above the rushes
    A load-star, or a light divine?

Brightened by the brisk March weather,
    Where brown mossy trinklets run,
Purple points of heath and heather
    Court the glances of the sun.

With an eye undimmed by trouble,
    Where its light the rigg illumes,
The daisy in the undug stubble
    Blushes ere in white she blooms.

Where the sunbeams to a focus
    Lately seem to have been drawn,
Bursts in flame the yellow crocus
    On the little patch of lawn.

Has the dawn stooped down and kissed her?
    Is the March wind overbold?

Or is her imperial sister
      Only purple with the cold?

Sung to by the sly black willy,
      Happy as a nymph can be,
That darling girl, the daffodilly,
      Nods and beckons in her glee.

Where the missle has been steady
      All mild February through,
The violet, from the bank already,
      Looks out with an eye of blue.

Close beside her the primrosie,
      Sweeter than a sacred nun,
Peeps out where the red breast cozy
      Has his foggy nest begun.

What is it can dull or deaden
      Tares still with the wheat at strife?
How these stragglin' briers redden,
      Lusty wi' the sap of life!

Telling all the folk how nearly
      Finished are the round mud walls;
Listen to yon thrush - how clearly
      From the bare ash tree he calls.

From the holly bush commodious,
      For his one note singing ten,
Answering him in bursts melodious,
      Hearken to wee Jenny Wren!

And, listen! listen! high in heaven,
      Where through light he seems to run,
The glorious skylark - doubling seven,
      Rolls a dozen notes in one.

There, O there with him one season,
      Just to scatter joy and sing,
Would surely rob me of my reason,
      Set me ravin' of the Spring.

THE PEARL OF PORTADOWN

Delightin' more than one townlan',
    The lark sings loud an' clear;
A dozen boats are on the Bann,
    An' summer's almost here.
Though carts of turf an' loads of fir
    Come trailin' into town,
The sunny day seems made for her—
    The Pearl of Portadown.

Oh, when in High Street she appears,
    Whatever chits may say,
Fine women feel their fifty years
    Have left them old an' grey.
Movin' as graceful as a swan—
    The simplest gingham gown
Looks fine as flowered poplin on
    The Pearl of Portadown.

Men at the stan'in's stop and stare,
    The very ragman tries
To get a glimpse of wavy hair,
    Red lips an' sparklin' eyes.
The nobby peeler heaves a sigh,
    The sub forgets to frown,
When like a vision passes by
    The Pearl of Portadown.

Fresh as a Bannside buttercup,
    So sweet - that I'll engage,
The busy clerk when he looks up
    Forgets to blot the page.
The carman, lookin' for a treat,
    Will bet you half-a-crown,
For beauty Ireland cannot beat
    The Pearl of Portadown.

The plants on every window still—
    Geraniums blushin' red,
Fuchsias an' monthly roses spill
    Their fragrance on her head.
Single petunias all in white,
    Win for themselves renown,
Exhaling odour to delight
    The Pearl of Portadown.

An' all the while upon the Bann
    The white sails flash an' fly;

Delightin' more than one townlan',
    The lark sings in the sky.
My dream - Och, wouldn't it be sweet!
    If where the bracken's brown,
In Ballyworkan I should meet
    The Pearl of Portadown.

Springfield Post Office where Moses Teggart posted all the poems he sent to the Portadown News. 'The Pearl of Portadown' was the first of many.

THE FLOWER OF DERRYANE

Oh, how I love the time of year
      When all the leaves are green!
When flowers, springing far and near,
      In robes of light are seen!
When little birds in every bower
      Sing o'er and o'er again—
Young Mary is the fairest flower
      That blooms in Derryane.

Oh, how I love the time of year
      When all the streamlets run
O'er golden sands, and run so clear
      They dazzle in the sun!
The west wind then at twilight hour
      Still whispers at the pane—
Young Mary is the fairest flower
      That blooms in Derryane.

Oh, how I love the time of year
      When earth and sky and sea
So beautiful they all appear,
      In Heaven seem to be!
Then 'tis I hear the sunlit shower
      Say to the growing grain—
Young Mary is the fairest flower
      That blooms in Derryane.

Oh, how I love the time of year
      When roses are in bloom!
When all the lanes, both far and near,
      Are full of sweet perfume!
Then 'tis that some bewitching power
      Sings to me this refrain—
Young Mary is the fairest flower
      That blooms in Derryane.

THE SKAY[7]

A Reminiscence of Old Ireland

Above the brace - I mind it well,
    The crumblin' scraws below
A place where odds and ends pell-mell
    Full often used to go.
Whip-crops an' sticks an' footy things
    When thrown out of the way,
Went up as if on lightnin's wings
    An' landed on the skay.

Rods neatly peeled, an' broken reeds,
    Old remlets, rags an' all,
A lowly household when it needs
    Will for them loudly call.
Birch wattles - prized an hour before,
    Green osiers from the Fay,
An' lots of trumpery loved no more —
    Went birlin' to the skay.

The heddles worn out in the maze
    Of the green linen yarn;
Old duds that had seen better days —
    Too old, indeed, to darn;
The stick that stirred the porridge pot
    When almost worn away,
Went flyin' up among the lot
    An' lit upon the skay.

The yellow slats of tough bog fir
    That bent but never broke,
The hangrails that no storm could stir,
    The purlines of black oak
Supporting scraws an' oat straw thatch,
    Made quite a cosy bay,
A rain proof loft you couldn't match,
    An attic snug - the skay.

The smoothin' irons in a row
    Hung each upon its nail,
An' seasoning the soot below
    A soople for the frail.
From foggy fums the soft blue smoke
    As up it made its way

[7] Type of loft built over hearth area of a jamb wall house, usually used for storage and occasionally for sleeping accommodation.

Stained blacker still the beams of oak
        An' dale boards of the skay.

Ah me! there are a thousand such
        In dear old Ireland,
Skays that you with your head could touch
        An' rake out with your hand.
An' yet how high an' dark they seemed
        In childhood's happy day!
How oft at night in torrents teemed
        The rain above the skay.

Below it often at the wheel
        Poor Mary's heart was wrung,
As with some plaything, spool or reel,
        She hushed Maria's tongue.
Below it oft a puny child
        Sick in the cradle lay,
Or opened its blue eyes an' smiled
        At forms beyond the skay.

Above the brace - I mind it well —
        A nook the roof below,
Where odds an' ends and all pell-mell
        In boyhood need to go.
Oh, there were hosts an' hosts of things,
        All useful in their day,
Went up as if on lightnin's wings,
        An' landed on the skay.

THE BELLE OF DERRYKEEVIN

The buttercups were sleepin' soun',
      The ragweeds they were dozin',
An' in the grazins all aroun'
      The daisies' eyes were closin'.
The blades o' grass wi' dew were wet,
      The lark the sky was leavin'
When walkin' out, by chance I met
      The Belle of Derrykeevin.

O, if blue eyes an' blushin' cheeks,
      An' sweet words sweetly spoken,
An' bashful glances when she speaks,
      A bonnie lass betoken—
Then she who there before me stood,
      Wi' bosom gently heavin',
Might well be in that neighbourhood—
      The Belle of Derrykeevin.

We listened to the trinklin' rill
      That through the sheugh was flowin',
We watched above McCulloch's hill,
      The star of evenin' glowin'.
One slender han' when I had foun'
      The fingers smooth with weavin',
Then of itself my arm went roun'
      The Belle of Derrykeevin.

Her lips were like the buddin' pinks
      When in the dews they're sleepin',
Her eyes like stars when through the chinks
      Of inky clouds they're peepin',
No thoughts had we of rainy days,
      Of grumblin' or of grievin',
No thought had I, but still to praise
      The Belle of Derrykeevin.

We wandered by the hawthorn hedge,
      An' down the sally loanin',
And every soft kiss was a pledge
      That come what might- disownin'
All footy talk an' blethers rife,
      An' foolish make believin',
I'd love an' cherish as my life
      The Belle of Derrykeevin.

An' now-however long the day,
      However hard my labour,

I still a kind word have to say
    To every thrifty neighbour.
An' when they hear me whistlin' sweet
    When light the sky is leavin',
They know right well I'm goin' to meet
    The Belle of Derrykeevin.

THE LILY OF LOUGH NEAGH

Do I remember Daisy Tennyson?
    Well! To be sure, I do!
Her hair was black as the clouds of night,
    Her eyes as heaven blue.
Her sweet face was the envy
    Of all the Milltown girls,
And when she laughed - then, you could see
    Her mouth was full of pearls.
A dear light-hearted Daisy
    In kirtle green and grey;
The colleen they were wont to call
    The Lily of Lough Neagh.

Her dad in Californy
    Had dug so hard for gold,
When he came home he had as much
    As Daisy's lap would hold,
Rich enough for a princess,
    She might have wed an earl,
But Daisy loved a fisher lad,
    And he adored the girl.
On Lough Neagh's banks at sunset
    Oh would these lovers stray—
Soft kisses were the dews that fed
    The Lily of Lough Neagh.

No useless shoes or stockings
    Would lovely Daisy wear,
Her feet were white as buttermilk,
    He shapely ankles bare.
Her namesakes in the dewy grass
    And on the rampers brown,
Outdone by Daisy's soft-white feet,
    Their rosy heads hung down.
But like herself in snowy white—
    On Daisy's weddin' day
They bloomed and blushed wherever went
    The Lily of Lough Neagh.

Do I remember Daisy Tennyson?
    Indeed, indeed, I do!
Her hair was black as the clouds of night,
    Her eyes as heaven blue.
A daughter or Hibernia,
    Sweet lass! I see her still.
No prettier colleen ever walked
    The wilds of Columbkill.
If in them parts you ever meet
    A grand old man and grey,
Just ask him if he ever knew
    The Lily of Lough Neagh.

DEAD AT THE BIRCHES

Sophia[8] of the red-gold hair
   And laughing eyes of blue,
Soft crimson mouth, and two cheeks fair
   As roses washed in dew—
      Sophia - one now with the wise,
      Dead at The Birches lies.

Be still, be still, thou bonny lark,
   Nor sing so loud and gay!
The lips are closed, the blue eyes dark
   That lately made my day.
      Sophia - one now with the wise,
      Dead at The Birches lies.

Sophia Jackson Palmer, c.1892.

Thou red rose in the garden, weep!
   My lily's cold and white,
And folded in her long last sleep—
   Alone with God and night.
      Sophia - one now with the wise,
      Dead at The Birches lies.

Cry, cry for rain, thou wet-my-lip;
   And when a teem comes down,
Thy young ones of their shelter strip
   Among the sorrel brown,
      Sophia - one now with the wise,
      Dead at The Birches lies.

No more together we shall see
   The lilies bloom and blow;
No more - O nevermore with me
   To Milltown church she'll go.
      Sophia - one now with the wise,
      Dead at The Birches lies.

The 'post' at morning comes across
   The moss with grief and moan—
The poor old man he feels my loss
   As if it were his own.
      Sophia - one now with the wise,
      Dead at The Birches lies.

---

[8] Sophia Jackson, born in Ballinary on 6 January 1859; married Thomas Palmer of Clonmacate, 1 June 1892; died 21 June 1899 as a consequence of drinking polluted water.

O Thou whose name is Life and Love,
   Two souls together twine!
O Liza, from they heaven above,
   Look down on me and mine.
      Sophia - one now with the wise,
      Dead at The Birches lies.

THE BOGLAND FARMER TO HIS WIFE

On the street while the childer are spinnin' their taps,
      While the light is still left in the sky,
Let us walk by the ramper and look at the craps,
      And see if the rickles are dhry.

That garden, dear Emily - some day when you've time
      I wish you would weed it, an' show
The naybors who pass - that it isn't the clime
      But neglect makes the chicken-weed grow.

This grass - to be sure it is needin' a shower,
      The chay-lady has clipped it so clean,
Small chance has the daisy - poor innocent flower,
      Like a smile on its face to be seen.

The people jaloused, it was so wet in June,
      That the summers were on the decline;
I didn't think so; for I knew by the moon
      That the month of July would be fine.

Myself as a prophet I've come to regard,
      For we're getting' good weather again;
An' yit it was only this mornin' I h'ard
      The wet-my-lip cryin' for rain.

One thing! there'll be lashins of fother, at least,
      An' I'm glad for the chay-lady's sake;
The hay's a good crap, an' the clover, and Wheest!
      I declare if yon isn't a crake.

The praties this year are a promisin' crap,
      The stalks they look healthy and sound;
If the blight ever touches the bloom at the tap
      They are sure to decay in the ground.

These cabbage are closin' (take care of that snail),
      Drum heads are beginnin' to fill,
An' look at those curleys - you never saw kail
      Any finer up there in the hill.

Bane-stalks in the rows are beginnin' to nod;
      An bloomin' an' fillin' beneath—
The pays are as even an' white in the pod
      An' as smooth as a purty girl's teeth.

This plat of white oats - they look very well,
      There's no mildew of which I may speak;
If this sunshiny weather houlds on for a spell
      They'll be ready to shear in a week.

Aren't these the fine turnips! A fortnight ago—
      You remember the big teem of rain,
Well, I thinned them that day. Dear me, how they grow!
      They're ready for thinnin' again.

These fitches are batin' the clover by far,
      See! the blooms are beginnin' to shut;
An' the rape and the force-grass - the whole of them are
      In the pink of condition to cut.

Last Lammas I deepened this runnin' march dhrain,
      I shovelled it out, an' I red
Up the banks an' the sides - till the water ran clane
      An' clear as the eye in your head.

The ould stack of turf it is near about done,
      But the new ones are dhryin' so fast—
These rickles (thank God for the wind and the sun),
      Are ready for stackin' at last.

It was here in the ling where the lark had her nest—
      Och! the dewdhraps - how aisy they spill!
Here's a sprig o' white heather, put it in your breast
      An' dhrame that I'm coortin' you still.

Why Emily, my dear! of course I can rhyme,
      Look there in the quag - on the floe,
The lave of the moss-gall are sweeter than thyme,
      An' the cat-tails are whiter than snow.

But let us go back. It is dark overhead,
      An' its time we were turnin', indeed,
For you have the childer to put to their bed,
      An' I've the chay-lady to feed.

THE HOUSE AT THE HEAD OF THE TOWN[9]

Many a change it has undergone,
    And many a tenant known,
Since my infant eyes first stared upon
    Its wall of lime and stone.
Since I, as a boy, the dwelling-house viewed,
    Where my humble life began—
The roof has been many a time renewed,
    And the rafters smoked to tan;
Lintels and porches, once so white,
    Are weather-stained, worn and brown—
All has changed but the air and light
    In the house at the head of the town.

Merrily there the shuttle flew
    Through the woof of linen green,
When I, as a child, looked up at the blue,
    Through the chimney, wide and clean;
Sweetly there the good mother sang
    In the long summer days of yore,
When father and she were blithe and young,
    And life's path lay fair before.
Now she has gone to a home above—
    She has gained her Heavenly Crown—
And naught remains of her but love
    In the house at the head of the town.

Well I remember the smooth, brown latch
    Made for the thumb to press;
The sharpened eaves and the roof of thatch
    Warm and light as a goodly dress;
The hawthorn tree, and the wallflowers red,
    That bloomed at the gable ends;
The marigold's flame, and the flower-bed
    That for rusticity made amends,
And well I remember the blue eyed girl,
    A rose in her rustic gown.
Who, dropping in rarely, seemed like a pearl,
    In the house at the head of the town.

O, dear old house, like a rough-coated shell,
    You held my pearl for an hour!
O, dear old home, many a sad farewell
    Takes place 'tween the frost and the flower;
But the sky is blue o'er the dear old home,
    And the grass is green there still,

---

[9] The area around Ballinary Methodist Church, sometimes referred to as Derryagh.

And happier children rest or roam,
      In the hollow or on the hill.
That home and that hill unknown to fame,
      I would raise to some renown,
Were the hopes realised that to me come
      In the house at the head of the town.

Like Noah's dove, sent forth at first
      From the ark and the one of her kind,
On the sea of life I pine and thirst,
      And no rest for my foot can find;
There are homes by the million in this fair land,
      Habitations good to see,
For the rich man there is a welcome hand,
      But no home and no heart for me.
And I long for the day the night to bring,
      When at peace I shall lay me down,
Where daisies spring and the song birds sing
      Near the house at the head of the town.

THE BRAES OF BALLINARY

Green are the hills where I was born,
      And fair the fruitful valley;
The hedges all are thick with thorn,
      The sedges set with sally;
And when the rowan-tree overhead
      Is covered o'er with coral,
The borders of the bogs are red
      With withered weeds and sorrel;
And there the bright stream and the brown
      In marches meet and merry,
While silvery rills still ripple down
      The Braes of Ballinary.

A lively place of whips and wheels,
      Of carts and ploughs and barrows,
Of spades and shovels, cribs and creels,
      Of baskets and of barrows;
A busy hive of honest folk
      As charming as they're cheerie,
Where wit and fun, and jest and joke,
      Win laughter from the weary;
Where lad and lass make love in rhyme,
      Where tired age can tarry,
And watch the bonnie children climb
      The Braes of Ballinary.

Were daisies, like a fringe of lace,
      Embroider all the byways,
Where brier, broom, and bracken grace
      The hillsides and the highways;
Where pillowed on the golden grain
      The scarlet poppy dozes,
Where every leafy, summer lane
      Is red and white with roses;
A land where larks for very love
      Their praise to heaven carry,
Build nests upon and sing above
      The Braes of Ballinary.

Within doors where the shuttle hums
      We enter, and - God save us!—
The weaver o'er his threads and thrums
      Is whistling like a mavis!
The lassie likewise doth rejoice,
      And winds her linen bobbins,
And there is something in her voice
      Reminds us of the robins;

Yet both would rather be without
    Where, stainless blue and starry,
The flax is flowering all about
    The Braes of Ballinary.

What time the wee ones run to meet
    Their dad from toil returning;
Upon the hearth, swept clean and neat,
    The turf fire's brightly burning.
At that fireside I'd rather sit
    And hear the children prattle,
Than dine where moths of mammon flit
    And tease me with their tattle.
My native hill is heaven to me,
    And ere with death I parry—
I hope my longing eyes shall see
    The Braes of Ballinary.

THE CRABTREE LOANIN'

Winds are moanin', trees are groanin'
Down the crooked Crabtree Loanin';
  Tell it not in Gath.
If lass and lover find a cover,
Where the hawthorn hangs high over
  This deep-pooled and stony path.

Where it bendeth, it not endeth,
But a rotten off-shoot sendeth
  Into still more dismal hole.
Oh! The dreary nights and weary
Road to travel to a dearie,
  And for lantern - blazing coal.

Yet together, through all weather,
Shod with brogues of tough bull leather,
  Have gone lovers by the score;
Ned and Owny, Tim and Tony,
Down this sloppy lane and stony,
  For a glance at their asthore.

Great attraction! feud and faction,
All are laid aside in action,
  When his bow Dan Cupid drew
Ah! the road was travelled over,
As if it were a lane of clover,
  Beauty only this could do.

Roses overhead are blowin',
When the flax her flower is showin',
  Now it is a wintry day;
Winds are moanin', trees are groanin',
Down the dreary Crabtree Loanin',
  Let them sigh away.

MEMORIES OF THE WEE MOSSCHEEPER[10]

As the hills of life grow steeper,
    And my burden wearies me,
How oft, O brown mosscheeper
    I pause and think of thee,
Joy of my happy childhood;
    The red bird and the blue
May warble in the wildwood—
    They memories none renew.

It might be in December,
    And dull the skies and grey,
But thy note - I well remember—
    Made music all the day.
On our hearts light sat our troubles,
    Our tasks were tasks of glee—
Mine to dig the oaten stubbles,
    And thine - to cheep for me.

Once more the ling and heather
    Blush to blossoming;
Again in April weather,
    I see thee rise and sing.
Once more myself I'm sunning
    Beside a turf-stack there,
Whilst thou art lively running
    Along the mossbank bare.

Where a daily round of duty
    Is still the common lot,
In the wild bogland thy beauty
    Is oft remembered not.
But as life's stern hills grow steeper,
    And my burden wearies me,
Full oft, O brown mosscheeper,
    I pause and think of thee.

Mosscheeper (alias the Meadow Pipit).

[10] The meadow pipit - a small brown streaky bird with a high piping call.

AT THE MOUTH OF THE OLD TURF STACK

When the icy breath o' the keen black frost
      Makes stiff the puddles all;
When the qua is crisp an' the moss is crost
      Lightly, if crost at all;
When the bitter blast, so hard to face,
      Drives the runnin' water back—
When the north wind blows, what a sheltered place
      Is the mouth of the old turf stack!

When snow lies around as lies the surf—
      Foam white, on Lough Neagh strand,
How black an' crackly looks the turf!
      How dry in the horny hand!
When peltin' sleet falls thick an' fast,
      When slush fills every track,
How glad we are to arrive, at last,
      At the mouth of the old turf stack!

The lumps an' the clods so light an' dry,
      The clinkers hard as bricks,
The mowl fine enough down on to lie,
      The black oak props an' sticks—
How cosy they look on a cold bleak day!
      How warm! When we pang an' pack
The crib or the creel, an' start away
      From the mouth of the old turf stack.

How bare the place is, an' how drear,
      How lost to love an' song,
Where we something cannot find to cheer
      Us life's rough way along.
When a curly lass comes 'round that way,
      With her rosy lips to smack,
Och, it's heaven, indeed, for an hour to stay
      At the mouth of the old turf stack.

THE BELLE OF BALLINARY

Before the lark has left the grass,
        Or green pewit the grazin',
She's up an' washed - the tidy lass!
        An' has the turf fire blazin':
For soda farrels the griddle hot—
        An' mim an' on her mettle,
The porridge plumpin' in the pot,
        An' puffin' steam - the kettle.
No bannock on the hearthstone burns,
        No little plans miscarry
When trig an' neat she does the turns—
        The Belle of Ballinary.

Above the flame the crooksticks flash
        Scoured by the hand of duty;
Out of the black bud on the ash
        The green leaf bursts in beauty.
Up from the bog rigg springs the corn
        By shine an' shower attended;
An' Mary on a Sunday morn,
        Is, as a blush rose, splendid!
Her little prayer book in her hand,
        No time to talk or tarry,
To church she goes, by zephyrs fann'd—
        The Belle of Ballinary.

The daisy blushin' in the grass,
        The bloom on ling and heather,
The gillyflowers see Mary pass,
        And all rejoice together.
The wee brown jinty on the brae
        Cheeps to her children seven;
The linnet trills upon the spray,
        The skylark sings in heaven.
Flits o'er the weed the butterfly,
        The bees the blossoms marry,
The birches bow as she goes by—
        The Belle of Ballinary.

Yet, Mary in her workin' frock
        Is sweet as any linnet;
An' deftly she can darn a sock,
        Or put a new toe in it.
Can glance up sweetly from the glakes,
        Sure that the butter's comin';
Kiss barefoot bairns, and cure their aches,
        As well as any woman.

In shinin' cans from the spring well
        A go of water carry;
An' milk the cows that snuff an' smell—
        The Belle of Ballinary

If love has ever touched the heart
        That still beats unbespoken,
Dear Mary of the honeyed smart
        Shows neither sign nor token.
An' if she has in school girl days
        Kissed under Cupid's banner,
Not the less kindly are her ways,
        Nor more demure her manner.
To haughty pomp she pay no tithe,
        An' none the heart may harry
Of simple joys that make so blithe
        The Belle of Ballinary.

An' when the lark has sought the grass,
        An' green pewit the grazin',
She seats herself - the bonny lass!
        Before the turf fine blazin'.
An' while the plates shine on the shelf,
        The day, with all its bothers,
Fades into happy dreams where self
        Is lost in love for others.
And, as fond thoughts make still more fair
        The stainless eyes an' starry,
Be sure kind heaven has in its care
        The Belle of Ballinary.

LIZA AND HER PLOUGHBOY

There's a lovely girl called Liza
      Sits weavin' on her loom;
Her blue eyes are like blossoms—
      They sparkle when they bloom,
The shuttle flies the faster,
      Her eyes grow brighter still,
When Liza hears her ploughboy
      Come whistlin' o'er the hill.

Her hair is like the raven,
      Her brow is broad an' low,
Her neat round chin it cannot hide
      The throat as white as snow.
The loom that runs so easy,
      Runs smooth an' lighter still
When Liza's happy ploughboy
      Come whistlin' o'er the hill.

Red is the sun-kissed cherry,
      An' ripe the brier hip,
But redder far and riper
      Is Liza's rosy lip.
A meltin' rasp untasted,
      It looks more temptin' still
When Liza's lucky ploughboy
      Comes whistlin' o'er the hill.

Like dawn upon the garden
      The look on Liza's face—
The dimples in the rosies,
      The pearls all in their place,
Her cheeks are like the mornin',
      Her smile is sweeter still
When she hears her merry ploughboy
      Come whistlin' o'er the hill.

Her voice - O she's not singin',
      She's listenin' to the tune,
The lively air that makes her feel
      Proud as the rose in June.
Then through the gable window
      She glances prouder still
As Jack, her jolly ploughboy
      Comes whistlin' o'er the hill.

Two white feet on the treddles,
      A white hand on the sleys,

An' the first that holds the pluckstick
 Is far too fine for praise.
She's movin' all to music,
 Her heart will not keep still
When she sees her curly ploughboy
 Come whistlin' o'er the hill.

MOUNTHALL[11]

On Mounthall hill, this ruin hoary,
      These pointed gables light and long,
Rose clothed with chords in childhood's story,
      And soared to heaven in boyhood's song.

Here in the goods days gone forever,
      The song and dance and mirth went on
Till man and maid and minstrel clever
      Closed their eyes by the light of dawn.

In this broad court o'ergrown with bramble,
      The skies forever throned above
Saw happy children sport and gambol
      While the lark in heaven sang of love.

Lady and chief and children ruddy,
      Babes on milk and slumber nurst
Sleep where the winding road and muddy
      Leads to the churchyard and the dust.

Sleep in that weed-grown wayside hollow,
      Where kings and queens so long have lain—
Strange fingers on green tombstones follow
      The letters rudely cut, in vain.

To them, Tartaraghan bell, deep tolling,
      At daybreak and at evening grey,
Sounds like a voice of heaven consoling
      Souls for glory passed away.

Driv'n forth by fire, or scorched in battle.
      And welt'ring sore through fen and fog,
The Hall's once sleek and well-fed cattle
      Are still intact in peat and bog.

Floating, as floats the air-filled bubble,
      Hid for ages the heath below,
Firkins are found beneath the stubble,
      And tubs of butter among the floe.

'Neath the teeth of time in silence crumbles
      This one-time fairest of Erin's halls;
Lost Echo alone it is that rumbles
      And wakes weird music within the walls.

---

[11] Former residence of the Hall family of Co Louth. The hill, aka Clonmacate Hill, at 133 feet high is the second highest in the area.

And now - to an ear attuned and subtle,
    Through an atmosphere as water still,
Comes the whirring sound of the weaver's shuttle
    And the herdboy's whistle sharp and shrill.

Gazing long on these grazing cattle—
    Sudden as if a bolt should fall
I hear the cry of hosts in battle.
    And the crash of hail on the burning hall.

I see the floods in the nearby mosses,
    The glaring flames reflected there,
And the hapless waif himself who crosses,
    And sends to heaven a hurried prayer.

I see the calf and the frenzied heifer,
    The wild-eyed kine and the lowing bull
Plunge to their deaths - in the quas forever
    To lie engulfed with the goose and gull.

I see the barrels and firkins rolling
    Adown the steep sides of the hill,
And the trembling steed - beyond controlling,
    Leap from the cliff and then lie still.

Here, ere the dreadful years of famine,
    The fatted ox was roasted whole;
The benches groaned under bream and salmon
    And poteen tasting of peat and coal.

Here in the dead and bygone ages,
    Robed in raiment white as foam,
Beauties who had for their pastime pages,
    Laughed till they wept when their lords came home.

Here while the wild and wandering harper
    Twanged the glories of Neil and Roe.
His shining eyes than the she-wolf's sharper
    Shot keen glances at friend and foe.

Then it was those glorious Dions—
    The Conns, the Obres and the Corrs,
Marched with the legions and fought like lions—
    Gideons all in the Gaelic wars.

Here where the rude north gales dishevel
    The glossy locks of this bonny birch,
The knights on the sward held courtly revel—
    Strangers to chapel and chime and church.

But - slow up-climbing, yon thin-clad peasant
      Bending below his load of peat
Recalls me back to the living present
      And the daisies blooming at my feet.

From this o'er-leaning and loosened gable,
      One ivy bud let me bear away,
To show strange peoples, how fact, not fable,
      Moulded the mind that thinks, today.

O crumbling pile, O ruin hoary—
      A joy and a wonder thou wert to me,
When sunset filled thy halls with glory,
      And the rising moon transfigured thee.

NED AND MARY

It was the spring-time of the year,
      An' all things looked like new;
The cuckoo called, an' far an' near
      The whiterump flashed an' flew.
Upon her rosy lip a song,
      An' mirth in her blue eye,
Bewitchin' Mary skelped along
      The ramper brown an' dry.

Where light of heart - a plat of oats,
      Young Ned was trenchin' in,
The briers were nibbled by the goats,
      The donkey cropped the whin.
"Good morra, girl! Lift up your head,
      An' bid me time o' day!"
"Good morrow, Ned!" sweet Mary said,
      An' passed upon her way.

But after seein' Mary's face,
      How rough seemed rigg an' fur!
The sunshine, too, that warmed the place,
      It must have gone wi' her.
The yellow willy seemed to know
      That something had gone wrong;
An' jinkin' through the turf below
      The jinty hushed her song.

Her linen web below her arms,
      How could poor Mary know
Daylight would leave the bogland farm,
      Or go where she would go?
If she had known such bitter moan
      Would shake the mosses brown,
A kiss to Ned she would have thrown
      Before she went to town.

"Keep up your heart, my boy," at last
      Unto himself he said;
"If that was blue-eyed Mary passed,
      Then I am still young Ned!"
An' trenchin' then in lively style,
      An' levellin' left an' right,
Into his grey eyes crept a smile
      That lit them up till night.

An' then along the footpad he
      Went hurryin' pell-mell

To where the leafy sally tree
      Leans over the spring well;
An' there - unseen by star or moon,
      Unknownst to sleepin' farms,
All out of breath, sweet Mary soon
      Was sobbin' in his arms.

MARCH IN THE BOGLANDS

The dark brown drains are flowin',
      An' where sappy rootlets stir
The winds of March are blowin'
      Over fallow, rigg an' fur,
Over qua and quickenin' heather,
      Over weed an' wiry ling,
Over wagtails fine of feather,
      An' larks that soar an' sing.

Buds are burstin' on the scions,
      An' at every dusty turn
Of the footpad, dandelions
      Bright as tallow candles burn.
Wi' their lace caps pink-bedighted,
      Never bashful, never coy,
The first daisies, sun delighted,
      Are full of life an' joy.

O'er the baytons dug an' dyin',
      O'er the plats where curleys grew,
The jolly whiterump's flying,
      A flash of white and blue.
Never hidden in the heather,
      Never ducked where rills run down,
He loves the wild March weather
      An' the bogland bare an' brown.

Leap to life the callow rushes,
      (An' how soon they will be green!)
Where the rosy, buddin' bushes
      O'er the sheughs, so shallow, lean;
Outdoor life wi' new life burneth,
      Mother Nature clasps his hand
When loved March, the rogue, returneth
      To the bonnie brown bogland.

A LOVER'S KNOT OF LOVE SONGS

'TIS ALL FOR THEE

The linnet's singing in the lane,
      The blithe lark in the blue;
And, with an eye to the growing grain,
      The bunting's singing, too.
However sweet to other ears
      These songs of love may be,
They're sweeter far to him who hears
      Them sung in praise of thee.

The flags are bursting into flower,
      In blue and orange they blow;
The rose is blushing in her bower,
      The lily's white as snow.
However these may others please,
      They're fairer far to me—
Thy lover, Mary, always sees
      The fairest bloom in thee.

REMEMBRANCE

I never see a wayside rose,
      Or a rose in any place
A rose that a trace of colour shows—
      But I think of Mary's face.
And I never see a crimson flower
      At which a brown bee sips,
Or rose-buds red in summer's bower,
      But I think of Mary's lips.

I never see soft violets blue
      Round which the zephyr sighs,
Sweet violets washed with rain or dew,
      But I think of Mary's eyes.
And I never see the dawn of day,
      And the sunlit skies above,
And evening fade into twilight grey,
      But I think of Mary's love.

SOLICITUDE

O Mary! when the night is drear,
      And when the rain comes down,
Do not come out to meet me, dear,
      In the loanin' down the town.
For I do not want the stormy night

    And the rain and wind to blow
Into your eyes so blue and bright,
    And wet your neck of snow.

But when the night on dusky wings
    Descends on your black hair;
And a little bird in the loanin' sings
    To the bird that listens there—
O come out then, my pretty pet,
    And meet your lover true;
I want no wintry skies to wet
    A blossom sweet as you.

NIGHT AND MORN

Oh, what a wild and stormy night,
    And how the rain comes down—
And yet there are two blue eyes bright
    As daylight down the town.
There are two lips as rosebuds red,
    And a face that's fair to see,
And when dear Mary goes to bed
    These in the dark shall be.

The storm may louder blow o'erhead,
    And the rain it may not cease;
But a flower, folded on her bed,
    My love shall sleep in peace.
The rain may not have left the skies,
    And grey the morn may be,
But Mary's blushes and blue eyes
    Shall make it fair for me.

ENDURING LOVE

My Mary's parents clasped my pearl
    And on me closed the door;
Well as they loved their little girl,
    They loved their riches more,
But fair as the blue sky above
    Her eyes still on me shine;
And in my dreams of youthful love,
    Dear Mary still is mine.

Her father sleeps the grass below,
    Her mother's by his side;
And Mary, years and years ago,
    Became another's bride.
For this, in spite of all the wrong,

And of heart-breakings sore,
Dear Mary in her lover's song
Shall bloom for evermore.

WHEN THE BUD IS ON THE THORN

They're ploughin' at The Birches,
　　The barrow's in the hill,
An' the land they cannot purchase
　　Is the land they're doomed to till.
The buttercups are springin'
　　Where the heifer's light feet fall,
An' the lovely skylark's singin'
　　Like a seraph over all.
On the brown twigs turnin' sappy
　　Raindrops sparkle night an' morn,
And the bog folk all are happy
　　When the bud is on the thorn.

They are crackin' long whiplashes,
　　They're full of life an' glee,
Where Lough Neagh floats an' flashes
　　Like a sunlit inland sea.
On a spad himself regalin'
　　The hardy fisherman,
Like a mariner is sailin'
　　From Blackwater to the Bann.
In the bogland they're preparin'
　　For trenchin' in the corn,
An' each child a smile is wearin'
　　Now the bud is on the thorn.

Than any pikeman bolder
　　At six the digger goes
Wi' his long spads o'er his shoulder
　　To work at Billy Rowe's,
An' the boy that herds the cattle
　　In the fields that face the Fay
Is full of the big battle
　　That was fought but yesterday.
To young Fancy of the Folly
　　There's an heir to nothin' born
Yet the big folk all are jolly
　　When the bud is on the thorn.

While the silver cloudlets dapple
　　The deep blue overhead,
Biddy's goin' to Maghery chapel
　　With a shawl about her head.

Och, the white feet of the crayter,
        An' the shamrocks in the grass,
Sure it seems to me that nature
        Is forever sayin' mass,
An' that Christ who reigns in glory
        Leaves none on earth forlorn
When the redbreast tell his story
        And the bud is on the thorn.

A BIRCHES BOY

When I out of infancy uncurled
  An' jumped right into joy,
'Twas the grandest thing in all the world
  To be a Birches Boy.

Hardship might stare us in the face,
  Newsmongers might annoy;
But on earth there was no finer place,
  No lad like a Birches Boy.

The wolf ne'er got inside the door,
  Nor a bailiff from the Foy;
The bogs wi' purple were covered o'er
  For the blue-eyed Birches boy.

There was always a milker from the Rock
  Or a madam from the Moy
To fill the can an' cream the crock
  For every Birches boy.

In barn an' byre, an' in the home,
  There was always top an' toy;
An' no matter where I then might roam,
  I was still a Birches boy.

There was aye some girl, a nice, wee girl,
  Now coaxin' an' now coy;
An' Morn still opened the gates o' pearl
  For her an' the Birches boy.

The skipper, when I crossed the sea,
  Just whispered, "Mate, ahoy!"
He told them all to be good to me,
  To be kind to the Birches boy.

Tell them at home in the motherland,
  That I'm pleased with my employ;
That the hand that writes this is the hand
  Of a brave old Birches boy.

SUMMER'S COME! SUMMER'S COME!

(On the Lough Shore, Co. Armagh.)

Honey up for winter layin'.
      Hear the bees how loud they hum!
Plain as can be they are sayin',
      "Summer's come! Summer's come!"

Gillyflowers in all the ditches
      From the far house to the Fay!
Kail an' clover, rape an' fitches—
      Oh, they're all in bloom the day.

The old birds are sentry keepin',
      Full of hope an' full of fear,
For the young ones all are cheepin'
      In the hedges far an' near.

See the craps, how well they're growin'—
      Healthy both at tap an'root,
A milky stalk the white is showin',
      As the oats begin to shoot.

Never mind - that goat is tethered.—
      Down this long fur follow me,
An' a nest of larks half feathered,
      Wattled in, I'll let you see.

If the lough the blue sky copies,
      Then this field of flax at rest
Is as full of blazin' poppies
      As of scarlet clouds the west.

Where that cow her calf is duntin',
      Just beyond them, on the tree,
Listen to the fat corn buntin'
      Singin' - oh, so lazily.

Skimmin' heights an' skimmin' hollows,
      Now they dip an' now they rise,
See that flock of wheelin' swallows,
      An' how fast they're catchin' flies.

Blackenin' the sky above us,
      Full of mirth an' merry tifts,
Och, Billy dear, Lord love us!
      Will you listen to the swifts.

Did you ever hear such skirlin'
      Or such sharp notes in your life?
Not since Jem wi' fingers tirlin',
      Learned to play upon the fife.

When the day an' night are meetin',
      In the dusk above the stripe,
Then our music is the bleatin'
      An' the maain' of the snipe.

Well may childer gather posies
      From dinner time till night;
Every bush is red wi' rosies,
      Every brae wi' daisies white.

Wi' their cheeks as red as cherries,
      Here's a little lad an' lass
Busy stringin' wild strawberries
      On a long green stalk of grass.

For the wee mouth or the muckle,
      For the golden-belted bee,
Such splendid honeysuckle
      Did you ever, ever see?

As I live, the crabs are shapin'!
      If the young ones only knew,
There'd be wee red purses gapin'
      For a juicy bite or two.

Where the blush is on the heather,
      Where the snow-white hawthorns stand,
Isn't it the lovely weather
      In the bogs, an' on the land.

Where yon wee moss grey is wingin'
      Over katty turf and fum,
Sure as death, if it's not singin'
      "Summer's come! Summer's come!"

THE CRABTREE CHAIR

In Derrytagh, where nettles thrive,
        And trees are neat and trim,
Where diggers sweat, and masters drive
        From dawn till evening dim.

A hedgerow runs between two fields,
        And growing greenly there
One bush that shade and shelter yields,
        Is called the Crabtree Chair.

Bent down and trained when green and young,
        A seat the branches form,
A summerhouse by leaves o'erhung,
        A shelter in the storm.

O'er it the lark sings songs of love;
        And when the noons are still,
Perched on the rounded roof above,
        The gay green linnets trill.

In days when daisies starred the grass,
        And sweeter than her name—
A bonnie, blue-eyed, barefoot lass
        Blithe up the car pad came.

(And O how oft her twinkling feet
        Illumed the well-known way!
How oft her dimpled smiles made sweet
        The February day!)

And when the crabtree budding green
        Made haste its bloom to show,
Full oft dear Mary must have seen
        The blossom blush and blow.

When praties planted in the plot
        First peeped above the ground,
In that green chair I often sat,
        Alive to every sound.

I heard the yorlin to her nest
        On wings expectant come;
And hovering o'er the daisy's breast
        The belted rover hum.

Full oft the blackbird skirling loud
        From hedge to hedgerow flew;

Full oft the braided silvery cloud
    Sailed o'er the breathless blue.

And the herd laddie noting these,
    And bud and leaf and bough,
Companions made of flowers and trees
    That are his comfort now.

In wakerife memory's musing dreams,
    The fields are always fair;
And Derrytagh a vision seems
    Seen from the Crabtree Chair.

CONEY ISLAND[12]

Coney Island in Lough Neagh
    Embosomed in the smiling bay—
Milltown Bay whose sandy shore
    Often I have gambolled o'er,
Burdened not by that I wore.

Furlongs seven from the strand,
    From the beach of silver sand,
Lies the round, romantic isle,
    Rich in antiquarian pile—
Ruin, cromlech, stone and stile.

There, the warrior knights of old,
    Or saintly men of finer mould
Bowed the knee in balmy bowers,
    Built their turrets, shrines and towers—
Shapes that now are crowned with flowers.

There, philosopher may find
    Food for retrospective mind;
There, the modern Earl may steep
    His mind in wisdom, or may sweep
His Helena at a glance - and weep.

There, the merry schoolboy may
    Roam at random, blithe and gay;
There, the hopeful lover sow
    Her name in wallflower that will blow
When love may be a word of woe.

Coney Island, far away,
    Fairest jewel in Lough Neagh,
You have got a namesake here[13]
    Which I've never gone anear,
Lest Nature outraged should appear.

Coney Island in Lough Neagh,
    Beauty spot of Milltown Bay!
I nor wave nor water note
    While around thee lone I float
By moonlight fair in Fancy's boat.

---

[12] A small island of approximately 8 acres, about a half mile from the village of Maghery on the southern shore of Lough Neagh. Formerly known as Sydney Island and allegedly used by St Patrick as a retreat.

[13] Coney Island, New York.

Coney Island, doubly fair,
      Since thy calm I cannot share,
One of Erin's islands blest,
      Oh that I in thee might rest
When old and weary of the West.

Though in other lands I roam,
      From the grassy height at home
Memory sees thee - than the hill
      Grander, fairer, greener still,
Dark 'neath skies of daffodil!

For the evening sun goes down
      And the light is like a crown,
And the winds are hushed the while
      Parting day doth beam and smile
On fairy-haunted Coney Isle.

Mouth of Blackwater River with Coney Island in the background.

THE BELLE OF COLUMBKILL

Where barefoot children toast their shins
      Before the kitchen fire;
Where roadsides thorny are wi' whins,
      An' brown wi' many a brier;
Where yellow mudwall cabins hide
      Each 'neath its spreadin' tree,
Where Lough Neagh flashes far and wide
      A mighty inland sea—
There is a purty colleen lives,
      An' finch and linnet trill
When she them her "Good Mornin'" gives—
      The Belle of Columbkill.

Oh, black as any crow her hair;
      An' as the vi'lets blue
The eyes whose silken lashes snare
      The heart that comes to woo,
An' red as moonicks in the moss
      When they their ripeness show,
The lips the zephyrs steal across,
      Then honey-laden go.
Sweet, sweet the meadow-pippet's song
      Piped o'er the peaty rill,
But sweeter sings the morning long
      The Belle of Columbkill.

Though many craft there are that float
      An' loiter within call,
Upon the lough her father's boat
      Is fastest of them all.
An' when round Coney Island he
      Brings home the catch so fine,
O then his net's a sight to see—
      So bright the pullens shine,
An' though this may our fancy stir,
      There's something brighter still—
It is the bonny face of her—
      The Belle of Columbkill.

As with her basket on her head,
      Across the bogs she goes,
The waitin' heather blushes red,
      The ling her footstep knows.
Kissed by the sun the whitewashed walls
      Of buildings low and bare,
Shine all the brighter when she calls
      To sell fresh pullen there.

An' mother still takes off the shelf
      A plate for her to fill,
Exclaiming, "Why, is this yourself?—
      The Belle of Columbkill!"

On Sunday - bright as any pearl,
      An' coloured like a rose,
She with a comely neighbour girl
      To Maghery chapel goes.
She sees the briers turnin' brown,
      The whin-bush an' the sloe,
The cold Kesh End, an' in Milltown
      The sights o' Sandy Row.
Green Coney Island, too, she sees,
      An' Derrywarrock hill,
The gravelhole, an' bogs that please
      The Belle of Columbkill.

Oh, happy is her simple lot,
      In maidenhood to dwell
Where Mammon's fingers meddle not
      Pink ling and heather bell.
Where linnets trill, an' daisies still
      Their shinin' faces show;
Where ragweed half the grazin's fill,
      An' pretty shamrocks grow,
Where Nature dreams in russet dress,
      When autumn nights are chill,
An' every mornin' wakes to bless
      The Belle of Columbkill.

Sandy Row, Milltown.

WHERE BLUE-EYED MARY DWELLS

If Mother Nature weeps to see
        A bonnie floweret blow,
Out on the cold and wind-swept lea,
        Where weeds and thistles grow,
She smiles when for our boyhood's bliss,
        One born to weave love-spells,
Blooms sheltered in a lane like this
        Where blue-eyed Mary dwells.

So heavy is the hawthorn bloom,
        So dashed with sparkling dew,
That oft the linen weaver's loom
        Is fresh and fragrant, too.
The rosie shows her blushin' face
        Above such placid wells;
It's easy seen this is the place
        Where blue-eyed Mary dwells.

Sometimes, but not so very oft,
        Out of her foggy bed,
All in the bank so green and soft,
        The cowslip rises - red.
Foxgloves, where deeper ditches sink,
        May ring their rosy bells—
There're fairy fingers, plump and pink,
        Where blue-eyed Mary dwells.

Below a tuft of violets pert,
        Or, it may be beside
A bunch of primroses alert,
        A robin sits, black-eyed.
And fie on him - the linnet green!
        He kisses and he tells,
Makes love to every saucy queen,
        Where blue-eyed Mary dwells.

Below the green and spreading ash,
        Below the alders brown,
Frogs in the horse-hole spawn and splash,
        And catkins drop and drown.
It may be finer far to roam,
        A nymph, in hazel dells,
But it was Nature chose the home
        Where blue-eyed Mary dwells.

Large as the children's flaxen heads,
        But flat and snowy white,
The blossoms which the boortree spreads

  Are targets for the light.
Disbanded bees and stragglers know
  How strong the honey smells—
It's droning drunk they often go,
  Where blue-eyed Mary dwells.

The woodbine twirls around the thorn,
  Enamoured twists and twines,
Dew-burnished, on a summer morn,
  The bell-shaped blossom shines.
The top shoot of the buckiebrier,
  With sugared sweetness swells;
Anemones are sparks of fire
  Where blue-eyed Mary dwells.

A trysting-place, where Jenny Wren
  Can in thick hedges trust;
Fine in the sunshine - finer when
  A shower has laid the dust.
A trysting-place where lovers meet
  And spin and weave love-spells,
And linger long and whisper sweet
  Where blue-eyed Mary dwells.

THE CHAY LADY

*"Come uppe, Jetty, rise and follow,
From the clovers lift your head."*
                    (Jean Ingelow)

I remember, and I think I ought,
   No matter where I roam,
When from the fair our father brought
   A 'pretty lady' home!
Chay lady, chay!
Pretty lady, chay!
It seems to me but yesterday
   He brought the new cow home.

And as she was both nice and new,
   He would the laddie tell—
"Be sure, my boy, whate'er you do,
   And treat 'the lady' well."
Chay lady, chay!
Pretty lady, chay!
It seems to me but yesterday
   She came with us to dwell.

We combed her and we curried her,
   With straw we rubbed her down
Till all her coat was smooth as fur—
   A shiny brindled brown!
Chay lady, chay!
Pretty lady, chay!
It seems to me but yesterday
   The new cow came from town.

We gave her drink, we gave her feed,
   And when we'd done our best—
Had given her all a cow could need,
   We let her lie and rest.
Chay lady, chay!
Pretty lady, chay!
It seems to me but yesterday
   She was nosing at my breast.

The Arab loves his bonnie steed,
   Beside him, too will bow!
And should not bairns love what they need,
   The pretty milking cow?
Chay lady, chay!
Pretty lady, chay!
It seems to me but yesterday
   I scratched her curly brow.

She gave us milk in foaming cans
    Full as the pail could hold;
And butter - that in mother's hands
    Was laughing lumps of gold!
Chay lady, chay!
Pretty lady, chay!
It seems to me but yesterday
    We cried when she was sold.

Expectancy at noon began—
    Far, far did fancy roam,
Till down the road at dusk we ran
    To meet her coming home!
Chay lady, chay!
Pretty lady, chay!
It seems to me but yesterday
    We met her coming home.

How the next morning we were up,
    Were up at peep o' day;
Were out to give the bite and sup
    Unto the pretty 'chay'!
Chay lady, chay!
Pretty lady, chay!
It seem to me but yesterday
    We fed the pretty chay.

Cow after cow to our byre came,
    For men will buy and sell;
But father's word was still the same—
    "Be sure and treat her well!"
Chay lady, chay!
Pretty lady, chay!
It seems to me but yesterday
    Ours came with us to dwell.

BEN THE THATCHER[14]

In my sleep, friends, am I walking?
    Do I doze, or do I dream?
By the hearth I hear you talking,
    Ben the thatcher, still the theme.

Once more 'tis the early morning,
    On each blade a drop of dew,
Roses every hedge adorning.
    Skylarks singing in the blue.

Soft smoke curling o'er the chimley,
    Tells of fum turf burning where
Blue-eyed Mary neat and nimbly,
    Milk and porridge doth prepare.

Hark! Is it the mated throstle,
    Is't the happy thrush I hear?
If not - then, no blackbird's whistle
    Ever rose so sweet and clear.

Molly says (and few can match her
    In bestowing mild reproof),
"That's no burrd! It's Ben the thatcher
    Whistlin' on M'Currie's roof."

Ben! How oft on mornings early
    Have I heard you far away,
Whistling sweet and whistling rarely,
    Making of hard labour - play!

Straight'ning straw and tending scollops,
    Doubling wattles tough and hard—
Cut where Master Willson[15] wallops
    Dunces - down in Derrylard.

Stretched along the leaning ladder—
    Wads of straw on every rung,
Tell me: Can a man be gladder
    Than is Ben of lip and tongue?

---

[14] Ben Simmons, born in Ballinary in 1839; married Elizabeth Millsop, 4 January 1864; died 4 March 1923 and buried in Tartaraghan Churchyard.

[15] Robert Henry Wilson, born 1860, the son of John and Elizabeth of Cloncore; died in Derrinraw, 29 April 1928. Master of Derrylard National School, 1884-1923.

Robert Henry Wilson, Principal, with pupils of Derrylard National School, c.1910.

O'er the saughs of silver sally,
    Sweetness to it giving wings,
Over all the verdant valley
    Ben's melodious music rings.

Picking, patching, mating, matching,
    Handfuls loose wi' handfuls long,
Thoughtful Ben delights in thatching,
    Loves it - as I love my song.

Careful - honest in his calling,
    Life may flow and life may ebb,
One straw keeps the drop from falling,
    On the cradle or the web.

No loose wisps behind him leavin'
    No tight bulges big as ticks,
Shows the boys - how smooth and even
    He will cut the eaves, at six!

Blust'ring breezes, March winds blowing,
    Spinning dust and spitting rain,
Still his tunes Ben keeps bestowing
    On the swaddie and the swain.

Under shining skies, or showery,
    Under skies of sober grey,

Now it is 'The Lass o 'Gowrie',
> Now "Old Derry walls away."

Well done, Ben! To make life pleasant,
> To crown with joy life's common things,
Lifts the poorest, humblest peasant
> Higher than the throne of kings.

The Simmons' cottage, Ballinary.

THE CATTLE COME FROM THE HILLS

In the drouth of the dry summer weather,
      When the moss is wool-warm on the stone,
When thistledown, light as a feather,
      Over by path and boulder is blown.
Its life from the fountain-head bringing.
      And sweet with the breath of the rills,
To the troughs how the water runs singing,
      When the cattle come down from the hills.

In the treetops asleep are the zephyrs,
      In the skies are the streamers of hope,
When the yearlings, the steers and the heifers,
      Like a picture illumine the slope,
On the bough, like a sunbeam alighting,
      The yellowbird - oh, how he trills,
Himself and his audience delighting,
      When the cattle come down from the hills.

The brindled, the brown, and the bright ones,
      The speckled ones, beef to the bone,
The duns, and the young black and white ones,
      The cherry, the red and the roan,
Make us think of the herd well attended
      When Jacob set store by his jills,
Oh, I tell ye, 'tis something quite splendid
      When the cattle come down from the hills.

The doves on the hen-house are cooing,
      The vine leaps a yard up the wall,
Little Beauty is Rover pursuing,
      The stallion neighs loud in his stall.
Higher seems the milk house by a storey,
      And, giving new strength to our wills,
The red barn takes on a new glory,
      When the cattle come down from the hills.

In the yard all the folk are assembled,
      Little Esther is whispering to me,
And the bantling that never yet trembled
      Is laughing and crowing with glee.
The stones and the rocks without number
      Feel something within them that thrills,
Even Churchill awakes from his slumber,
      When the cattle come down from the hills.

Is it rest, is it wonder, or is it
      Some longing we cannot quite name,

Makes the farm so well work a visit
      When summer's tanned cheeks are aflame?
Be this as it may, the great Mother
      Life's cup with delight overfills,
And sets us to pledging each other,
      When the cattle come down from the hills.

ABOVE THE BOGS IN IRELAND

They tell us how the mocking bird
      Where southern roses blow,
Pours out such tuneful melodies,
      No sweeter songs they know.
But who can tell, Oh who can tell
      How sweet it is in spring,
Above the bogs in Ireland
      To hear the skylark sing?

Full brother to loved Shelley's bird
      Lost in Italian skies,
How oft from thy sweet heather couch
      At dawn I've seen thee rise
And sing, and soar, and carol,
      Till all the quiv'ring blue,
With thy delight and rapture
      Was quickened through and through!

Own brother to good Wordsworth's lark,
      How oft in early spring,
I've heard thee down from heavenly heights
      Love's tender twitterings bring
To her thy pretty dark eyed mate
      Who ran the paths along,
Won more by soft endearments
      Than by love's divinest song.

They tell us how the nightingale
      When summer sights are still,
Doth with her wondrous music
      The dusky woodland fill.
But sweetest of all earthly joys
      It is in tuneful spring,
Above the bogs in Ireland
      To hear the skylark sing.

THE SALLY TREE

O'erlooking Mary's loved abode,
      A lusty tree, and full of sap,
A landmark by the country road,
      Long may it stand without mishap.
Enjoying now its winter nap,
      Where woodmen none their axes wield,
It stands beside the hawthorn gap,
      That leads into my father's field,
Unto the task their sinews steeled,
      Full many a time the boys wi' glee
Spat on their dusty hands and speeled
      Like wild cats up the sally tree.

Among green leaves that interlaced,
      High up as any linnet flies,
With knees and elbows firmly braced,
      Let none their airy perch despise.
From it outstretched before their eyes
      The level waters of Lough Neagh,
Glassing the blue of laughing skies,
      Large as a summer ocean lay.
They saw the lights and shadows play
      On emerald field, so fair to see,
Tyrone grew dearer every day
      To those who climbed the sally tree.

But unto me, than field or lake,
      The sally tree, however bare,
Was ten times dearer for the sake
      Of her who often met me there.
Her kind blue eyes, her coal-black hair,
      Her feet and ankles bare and brown,
Her bonnie lips and blushes were
      Fine offsets to her tattered gown.
At dewy twilight 'down the town',
      When coming from the well was she,
Full often were the cans set down,
      And rest took 'neath the sally tree.

O'erlooking Mary's hushed abode
      A silent tree, though full of sap,
A landmark by the country road,
      Long may it stand without mishap
Enjoying its long winter nap;
      Though not a twig on it doth stir,
Around it I my arms could lap
      A thousand times for sake of her.

The cold blue day seems but a blur,
        Since Mary meets no more wi' me
Where hangs the gate on spur and spur
        Spiked in the lonely sally tree.

THE OULD STRAW STACK

Bundled up sometime when autumn
        Laves a shafe at every gap;
Fum turf below the bottom
        And a fod upon the tap.
When the bitin' frosty weather
        Fills with ice the shilty's track,
How the yelties love to gether
        Roun' the new straw stack!

Then it is we hear the mother
        Every night an' mornin' say
"Go an' pull a bite of fother
        For the poor ould chay."
An' when the sleety weather
        Sends the shivers down our back,
How the linnets love to gether
        Roun' the dry straw stack!

When the ditcher an' the digger
        Are slavin' for a meal;
When the boys wi' bow an' trigger
        Set the ould bird creel,
In the wild an' stormy weather,
        When the clouds wi' snow are black,
How the white wings love to gether
        Roun' the rough straw stack!

When the winds have quit their blowin'
        Over moor an' mountain tap;
When the tenant thinks of sowin'
        For the rent, another crap
In the charmin' April weather
        When the ropes are hangin' slack,
How the childer love to gether
        Round' the ould straw stack!

LIZZIE WALL[16]
A Song of Cork City

In fair Cork city, where many a ditty
        And rhyme delightful is penned and sung,
Life was worth living, and love worth giving,
        And worth revering, when I was young.
Where bells chimed daily, now grave now gaily,
        In the schools they after St. Nicholas call.
Among the fair ones and rosy rare ones,
        No maid was sweeter than Lizzie Wall.

Oft in the gloaming, when we went roaming,
        The round moon rising o'er the hills to see,
We'd our walk abandon when the bells of Shandon
        Pealed out sudden o'er the rippling Lee.
Oh, as if still near them, I think I hear them,
        I seem to listen to each rise and fall
Of their silver chiming, till I'm once more climbing
        The dusky hillside with Lizzie Wall.

Loved scenes inspiring I'm still admiring—
        And forever never from memory fade—
Spurs their heels adorning, when each bright morning
        The troopers cantered up the Grand Parade.
Would I were there now, without a care now,
        To leap soul-gladdened to the bugle's call,
See the horses prancing, and the blue eyes glancing
        'Neath the bright, arched eyebrows of Lizzie Wall.

Relieved from duty, nor blind to beauty,
        Once more enraptured at eve I meet
Enchanting graces with Spanish faces,
        Their light feet twinkling on Patrick Street.
And though one grand creature, her plainest feature
        Enough to hold a saint in thrall,
Bards captivated, yet I estimated
        Far and above her sweet Lizzie Wall.

Peace left her arbour to seek the harbour
        Joy clapped his wings and crowed with glee
When nor let nor staying kept the bands from playing
        On the steamers plying down the sun-lit Lee.
Over there was Blarney, and behind Killarney,

---

[16] Elizabeth Wall was appointed assistant teacher at St Nicholas National School, Cove Street, Cork in 1867. She was a colleague of the poet who also taught in this school.
The poem, with its swinging rhythm and internal rhyme, is somewhat similar in style to an earlier work by Francis Mahony, (1805-66), *'The Belles of Shandon'*, with which Teggart was doubtless familiar.

And there was Passage, and blessing all
The blue sky smiling, and me beguiling,
And the brogue and banter of sweet Lizzie Wall.

Oh, fair Cork city, the wise, the witty,
Bards and poets have thy praises sung,
But the Lee raced after its own sweet laughter,
And love was real when I was young.
For I knew no sorrow, and each golden morrow,
Climbed till it kissed the towers tall,
And filled with glory the trellised storey,
Where bloomed and blossomed sweet Lizzie Wall.

The Grand Parade, Cork.

THE BLACKTHORN BLOSSOM

Have you ever seen it - the blackthorn blossom
    Snowy white on the dingy bough,
No tufts of green where it may embosom,
    The bush leaf-bare as the trees are now?
My boyish bosom with ne'er a care in,
    My face with gladness all aglow,
How oft it charmed me in changeless Erin—
    The blackthorn blossom white as snow.

Up the green hillside where hawthorns hoary
    Leaned o'er many a fairy ring,
The sloe was the first to tell the story
    Of love eternal as told by spring.
House-sparrows mad o'er their mates were quarrelin',
    The brown hedgesparrow chirped below,
But aflame in yellow the joyous yorlin
    Flooded with music the blossomed sloe.

Hard and high rose the hawthorn hedges,
    But here and there the gaps between,
Illuming the sprigs - tops, sides and edges,
    The freshly opened buds were seen.
On old mossed stones the shamrocks shining
    Spoke to a heart untouched by woe,
Of budded woodbines above them twining,
    And rough among them the blossomed sloe.

Oh, days departed! No more for ever
    May I my home in Ireland see,
But nor time, nor fate, nor seas can sever
    One happy memory from me.
No listless crowd may my song embosom,
    In vain may my numbers flash and flow,
But what care I while the blackthorn blossom,
    Spreads out before me, white as snow.

THE WHITERUMP[17]

Where the mossy runlet trickles,
    Where in cakes the clabber dries,
O'er the futtins, rows and rickles,
    All agog, the whiterump flies.
Now he's in the stubble bayton,
    That sweet "Cheer-up" is his song;
Now upon a clod he's waitin'
    Till his wifie comes along.

Nothing seems to daunt or tire him,
    Blue an' white - the bird of morn,
How the lusty lads admire him
    When they're trenchin' in the corn!
O'er the wee lump an' the muckle,
    O'er the wiry stalks o' ling,
To us all his cheerful chuckle
    Is the very laugh of spring.

The Whiterump - alias the Wheatear
(Courtesy Breffni Martin)

O'er the furrows sloped and slanted,
    O'er the little trinklin' rills,
O'er the plats wi' curleys planted,
    O'er the rough potato drills;
O'er the bogs, no more benighted,
    Under grey or shining skies,
All day long the bird delighted,
    Happy rover! flits an' flies.

Ere the bees whose nests are legion.
    O'er the tufts of heather hum,
Pretty bird, from what far region
    To loved Erin, do you come?
"Cheer up!" "Cheer up!" O romancer,
    You've just come across the sea,
And your song's a fitting answer
    For a moping bard like me.

---

[17] The wheatear, a small mainly ground-dwelling bird. It is blue-grey above and white below with an orange flush to the breast. In flight it shows a white rump and a black 'T' shape on its tail.

IN DEAR OLD IRELAND

They made her grave in Erin's Isle,
      They dug it dark and deep,
That she with ne'er a thought, the while,
      May through the ages sleep.

With grassy sods they happed it up,
      And wandering winds avow
The daisy and the buttercup
      Are blooming on it now.

The fields and farms around are fair;
      And every morn in Spring,
The red breast and the chaffinch there
      Their matins chant and sing.

The yorlin, perched, repeats his rhyme,
      The purple violets blow,
The primrose peeps, and there, in time,
      The shamrock green will grow.

The dew at dawn impearls the grass,
      The wildflowers o'er it wave,
And barefoot children when they pass
      Say "There's poor Mary's grave."

God bless the wildflowers and the weed,
      And all the blooms that shine;
Poor Mary's grave it is, indeed,
      Her humble grave and mine.

For all my hopes lie buried there,
      The dreams I dreamt when she
With blushes made the whole world fair,
      And life a joy for me.

And now my only comfort's this,
      When soft airs round me blow,
Soul currents from some land of bliss
      Make me, thank God, to know

The grave was never dug so deep
      But love could understand,
Though one wakes here, and one's asleep
      In dear Old Ireland.

THE TURF CUTTER

Don't stand there with your mouth agape!
      Find somethin' else to do!
Come, get the turf spade an' the graip,
      An' the turf-barra, too.

My back is not too stiff to stoop
      To work - no matter what;
So I'll clane out the cow-house groop
      While you are doin' that.

Oh, no! I'm not the laste bit cross—
      But now when labour's throng,
The turf bank I've pared up the moss,
      Will crack if left too long.

Now get your old Glengarry cap—
      The sun's so hot the day,
Most boys would rather peg a tap
      Than fork wet fums away.

Put in the fut boards, graip an' all,
      The turf-spade, too, I'll wheel;
From your wee showlder should it fall
      It might chip off a heel.

Wi' sods filled up its every pit
      That deep last winter showed
This ramper - since they gravelled it,
      Is like a county road.

That corn is showin' a fine braird!
      These early sprouts 'll do!
An' here's the bank that I have pared,
      An' shovelled smoothly, too.

Wheest! there's our friend the mosscheeper,
      Untouched by cant or care,
Och, how the lark-like notes of her
      Make sweet the throbbin' air.

These katty turf in the tap graft—
      So tough, fill me with hope,
The bottom ones, if not too saft,
      Will cut like yellow soap.

Ye might as well cut through a rug,
      Or grazin' closely clipped!

My fut, just now, off the spade lug,
      Wi' heavy pouncin' slipped.

Wheel these ones out - but not too far—
      That heather height 'll do!
(Those bells of ling - how sweet they are!
      How fresh an' rosy, too!)

You do not like to cover them
      Wi' wet turf or wi' dhry?
Go on! an' think how many a gem
      Gets hidden from the eye.

Think, too, of the cowld winter nights,
      The fine warm fireside,
The shadows and the shinin' lights
      No book from you can hide.

If I could cut down to the clay
      Through buried sprig an' bell,
My summer labour would repay
      Me in the winter, well.

But for the brown moss water here,
      There isn't half a fall!
Indeed, that march this many a year
      Is no march dhrain at all,

When in the hole that lump of bog
      Fell with a sudden splash,
How fast the sickly yellow frog
      For safety made a dash!

Ah! these are fine ones! from the spade,
      How smooth an' clane they slip!
Take care! The turf-graip wasn't made
      Their shinin' sides to rip.

Dear me! How long that skylark sings!
      He's surely in good tune!
No dinner-bell his wifie rings,
      An' yet it must be noon.

Wheest! isn't yon your mother's "hoagh"?
      The mugs are on the shelf!
Run on, my boy, an I'll bring Coagh—
      The craythur, home, myself.

WHERE THE BOG BEAN GROWS

O ye who prize the goldenrod,
      And ye who love the rose,
Come visit us and see the sod
      Where green the bog bean grows.
The bonnie lark will welcome you,
      And bogland orchids sweet—
Is yellow some, and some in blue,
      Will blossom round your feet.

White oat tails, too, will wave their plumes
      And where the quagmire lies,
Bough saggins flash their iris blooms
      Before your laughing eyes.
O'er ling and heather you may stray,
      In brown pools dip your toes,
Or rest beside the tammocks grey
      Where green the bog bean grows.

O ye who o'er your ledgers nod,
      And ye o'er desks who doze,
Come visit us and see the sod
      Where green the bog bean grows.
Come taste ye of its bitter leaf,
      And while the skylark sings,
Bethink ye peasants have their grief
      And joy, as well as kings.

See Erin for yourselves, and then
      Her boggy wilds shall be
Vast purple prairies, oft again
      In life you'll long to see.
Wide moorlands where the hand of God
      It is that paints and sows,
And waters well the brown turf sod
      Where green the bog bean grows.

THE VOICE OF MARY

Mary's only passing fair,
    Yet her melting voice and mellow
More than beauty doth ensnare,
    As with magic, me - poor fellow!

In her throat a flock of birds
    Wildly warbling all together,
Makes the music of her words
    Sweeter than the fair June weather.

Heavens! When I met her first,
    Such a rush of joy came o'er me,
All the wide world seemed to burst
    Into sudden blooms, before me.

Sparrows chirruped, skylarks sang.
    Twittered sweet the darling swallow,
Music rolled and music rang
    Over hill and over hallow.

Rapt upon her speech I hung,
    Till, as if our souls were mated,
To the music of her tongue,
    Every pulse in me vibrated.

And today, in life's calm hush,
    Linnets green in uplands airy,
Mavis, merle and mountain thrush
    Woo me in the voice of Mary.

This, and something in her eyes,
    Something melting, warm and mellow,
To her silken girdle ties,
    As with magic, me - poor fellow.

LILLIAN MARTIN[18]

Loose locks - black as the raven,
    The wind delights to blow
About her pulsing temples
    White as the driven snow.
And moon-white in its beauty
    Where'er I go or stray,
The sweet face of Lillian Martin
    It haunts me night and day.

Glad when on me she glances,
    And saddened when I see
Her silken-soft eyelashes
    Love's dawning hide from me.
Like stars forever beaming,
    On life's grief-trodden way,
The grey eyes of Lillian Martin
    Are shining night and day.

Spirits unseen around me
    Strike fancy's finest strings,
And still at tender twilight
    Play the divinest things.
Though these oft give me pleasure,
    And sweet it is they play,
The loved voice of Lillian Martin
    I hear it night and day.

Above the dark-brown water
    The lily holds her hands;
When day stoops down to kiss them,
    The star-flower understands.
The tremulous water-lilies,
    Though much beloved are they—
The white hands of Lillian Martin
    I kiss them night and day.

The leaves - how light they rustle!
    How sweet they dance along
When brown October's breezes
    Break into mirth and song!
O mild autumnal music
    In my heart, no longer gay,
The light feet of Lillian Martin
    Are dancing night and day.

---

[18] Possibly, Elizabeth Martin of Derrylard, born 1845; died 10 November 1879.

So charming is her manner,
    So sweet her winning ways,
She has a hundred lovers
    All proud to sing her praise.
And one - a friendly stranger,
    Full oft I hear him say,
"For the love of Lillian Martin
    I'm dying night and day."

LIGHT AND DARKNESS; OR THE BIRCHES BOY'S FATE

There was a boy - a Birches boy,
    Stout both of heart and limb;
His mother in him took no joy—
    The stranger needed him.

Blue were the eyes below the brows
    That brightened broader still
What time he herded calves and cows
    Upon the gravel hill.

In shine and shower, in light and shade,
    At morn, at eve, at noon
Upon his yellow fife he played
    Full many a merry tune.

His face was far from being fair,
    Sunburnt and brown was he;
Yet would that city scions were
    As manly and as free.

Nature was mother to the lad—
    Upon her breast he lay,
And many a golden vision had
    Of fair lands far away.

For to that green and grassy hill
    Some rover still returned
From over seas - and list'ning still
    His heart within him burned.

Yet knew he every bonny bird
    That o'er that hill did roam;
Each leaf and twig on it that stirred
    Was music made at home.

The yorlin sat upon the brier,
      The linnet on the thorn;
Each evening sun went down in fire,
      Rose red each dewy morn.

He loved the gently arching boughs
      That bended o'er the rill;
He loved the heifers, calves and cows
      That grazed upon the hill.

But ere he ceased to be a boy,
      Away from home he ran;
The world was wide - it gave him joy
      To think himself a man.

Where coalpits - black as night, deface
      Earth's radiant robe of green
He found employ, he got a place
      Where daylight was not seen.

Down in the bowels of the earth,
      In a darksome pit deep down
Where was no music and no mirth,
      No country and no town.

Shut out from sun and rain and dew,
      Shut out from balmy air,
His eyes in that black pit were blue
      As ever jewels were.

There, with three hundred more, one morn
      Through all that cavern's gloom,
He found his fate - with none to warn,
      He met, poor lad, his doom.

The explosion in a moment turned
      The black pit into hell;
The mangled bodies while they burned
      Made horrible the smell.

Two hundred blackened corpses brought
      They to the upper ground;
For trunks they searched, for bodies sought,
      For limbs they never found.

He who upon earth's grassy breast
      His couch had often made,
Brought to the pit's mouth - with the rest,
      In the dead row was laid.

Death sudden unto him had come,
      Had blanched the bright blue eye,
Had struck the dusty toiler dumb
      Where was no smiling sky.

But while it came - in some red dawn
      That never saw the day,
The collier lad was thinking on
      The green hill far away.

They laid him on the coal dust - sad—
      Even that was their annoy—
They never knew the dreams he had
      What time he was a boy!

But those poor widowed ones beheld
      Upon his upturned face,
A light that half their sorrow quelled—
      Peace from another place.

As pure a light was on the brows
      That now, alas, were still,
As when at home he herded cows
      Upon the gravel hill.

THE BELLE OF DERRYAGH

These boys from up the country,
      They boast about their girls
Wi' cheeks as red as rosies,
      An' teeth as white as pearls;
An' then they tell how fine it is
      To sue for favours - Bagh!
They never coaxed at milkin' time
      The Belle of Derryagh.

The ould men laugh an' listen,
      An' then wi' them agree;
The young blades sit an' snigger
      Then slyly wink at me.
These boys from up the country
      Have been enchanted - Bagh!
They never lapped their arms aroun'
      The Belle of Derryagh.

An' while they're busy talkin',
      A crowd soon gathers roun',
Some chaps from the far houses,
      An' some from down the town.
The strangers tell of lightsome heels
      An' twinklin' ankles - Bagh!
At dance or ball they never met
      The Belle of Derryagh.

These boys from up the country.
      When down for turf they come,
About the beauty of their girls
      They'd talk ye deaf and dumb.
They'll tell ye they have tasted lips
      As sweet as honey - Bagh!
They never kissed at milkin' time
      The Belle of Derryagh.

UP THE RAMPER

Up the ramper - wee white houses
    Dot the narrow, winding way;
Picks the tethered goat and browses
    In some wet ditch all the day.
Up the ramper - blooms the heather,
    Blushes on its stem the ling;
Moss-bred birds of modest feather
    Mate and marry, pipe and sing.

Up the ramper - Mary's shuttle
    Through the woof delighted hums,
Clicks the loom - that trig and subtle
    Life of years and threads and thrums.
Up the ramper - blue eyed Mary
    Weaves a cambric web so fine,
People come to Ballinary
    Just to see the borders shine.

Up the ramper - birches buddin'
    Blush wi' shame what time they see
Some barefooted gossip scuddin'
    Home to her wee children three.
Up the ramper - mirth and sorrow
    Scarce divided by a drain,
Change so quick, that by tomorrow
    Woe has mirth and mirth has pain.

Up the ramper - leaves like ribbons
    Shine upon the rowan tree,
When wi' turf the creels and cribbins
    Are as full as full can be.
Up the ramper - when together
    Saunter happy girl and boy,
Sings the skylark o'er the heather
    Songs of gladness and of joy.

TO THE ROBIN RED BREAST

Robin Redbreast! Never wildwood
      Thou with song were meant to fill;
Poet of my happy childhood,
      Thou art dark-eyed Robin, still.

Ah! what haps my life have hinder'd
      Since with book in hand I stood,
Moved to tears about thy kindred
      And the Children in the Wood.

Now when 'round the house I labour—
      Footrin' with a cutty spade,
Thou art aye my constant neighbour,
      One whose friendship I have made.

Daytime songsters, idly roaming,
      Give to wilds their warbling glee;
Thou, sweet minstrel of the gloaming,
      Say'st thy melodies for me.

Scarce has evening soft descended,
      Day's faint footsteps scarce depart,
Till thy song, with sorrow blended,
      Reacheth to my inmost heart.

Daylight's fervid clash and riot,
      May set louder fancies free;
Twilight's hush and holy quiet
      Suits alike both thee and me.

Listless whilst the skirling thrushes
      Jinked among them all day along,
Thou but chirped, and these thorn bushes
      Hushed themselves to hear thy song.

Sheltering more than one wee ant hill,
      This young birch, white limbed and tall,
Gathers round her her green mantle,
      Weeps, and listens to it all.

Robin Redbreast, art thou bringing
      Back the dead and gone to me?
Or art thou, as some think, singing
      Of the peace that is to be?

Thou hast sung for him - my brother
      Homed now in the Hebrides;

Thou hast sung for my poor mother,
      Sung for all, in these same trees.

One repines and one rejoices,
      One has dool and one delight,
Yet, love-circled, all their voices
      Melt in thy sweet song tonight.

Not a sound of joy or illness
      Stirs the bogland ramper's rim;
All the place is hushed to stillness,
      Listening to thy holy hymn.

No lamp twinkles in the valley,
      Darkness hides the further hill,
Sleeps the finch in yonder sally,
      Yet thou'rt softly singing still.

Long time standing at the gable,
      I have listened to thee, now,
Till the night's soft wings and sable
      Hidden have both twig and bough.

Wet the weed is, wet the wallflower,
      Dampened well the dew doth keep
Sage and mint and e'en the tall flower
      Kissed by me and sent asleep.

Soft! A lull! Ah! Is it ending?
      Is it hushed, that song of thine?
No! Once more I hear it blending
      With this pensive warble mine.

Robin Redbreast! Never wildwood
      Thou with song wert meant to fill;
Pet and poet of my childhood,
      Thou in this art singing still.

WHERE DARLING SALLY DWELLS

The borough slumbers on the brow
    Of a most ancient hill;
The storied keep - a ruin now—
    Has one round tower still.
The dust of Hengist heareth not
    The gentle vesper bells,
The sounds that circle round the spot,
    Where darling Sally dwells.

No sea-breeze there the traveller sniffs,
    Far inland it is set,
Where breathes her balm among the cliffs,
    The yellow violet!
The rarer blossom and the blue
    Mingle their fragrant smells,
And, like the primrose, feed on dew
    Where darling Sally dwells.

Their chairs the gentle dames forsake
    What time the day is fine,
Pick posies, herbs and buds, and make
    The fragrant cowslip wine.
The partridge winters on the wold;
    And when the green bud swells,
The lambs bleat loud in every fold,
    Where darling Sally dwells.

What time the cuckoo from afar
    Comes to the wooded hills,
The fine old-fashioned gardens are
    Ablaze with daffodils.
From banks that frame the sloping fields,
    Peep out the pimpernels,
The wildest copse some floweret yields,
    Where darling Sally dwells.

The molten sun of autumn gilds
    With gold the glossy leaves;
In May the twittering swallow builds
    Below the hallowed eaves.
Grey - in a wilderness of green—
    The distant grange compels
The bard to come back to the scene
    Where darling Sally dwells.

When he in his demesne lies down,
    Sleep comes to him at will;

And in his dreams the little town
        Seems nodding on the hill.
When twilight silence o'er it falls,
        He hears the vesper bells,
And sees, once more, the ivied walls
        Where darling Sally dwells

BRANNON'S BRAE

(Grandma's Version)

It lies fornenst the sun at noon,
        A rough and stony height,
Where all the bushes bud as soon
        As Winter takes his flight.
The lark may like the dewy lea,
        But on a Summer's day
There's no place nicer you could be
        Than up on Brannon's Brae.

The hedges they have not been clipped
        For two or three years an' more,
Nor ivy from the hawthorns stripped—
        I'm sure since fifty-four.
In air that is as sweet as wine,
        Pink honeysuckles sway;
The very whins wi' blossoms shine,
        And blaze in Brannon's Brae.

The dandelion an' the broom
        Are lovely to behold,
Though groundsel, when it is in bloom,
        You couldn't match for gold.
An' these wee yellow flowers - these
        On threads of pink, so gay,
Are courted by each coolin' breeze
        That comes to Brannon's Brae.

A blink of sunshine warm an' bright
        Upon the thorny sloe,
An' then the blossom comes as white
        As comes a shower of snow.
June breathes upon the brier bush,
        The rosebuds nothin' say,
But it's wonderful the way they blush
        An' bloom on Brannon's Brae.

A posy here you aye may pick,
    It's Nature them that owns;
Larkspurs an' lupins blossom thick
    Among the gravel stones.
An' a nicer place you never sat
    An' whiled an hour away
Than by the spring that rises at
    The foot of Brannon's Brae.

Between the foggy stones - in Spring—
    The bonny vi'lets rise
So backward-like, they often bring
    The tears to granny's eyes.
Primroses they fill every nook
    Wi' fairy gold in May,
An' nowhere finer do they look
    Than up on Brannon's Brae.

When comes the cuckoo from afar—
    The shower and shine between,
In sheets the beds of daisies are
    Spread out upon the green.
An' white as hailstones, in their hoods,
    An' lovely hoods are they,
On slender threads the sorrel buds
    Just melt on Brannon's Brae.

Then, it's the haunt of all the birds
    Aroun' the country side;
From them the ploughboy learns the words
    That please the blushin' bride.
The yellow yorlin an' the finch,
    The linnets green an' grey
An' hedge-sparrows know every inch
    Of groun' on Brannon's Brae.

The roguish blackbird an' the thrush,
    The wren an' all the rest
In pairin' time on every bush
    Just sing their very best.
At Candlemas if cold rain falls
    A shower-bath on the jay,
Then you should hear how loud he calls
    The Spring to Brannon's Brae.

When from the briers breathin' musk
    The honey bee has gone,
Wee robin redbreast in the dusk,
    An' in the early dawn.

Wi' th' dewdrops rolling off his wing
    Warbles his roundelay;
And nowhere softer does he sing
    Than up on Brannon's Brae.

A darlin' place it is, indeed,
    On which your limbs to rest;
Or, if you like it, learn to read
    In Nature's book - the best.
When all the twigs are hung wi' pearls,
    It's there that you should stray;
An' where will you meet nicer girls
    Than those on Brannon's Brae?

Who is it that would not be fond
    Of this - the poet's hill?
The fields are fair, an' those beyond
    Are green and fairer still.
Yes, these wild rosies they remind
    Me of my weddin' day!—
You'll know the feelin' when you find
    A wife on Brannon's Brae.

Brannon's Brae, as it is today.

A LOUGH NEAGH LAMENT

Upon thy naked shores, Lough Neagh,
      No more a boy I wander,
But on thy waters wide and grey
      Full many a time I ponder.
In dreary dreams, at midnight seen,
      Me of my rest they're robbing;
There still beside a graveyard green
      I halt and hear them sobbing.

For there my darling mother sleeps,
      And o'er her grassy pillow
The dewy star of evening weeps,
      Or beams upon the billow.
There she at rest, all lowly laid,
      Hears not the wan wave sobbing
Around the blossom or the blade
      That it of rest is robbing.

She does not hear the church bell ring
      On Sunday morning holy;
Nor does she hear - like cherubs sing—
      The loved ones of the lowly.
She sees no more the heather bloom
      That bees of sweets are robbing;
Both day and night beside her tomb
      The weary wave is sobbing.

The fisherman, far, far away,
      Takes a delight in sailing
His boat into the dying day,
      Into the dim light failing.
At red dawn he returns and hears
      The same grey water sobbing;
And touched - in his blue eyes the tears
      His heart of hope are robbing.

The yew trees at the churchyard gate
      Are dark in spring and summer,
Are dark when autumn, lingering late,
      Leaves them to the next comer—
Leaves them to winter, who would not
      Them of their gloom be robbing;
The seasons seem to have forgot
      The yew tree used to sobbing.

Ah! many in the years that fly,
      Between the yew trees, slowly

Pass inward, borne shoulder high,
      There to be laid so lowly.
Grey Time - a thief by day and night—
      Though mourners sad are sobbing,
Brings through that gate the brave and bright
      From homes he has been robbing.

Thou art my mourner, loved Lough Neagh,
      Lone watch for me still keeping;
Though from thy banks I'm far away,
      I see and hear thee weeping.
Tonight wan Memory walks the wave,
      Of my repose me robbing;
Lough Neagh and I beside one grave
      Meet, and we both are sobbing.

A SHEAF FROM THE BOGLAND

A LITTLE THORN

The little thorn on Brannon's road,
    How dear it is to me!
Rose-pink the buds in spring it showed,
    And rain-pearls on it gleamed and glowed
And glanced when I was wee.

What though red brambles from it hang,
    What though it suffers dree,
How oft on it the yorlin sang
    Till all the banks and borders rang
With bogland melody!

The little thorn on Brannon's road
    Grew up along wi' me;
And near my father's thatched abode,
    From morning glanced till evening glowed,
Watched us the little tree.

A CHANGE

The wind among the sally trees—
    Its melancholy roar
Sounds loud as sound the dashing seas
    Upon a dismal shore.
Yet safe below the sally trees,
    Before a turf fire bright,
The kitten purring on her knees,
    Sits my true love, tonight.

The wind among the sally trees
    Oh, how it loves to sing
Of hope and joy, and, me to please—
    Love, innocence, and spring!
But cold below the sally trees
    One hearth's no longer bright—
My blue-eyed love on foaming seas
    Is far from home tonight.

THE LOUGH AT DERRYADD

Around its edge thick grows the sedge
    And though they it befriend,
For which shall fill its borders, still
    The fir and birch contend.
When through the trees the summer breeze

   Blows wistfully and sad,
'Neath leaden skies how dark it lies—
   The lough at Derryadd.

When smiling May brings insects grey
   To feed her feathered ones,
Along the edge, among the sedge,
   The wee mosscheeper runs.
When through the trees the summer breeze
   Blows musical and glad,
'Neath laughing skies how blue it lies—
   The lough at Derryadd.

The Lough at Derryadd

THE BLACKCAP[19]

Outringing from his muffled throat,
        And echoed far and near,
In winter time the blackcap's note
        Is joyous, loud and clear.
Perched on a jointed, rush-like reed
        Beside the river Bann,
So spry he is, he seems to need
        No charity from man.

And in the bogs, among the riggs
        So blithe he seems to go,
The burdocks and the birken twigs
        His presence seem to know.
And all the time from muffled throat,
        Be it or far or near,
He sends the ringing joyous note
        That does us good to hear.

UPON THE STUBBLE RIGG

At shearin' time a little lad
        Was wont around to run
An' jump the furs, until his dad
        Would call him and say, "Son,
Pick up the ripened heads that fall,
        The little and the big,
An' leave no stalk of corn at all
        Upon the stubble rigg."

I picked them up, the great an' small,
        The little an' the big,
Nor left a stalk of corn at all
        Upon the stubble rigg.
But knowing well the sunlit hours!
        For growth were all too few,
I always spared the bonny flowers
        That in the furrows grew.

LIZA

When Liza love of loves, to me,
        Is seated on her loom
Her lip is like the strawberrie,
        Her eyes like lint in bloom,
Crowned by a mass of coiled-up hair,

---

[19] A distinctive greyish warbler. Its delightful, fluting song has earned it the name 'the northern nightingale'.

        Black as the raven's wing,
Her face, with lights and shadows fair,
        Is like a morn in spring.

When Liza - love of loves lets me
        Round her my arms entwine,
Her lip tastes like a strawberrie,
        Her eyes like blossoms shine.
Close to my bosom fondly prest,
        Soon as I set her free,
With love's tumult her little breast
        Is heaving like the sea.

BOG FIR

In what dim ages of the past
        Was this fir stump a tree?
What awful floods, what torrents vast
        Engulfed it like a sea?
We know not, though we know that now
        Dragged out of mud and mire,
Cut up and dried and stocked, somehow,
        It makes a rousin' fire.

Nodding and dreaming, lovely once,
        Upon some mountain side,
A splinter now stuck in the sconce
        Lights up the kitchen wide,
Have vanished floods and torrents vast,
        But still where mortals stir,
The pent-up light of ages past
        Burns in the tough bog fir.

IN MILLTOWN CHURCHYARD

These green mounds in the churchyard
        Are graves my little son:
The graves of men and women
        Whose earthly tasks are done.
The graves of pretty boys and girls,
        And little children too,
Whom God, in love, has taken
        To dwell beyond the blue.

You think, as scores of others think,
        At service who appear,
That, rested from their earthy toils,
        They all are sleeping here,
But in fields that lie around

>   The New Jerusalem
> Some reaping are, some gleaning are,
>   And God still feedeth them.

OVER AT MITTON'S[20]

> Over at Mitton's - our neighbour's white house
>   The words how familiar to me!
> For in childhood if only the cat caught a mouse
>   We were sure to run over to see.
> But 'Over at Mitton's' full early meant more,
>   For up to the house was a lane—
> A dear little loanin' by birches hung o'er
>   And oft at the end of it - Jane
>
> 'Jane' to her people, but Jenny to us,
>   A sweet little Quakeress she,
> Blue-eyed and red-lipped and bewitching, and thus
>   A mark for Dan Cupid and me.
> Alas for the heart when the arrow is sped;
>   Alas for the throbbing of yore!
> Her parents are dead, and wee Jenny is wed,
>   And I 'gwover' to Mitton's no more.

---

[20] James and Rebecca Mitton occupied one of the largest cottages in Ballinary. It had seven front windows, nearly twice as many as the townland average.

MORE BITS FROM THE BOGLAND

DIVIDED

She feels her face the zephyrs fan;
    And when the south wind swells,
Floats to her ears, across the Bann,
    The sound of Lurgan bells.

At dusk, subdued unto her comes
    The sough from wide Lough Neagh;
And oft, abed, she hears the drums
    Beat, miles and miles away.

But never do her hungry ears
    Thrill with the joyful cry
Of one whose foot for twenty years
    She has not heard go by.

Far in the wild Australian bush,
    The bell-bird's ringing call
Delights the ears to which the thrush
    Once piped in Derryall.

The feet that once to Mary's eyes
    Were shod as with the sun,
In Kangaroo[21] now fall and rise
    Across a shepherd's run.

His schoolmate still by Kerrib bog
    May herd the brindled cow,
But in his hut his collie dog
    Is his companion, now.

And though in many a happy dream
    He sees his boyhood's home,
His horse and he, by scrub and stream,
    Comrades together roam.

Instead of, as in seasons gone,
    Belauding yellow broom,
His fine blue eyes now feast them on
    The wattles' matchless bloom.

---

[21] South Australian island, seventy miles south-west of Adelaide. The subject of the poem is probably William Francis Teggart, brother of Moses, who emigrated to Australia in the early 1880s.

He hears his sheep the herbage crop,
    And nigh the lonely springs,
Perched on a towering gum tree top
    For him the magpie sings.

His beard falls black upon his breast,
    His Melbourne jacket's grey,
Yet Mary always sees him dressed
    Just as he went away.

For him the Murray gleams and glides,
    For her moss trinklets run,
And thus a whole round world divides
    Two lives that might be one.

THE STONECHECKER[22]

'Whinchat!' Isn't that your name,
      Your book name, pretty bird?
Though 'stonechecker' the gorsons claim,
      Is just as good a word.
Through whin bushes jink you may
      When they're blossom lit;
But here through futtins, half the day,
      Like a flame you flit.

Those who've seen your velvet hat
      And your red-brown wings,
Must have heard your "checker-chat"
      And how harsh it rings.
No matter! you're a nice wee bird!
      Cock your tail and go!
A chat whose note's a double word.
      Must some bird language know.

BELLA[23]

She's neat an' she's smart, an' her sharp piercin' eyes
      Are as black as the sloes on the bush;
An' further, the Derryagh dames to surprise.
      In her long yellow throat there's a thrush.

A slip best forgot, in her face when they fling,
      They cast on her good name a slur;
An' in all the wide parish there's no one can sing
      'In green Caledonia' like her.

THE TURF BUMMER[24]

"Never mind the shilty's winkers!
      But if somethin' you must do,
Throw me up those clods an' clinkers,
      Pitch me up those black ones too.
This load's for a man in Lurgan;
      An', to-morrow, Tandragee
Will see me in the market stan'in'
      Hagglin' for three bob an' three."

---

[22] Small perching bird that hops or runs on the ground. It has a prominent white stripe above the eye.
[23] Bella Bearns (Barnes), Ballinary but originally from Scotland. She married Thomas McAnally, Ballinary, 11 January 1873.
[24] One who travelled the countryside selling turf.

Rain an' sleet an' hailstones scornin',
      A master of the bummer's art,
Many a cold an' hasky mornin'
      Has poor Jemmy panged the cart.
Many a night, between the cribbins,
      Studyin' the starry dome,
He, foot-sore, has brought the shilty
      An' the three white shillin's home.

THE BLUECAP[25]

See the bluecap! blithe and jolly
      On the blossomed apple bough,
Naught he knows of melancholy,
      Twig him! Watch him! See him now—
Head downward to an offshoot clinging,
      His sharp eyes looking every way.
And now, in blue and white, he's swinging
      From a rosy-tufted spray.

Happy bird! Boy with a new cap
      Never was one half so gay,
As in summer time the bluecap,
      With new antics every day.
In winter - round the barns he dodges,
      Flits among the ivy leaves;
And on frosty nights he lodges
      With some sparrow 'neath the eaves.

Bluecap

ON THE WEE GREEN RAMPER

Up and down the wee green ramper,
      Blithe it was when I was wee,
Half the day to skip and scamper,
      Roll and tumble jollily.
Nothing there to hurt or harm me,
      Fairy none, nor elfish fay,
Birds and bees and flowers to charm me,
      And the night time far away.

But when dusk came, the green ramper
      Was, indeed, no place for me!
Fairies, there were known to scamper,
      Fays to foot it merrily.
So feared was I of elves and witches,
      And, of boogles, bleary eyed,
Nor twilight star, nor untold riches
      Could tempt me from the fireside.

---

25 The bluetit - its plumage is a colourful mix of blue, yellow, white and green.

A BLACK FROST

This keen black frost the daisy nips,
        The poor wee rosy thing!
It makes us blow our finger tips,
        So sore they stoun' an' sting.
The stubble rigg's inch thick wi' crust,
        Through which a Newry spade
Must bite before the sod will 'brust'
        An' break, an' mould be made.

There's ice upon the drains hurrah!
        Come on an' have a slide,
Down on your hunkers! Jack agra.
        How swift we swirl an' glide!
An' wait till night - the moon will shine,
        An' then upon the pool,
Wi' Mo an' Joe - all in a line,
        We'll start the three-legged stool.

Worse than the frost, the keener wind—
        Oh, how it cuts an' stings!
The shelter's thin the linnets find,
        The poor wee chitterin' things.
An' now, back to the stubble rigg
        Where daisies - star an' stem,
Are all laid out - I like to dig,
        But hate to bury them.

BOGLAND PICTURES I

WEE JERRY

When my daughter set sail on the big boat at Derry,
    To be sure I was lonesome and sad for a while,
I was dwamy, indeed, till my brother's wee Jerry
    Came in an' lit up the whole house with his smile.

An' he says, "Uncle Rabert, what is it that ails ye?
    Are ye frettin' for Peggy, the sonsy an' true?
Ye must cheer up your heart, an' if everything fails ye,
    I'll be both a son and a daughter to you."

I got him last night to write me a wee letter,
    Tellin' Peg in the States I was happy and well;
For a boy, to his uncle, there isn't a better
    In the sound of the ring of Tartaraghan bell.

He'll run a wee errand for me to the Birches,
    He brings me my milk every morn in a can;
An' on Sunday he knows, like his da, where the church is,
    God send him his health, an' befriend him - a man.

IN THE BIG MOSS[26]

Far in the wilds of the Big Moss,
    Unwinnowed and unwon,
Where bogholes one another cross,
    And drains like rivers run—
The shy and lately hunted hare,
    Snug in her sheltered form,
Of coming danger unaware,
    This winter day sleeps warm.

Hark! 'tis the fowler and his dog,
    And eke his deadly gun!
He shoots whatever thing the bog
    Sees fly, or rise, or run.
One moment and poor puss across
    A tammock bound she may—
The next, and lone in the Big Moss
    Her life-blood ebbs away.

---

[26] Name given to Columbkill Moss, Derryland.

MY FATHER'S BIRCHES

This row of birks along the ramper,
        Rough of twig and round of stem,
Touch them not with tools, nor tamper
        With the tassels green on them.
But while Spring around them lingers,
        Making whole what urchins mar,
With the pink tips of your fingers
        Feel how smooth their white skins are.

On their tops the twait - spry fellow!
        Is our red-crowned springtime bard;
And their long, tough roots and yellow
        Help to make the ramper hard.
Harm them not, my comrades! rather
        Deem them sacred - twig and stem,
For 'twas he, my thoughtful father,
        Years ago, who planted them.

TREASURE-TROVE

Our Mary (light be now her troubles!
        By her help it was we throve)
Digging, one day, in the stubbles,
        Lit on bogland treasure-trove.
Digging - not with spurt and splutter!
        To the quick, and deeper far,
She dug up a tub of butter,
        Axle grease as black as tar.

Whence, oh whence, and from what region,
        Did the hoard, once yellow come?
Ask the winds - their name is legion,
        Yea, beseech them, and they're dumb.
Shouldered home - an awkward bundle!
        And the black staves knocked apart,
No longer squeaked the barrow trundle,
        Creaked no more the old turf cart.

THE MEADOWPIPIT

See how quickly she can trip it
        O'er these bogland banks so bare!
Shy she is - the meadowpipit,
        Sombre-hued and yet how fair.

Poor mosscheeper! We have known her
        Since our bogland life began,

And to clod her, or to stone her,
        Were a sin, in boy or man.

As the 'tit-lark' too, her ditty
        Piped and poured out in mid-air,
Seems to make the bogbean pretty
        And the ling bells, twice as fair.

See how red her shanks are, running
        Down the long wheelbarrow track!
See the speckled breast she's sunning
        Now, upon the old turf stack!

Oh, thou light brown meadowpipit!
        Moss-lark still to mine and me,
Would that I once more might trip it
        O'er the bogland banks with thee.

YELLOW BROOM

'Twas that delightful season when the broom,
Full-flowered and visible on every steep,
Along the copses runs in veins of gold.
        (Wordsworth)

Wizard of Windermere! Steeps and copses
        Almost are unknown to us!
Nature, in the bogland, stops us,
        Saying, "Stoop! and see me thus.
Here along the moss-plat edges
        Are little springs of yellow broom,
Fine as ever mountain ledges
        Sheltered, in or out of bloom."

Broom.

And we stoop, or e'en upstanding,
        Here and there, sun-lit behold
Blooms that in an hour expanding,
        Show their wings and hearts of gold,
Bare and bleak the bogland may be,
        Colder, too, than Cumberland;
But if only bright the day be,
        Broom is broom in Ireland.

THE LOVED ONE

On that sad day they sent me word
>That Mary, the beloved, was dead,
My heart, like some poor wounded bird,
>Helpless and hopeless - how it bled!

To think that Death had shut the door
>And left me shattered among men,
Never to see my darling more,
>Or meet her on this earth again.

No more - not e'en at dusk, by chance
>To hear her laughter in the lane,
Or see those eyes whose briefest glance
>Was ne'er bestowed on me in vain.

And then how quick did I recall
>The favours giv'n in days gone by,
The kisses, glances, smiles and all
>That could not with dear Mary die.

The looks that sweeter made the day,
>The charms that most a poet please;
These things could never pass away,
>And Mary was made up of these.

These still were mine, and so my heart
>Built up the old-time love anew;
Nothing had rent our souls apart,
>That she was dead - it was not true.

Still met we in the land of dreams,
>And still whene'er I wandered wide,
By moorland or by mountain streams,
>I found her walking at my side.

Still fell the same sweet, winning voice
>Upon a heart that thrilled to hear;
Nor could my spirit but rejoice
>Knowing its other self was near.

And so from day to day there grew
>No memory Mary, but the same
Blest creature from whose eyes of blue
>Love first into my being came.

And many a bitter day I brooked,
>Nor failed to conquer grim despair,

For still when in my heart I looked
    It was to see her happy there.

And she is there, nor has black Death
    Upon her shut the iron door;
Against my cheek I feel her breath.
    She's by my side for evermore.

She speaks at morn in every bird,
    Her blushes fill the day with bloom,
By her the twilight boughs are stirred,
    Her looks of love the night illume.

Love's first ungathered dewy rose
    Breathed on by God and made divine,
She's still the influence sweet that flows
    Into this quiet life of mine.

She has not parted from me yet,
    Her face bends this sweet line above,
Nor can she die till I forget
    The meaning of eternal love.

THE BELLE OF CLONMACATE

The carts are comin' home from town,
    The day in glory dies,
An' o'er the mosses bare an' brown
    The pretty pewit flies.
The crested pewit flies to feed
    In meadows where the cows,
Wi' none to drive an' none to lead,
    All day in freedom browse,
But who is she who comes this way,
    Light-steppin' to the gate?
Hush! That's - the Birches' boyos say—
    The Belle of Clonmacate.

You cannot see her colour now,
    But sure as this I sing,
The locks around her lily brow
    Are like the raven's wing,
The rose that blossoms on her cheek,
    If it e'er kissed has been,
Would tell us - if it could but speak,
    Love's sweet at seventeen,
An' so it is, O so it is,
    God knows it's so of late,

Yet where's the lad can call her his—
      The Belle of Clonmacate?

Light-hearted, too, she is the girl,
      A maid who loves the moon,
A blue-eyed lass, a blushing pearl
      Some lad will gather soon.
Yet rest from toil she seldom takes,
      For even in July,
From early morn till night, she makes
      The yellow shuttle fly.
She with her web on passin' day,
      The dear, is never late,
She has no time to spend at play—
      The Belle of Clonmacate.

The curleys grow, the roses blow,
      Her mother's place is small,
The rent, too, must be paid, ye know,
      But Mary's all in all.
An' though for higher things she yearns—
      The desk, the scholar's pen,
'Tis on her linen loom she earns
      The needed two pound ten.
Avaunt, avaunt, ye wordly cares!
      She's leanin' o'er the gate,
And Love and Song have crowned her theirs—
      The Belle of Clonmacate.

STILL MORE BOGLAND PICTURES

THE SHOVEL AND THE SPADE

Let laureates sing of belted lords
      And dames of high degree;
Or, flushed with sherries, strike the chords
      Of mirth and revelry.
A humbler song, a lowlier lay
      Suits him - the nobler made,
Who sings the lords of loam and clay—
      The Shovel and the Spade.

Stern is the muse when laurelled bards,
      With languor in their eyes,
And greedy of their king's regards,
      Our rugged tools despise.
Winsome the muse, when some poor wight
      Whom toil can not degrade,
First sings, with all his valiant might,
      The Shovel and the Spade.

The thews of manhood - how, like steel,
      They strengthen at the song!
From fist to foot, from head to heel,
      They brace them, giant strong.
They feel that they had not been thews,
      With muscle overlaid,
Had hand and foot not learned to use
      The Shovel and the Spade.

The mind itself, it feels a force,
      It had not had but for
The ready tools, however coarse,
      With which the hands make war,
On rough hillsides and heathy wolds,
      On glen and rocky glade,
And to its larger heart enfolds
      The Shovel and the Spade.

What frowning shores, what marshes grey,
      What wastes on beach and isle,
What dismal bogs, what deserts they,
      Well handled make to smile!
What gardens in the wild have bloomed
      And blossomed by the aid
Of those two bruisers, still undomed
      The Shovel and the Spade.

All honour to the horny hands
    That dig and delve and toil,
And make to laugh the niggard lands,
    And plant with seed the soil,
No palsied poet, shunned by Pan
    Is he - the nobler made,
Who sings, with all the might of man,
    The Shovel and the Spade.

MORN

Morn! an' the elves an' witches
    An' the folk from the land of Finn,
At a bound have cleared the ditches,
    An' gone back to their kin.

The boogles have changed to bushes,
    Sparklin' with sunlit dew;
Robin Goodfellows turned to rushes,
    And the fays to violets blue.

The goblins have washed their faces,
    And now as ragweeds shine;
And the ghosts that in lonesome places
    Did nought all night but pine

Have gone, like children chidden,
    To hide their griefs and ills;
An' the fairies all are hidden
    In the hollows of the hills.

The maid is the milk in-bringing,
    Foaming and sweet and new;
And the lark, for joy, is singing
    Blithely in the blue.

Morn! an' our last misgiving
    In the cock's loud crow is drowned;
And the boy is once more living
    In a world that's safe an' sound.

NIGHT

Night! an' adown the loanin'
      An elf with a green-plumed cap;
An' a big black boogle groanin'
      At every hawthorn gap.

A ghost at the horse-hole walkin',
      Another on Brannon's brae;
An' the wraith of Tam, the balkin,
      Haunts Poyntzpass, so they say.

To walk to the road undaunted,
      Were worthy of praise galore.
An' Koosh big house is haunted
      From the attic to the floor.

Something dunders against the gables,
      So rough up at the Street;
An' a black man haunts the stables—
      Take care ye don't him meet!

There's a will-o-the-wisp swift skippin'
      Over the wet bogs, now;
An' wheest! There's somethin' trippin'
      Itself over that ould plough.

There are so many scaresome places,
      A little boy at night
Has to put licks in his paces,
      Or die on the road with fright.

Koosh House.

THE FISHER GIRL

With ruby lips and teeth of pearl,
How fair she is, - the fisher girl!
  Out of her covered sally basket,
  She'll give you a pullen, if you ask it,
And laugh and show her teeth of pearl,
The bonnie, blue-eyed, fisher girl.

Slim below her skirt's dark line,
Her shanks - as Aphrodite's fine—
  Bear up a lithe and supple body,
  Clad it may be in vulgar shoddy,
But the bosom beating there
As Aphrodite's own is fair.

Rich of speech, and sprightly, too,
Straight as a queen she looks at you,
  You who now forget to be sullen,
  And warbles how her fine fresh pullen
Are caught in nets when deep Lough Neagh
Slumbers below the night cloud grey.

Smelling of dulse and osier slips
Swaying and swinging, waist and hips,
  Here she comes with her shallow basket
  Perched on her head, and if you ask it
She'll sell you a tench without demur,
And kiss the coin with a "Thank ye, Sor."

Kinked and curly, coal-black hair,
Firm white neck - as a lily fair—
  These and her shapely ankles twiggin',
  The burly boys in the bogland diggin'
Think of her as a Milltown pearl,
The bonnie, blue-eyed, fisher girl.

THE OLD STONE-BREAKER

A bulky pile of stones before him,
      By the roadside lorn and lone,
Soft grey skies, low bending o'er him,
      Sits old Neddy, breaking stone.

Aloof alike from clash and clamour,
      And the pride that stoons and stings,
In the hands the stout stone hammer,
      Iron hammer raps and rings.

Rings on every stone he places
      Plump before him in the pile,
Some with smooth and flattened faces,
      Some with backs that him beguile.

Whack! and that big thumper's broken;
      Crack; and there's another gone;
Smash! And flint - of fire the token,
      Shattered lies the pile upon.

Passing in your carriage, madam,
      Do you even pause to think
How this toiling son of Adam,
      Needs must through his goggles blink.

When the spark, rough-startled, flashes,
      Out of the astonished stone—
Hit so hard, the tool that smashes
      It, dinnels like a living bone?

Poor old Neddy! there beside him;
      In the grass, his cutty pipe,
Never for a day denied him,
      Is of him and his a type.

In the bundle, tied and knotted
      Up in that old handkerchief—
New and glossy once and spotted—
      Is his noontime dinner - if

You can call dry bread a dinner—
      Yet, this, and a little tea,
And then a smoke makes him a winner
      Of content and pleasantry.

For he'll crack and joke, and tell you,
      Shifting with one hand his cap,

How 'wee Spotty', just to smell you,
      Woke up from a cosy nap.

Or, with tears his cheeks down streaming,
      Inform you how last Holland-tide,
Love still in her old eyes beaming,
      Molly stretched her arms, and died.

Harsh, for Ned, the drastic measures
      Fate deals out, in wet and dry!
Joyous life and all its pleasures,
      On the roadside, pass him by.

Yet for him the yorlin raises
      Such a pretty wayside song,
In his heart he silent praises.
      God for it, the summer long.

This, and in the briery ditches,
      Buds, like yellow gold, that bloom,
And rude health, are all the riches,
      Neddy knows this side the tomb.

Whether bends a blue sky o'er him
      Or above him all is grey,
Still at the rough stones before him,
      Stout of heart, he pegs away.

A MONODY FOR MARY

Not in the calm autumnal weather
      Not while winds did wildly rave,
Not till loved spring had knit together
      The sods upon thy grave—
Dear Mary, did thy lifetime lover
      Dare to lift his note of woe,
Or wail as wails the widowed plover,
      What time the fowler turns to go.

Not till the month that mildly closes,
      Had decked thy grave with tender care,
Starr'd the green grass with pale primroses,
      And worked the blue-eyed violets there—
Did I dear Mary, dare to darken
      Hope's pearly crescent with my pain;
Or ask a hurrying world to hearken
      To this my sorrow's hopeless strain.

But now that April - handmaid cheerie,
      Has fringed the daisy's cap with red;
And set, and lit, like gold lamps, dearie,
      These buttercups around thy bed—
And sent, for thee, the skylark singing
      Far up in the blue above,
I, in the grass myself down-flinging,
      Sob out my sorrow and my love.

Nurslings we of kindred mothers,
      Playmates, and - O thought divine!
Long ere might made thee another's,
      Virgin love had made thee mine.
Dream not, dear, my hopes were blighted
      When the joyless rites were o'er—
Souls like ours once pledged and plighted,
      Mated were for evermore.

Whilst thou lived, the darkest morrow
      Terror none could hold, for me;
Purified by patient sorrow,
      Life, God-hallowed, still held thee.
Still had I hoped some day to meet thee
      In the fields beloved of yore;
Hold out a kindly hand and greet thee,
      Call thee "Mary" just once more.

SUMMER IN THE BOGLAND

TO BE A BOY AGAIN

O would I were a herd-boy still,
      In jacket coarse and brown,
Tending the cows, on yon green hill,
      That overlooks the town,
Then might I every morning see,
      And every night enjoy
The smiles of Minnie Annesley[27]—
      The Hebe[28] of the Foy.

O would I might, where yorlins sing,
      Watch the milk cattle roam;
And every eve, at sunset, bring
      The patient creatures home.
Then would I every morning see,
      And every night enjoy
The smiles of Minnie Annesley—
      The Hebe of the Foy.

WORKING AND DREAMING

When daddy's cuttin' turf, an' I
      Am forkin' them away,
How slow! how slow! the time goes by,
      How burdensome the day.
In vain it is the skylark sings,
      In vain the red-brown peat,
Smelling of all delightful things,
      Fall wet around my feet.

When daddy's stackin' turf, an' I
      Am pitchin' up to him,
How slow! how slow! the day goes by,
      How tired my every limb.
Yet he, no doubt, in dreams of bliss,
      Dreams that I can't enjoy,
Is helping grandda, just like this,
      A happy, happy boy.

---

[27] Mary Annesley, daughter of Michael and Ann Annesley, baptised in Drumcree 27 December 1845, or possibly the Mary Annesley who married Francis Ford in Drumcree Parish Church, 3 December 1894.
[28] Daughter of Zeus and Hera, the goddess of youth in Greek mythology.

SUMMER NIGHTS

These are the nights, the dusky nights,
    When o'er the wild morass,
The jack snipe bleats in downward flights,
    And in the lush wet grass
The corncrake cries, and homeless wights
    The hours in hayricks pass.

These are the nights, the lovely nights,
    When by the bubbling springs,
In hedges, and on hawthorn heights,
    Fluttering unseen wings,
For lovers and meandering wights—
    "Jug-jug!" the night jar sings.

These are the nights, the dewy nights,
    Nor moonlit nights nor dark,
When, dreaming of his skyward flights,
    The nodding, earth-couched lark
Twitters a stave for those fond wights
    Who love the summer dark.

These are the nights, the ambrosial nights,
    When muse and poet meet,
Not on cold Olympian heights,
    But where the whisp'ring wheat
Disturbs not, with its hushed delights,
    The poppy slumbering sweet.

DOWN THE LONG ROAD

Rachel dear, put on your hat,
    Come out along with me,
And wander where the brown whin-chat
    Chuckles wild and free.
Their thorns as sharp as shining pins,
    Their odour all divine,
Like blossomed gold the ragged whins
    Along the roadside shine.

Ah, little thought we how the sough
    Of winds, three moons ago
Would wake to life in every sheugh
    The saggins here that show
So bonnily their iris blooms,
    That, beamed on by the sun,
Fill, with their delicate perfumes,
    The ditches every one.

Look at these purple thistle tops,
    Nor wonder why, my dear,
The Derrykerrib donkey crops
    The scanty herbage here.
An outcast the poor cuddy is,
    And thistle, heath and whin
Are oft the only fodder his,
    When hay is hard to win.

There in the moss are the turf stacks,
    They stand on lower ground,
And in this bank the fairy flax
    Long years ago I found.
And here was one wee rosie bush,
    Its blossoms wet wi' dew,
From which - I plucked, and with a blush,
    One blossom kissed for you.

But 'twas the whin-chat and ablaze—
    The whins we came to see,
And there's the bird whose antic ways
    So often tickled me.
See! there upon that blossomed gold
    He sits, and his black eye,
Now upwards, and now sideways rolled,
    Sees all that passes by.

BOGLAND PICTURES FIFTH SERIES

GRANDA'S LABURNUM

One laburnum - that was all,
        Among the trees that grew
At grandda's doorway, rose roof-tall
        A joy against the blue.

And when the bogs with snow were white,
        Still as the night drew nigh,
Its leafless twigs, for our delight,
        Traced pictures on the sky.

If thus it looked while winter's sting
        All patiently it tholed,
How beautiful it was when spring
        Clad it in green and gold—

Strung it with leaves, and blossomed chains
        That bobbing in the sun,
Or, wet with laughing April rains,
        Like gold thrice burnished shone.

So fair it was, poor working folk
        On Sundays came to see
(And quietly of love it spoke)
        Grandda's laburnum tree.

FINE GROSBEAKS[29]

From Norway 'twas, no doubt, they came,
        A dozen birds or more,
Fine grosbeaks with their crests aflame,
        And bills cross-lapped o'er.

The days they did in pine trees pass,
        But ere a month had flown,
The fowler's cruel eye, alas,
        Had marked them for his own.

Scarce had their visiting begun,
        When, woe and sad to tell,
Bang! went the gun, and one by one
        The handsome fellows fell.

Grosbeak (Courtesy of Joe Kosack).

---

[29] Member of finch family, with large bills, they make a rich warbling sound similar to the American robin.

No more to Norway o'er the foam,
      Back might the grosbeaks fly;
They came to seek a winter home,
      They came, alas, to die.

Pity it is, each plumaged thing
      If rare it be at all,
With blood-closed eye and broken wing,
      Must, for its beauty, fall.

A truce, I cry, to all such deeds!
      On him the prophet's ban,
Who glories when some creature bleeds
      That useful is to man.

A FINE CROP OF TURF

On the banks, this sun-bright weather,
      In the brown bogland,
In rows, but not too close together,
      Neat the turfstacks stand.

Need no longer now for worry,
      Or for aching back,
Pitched up often in a hurry,
      Topped is every stack.

For weeks, indeed, the broken weather
      Spoiled some odd jobs planned,
But sun and wind, in time, together
      Dried the brown bogland.

Happy now the blithe young farmer,
      Hale, and weather-tanned,
Chucks below the chin his charmer,
      In the brown bogland.

Sold can be the turf where standing,
      Marled, and black, and brown;
Or, a better price commanding,
      Carted to the town.

Wise he was, the blithe young farmer,
      Who, while others planned,
Stacked up turf and wooed his charmer,
      In the brown bogland.

THE OLD FOOT-STICK

A plank o'er which the neighbours pass
    From New-year's day to Yule;
A board o'er which the barefoot lass
    Skips on her way to school.
Soaked with the cold November rain,
    And bleached 'neath summer skies,
Across the shallow bogland drain
    The old oak foot-stick lies.

How oft it has - when white with frost,
    The marks of boot-tacks bore!
How oft! By little feet been crossed
    Will never cross it more.
The old turf barrow, too, how oft
    O'er it has trundled been,
In winter - when the roads were soft,
    In spring - when pads were green.

And many a dark and rainy night
    O'er it the old man came,
At Palmer's not a styme of light,
    In heaven no star aflame.
And still on hands and knees 'tis crossed,
    After the night-school door
Has closed on lads who, seldom lost,
    Laugh as they scramble o'er.

Bleached by the winds of rugged March,
    And wetted with the rain,
How hot it is when fierce suns parch
    The grass and growing grain!
Astride on it who cares may sit
    And watch the tadpoles race
Through water not too dark a bit
    To show his own red face.

A plank o'er which the neighbours pass
    From New-year's day to Yule;
A board o'er which both lad and lass
    Skip on their way to school
Stepped on with joy, or crossed with pain,
    A mark for many eyes,
Year in, year out, across the drain
    The old oak foot-stick lies.

BOGLAND PICTURES SIXTH SERIES

COLUMBKILL

Mudwall cabins - their rough fronts
      Turned to wide Lough Neagh;
Little plats where blue kail runts
      Dream of blossoms gay.
Old white buildings thatched anew,
      Sheds and shanties brown,
Fine white farm-houses, too,
      Neat as those near town.
These, at Candlemas, are still
Sights to be seen in Columbkill.

Nets spread out upon the shore,
      Sandpiper and gull,
Fishermen around the door,
      Stagnant pools and dull.
Ragged urchins minding cows,
      Boys with measled shins,
Leading goats to pick and browse
      In the roadside whins.
These, at Lammas-tide, are still
Sights to be seen in Columbkill.

Hawthorn bushes red with haws,
      Bulging barn and byre,
Pussy licking velvet paws
      By a hearthstone fire,
Turf stacked up at gable ends,
      Ricks of oats and wheat,
Friends out talking with their friends,
      And men to men they meet.
These, at Michaelmas, are still
Sights to be seen in Columbkill.

Silver pullen in the net,
      Sail and rattling oar,
Fishermen in oilskins wet,
      Boats pulled to the shore.
From Ardbo a sudden squall,
      Lough Neagh tempest-torn,
Lull and lash, and over all
      The wild grey light of morn.
These, at any time, are still
Sights to be seen in Columbkill.

HOW THEY MANAGE IN DERRYAGH

When Billy's diggin' in the hill,
    An' Mosey's down the town[30],
The donkey carts keep passin' still
    Wi' turf to Portadown.
The wear an' tear upon the road,
    The wild an' stormy days
An' one bare shillin' for the load,
    You'd wonder how it pays.

But where the bogland scarce supplies
    The things that needed be,
It is the smooth white shillin' buys
    The sugar and the tea.
An' so while Billy, in the hill,
    An' Mosey down the town,
Are workin' hard, the turfcarts still
    Trail into Portadown.

THE BLUE CORNFLOWER

Dearest of summer's wilding gifts,
    Offspring of sun and dew,
Lone in the oats the cornflower lifts
    Her lovely disk of blue—
Her blue-fringed disk all dewy wet
    When falls the evening grey;
Deep blue at noon, and - who'd foget?
    How blue! at op'ning day.

Where early flits the humble bee
    O'er some head-rigg of corn,
With only ruddy dawn to see,
    The pretty flower is born.
There, where nor care nor trouble drifts,
    And soft airs sing above,
Up to the light her face she lifts
    Lost in a dream of love.

THE BULLFINCH

As all agog he flits about
    The Birches and the Gall[31],
The bullfinch is, without a doubt,
    The biggest finch of all.

---

[30] Billy Roe and Moses Teggart, the poet's father, both lived in that part of Ballinary, known as Derryagh.
[31] Townland of Gallrock, Parish of Tartaraghan

          On a thistle top,
          Filling his crop,
"So sweet!" "So sweet!" he cries;
          Then o'er the bog.
          To some thick scrogg,
On flashing wings he flies.

His colours all the loveliest are;
    And black and reddish brown,
And roseate hues - unseen afar,
    Look well on dark grey down.
          On a ragweed top,
          Filling his crop,
"So sweet!" "So sweet!" he cries;
          Whistles it clear,
          And then, through fear,
To some far thicket flies.

THE SPEY-WIFE[32]

She'll sit on a turf, and tell you the charm,
          The secret that she only knows,
To cure a strained arm, or shield you from harm
          When the wind out of blinkerdom blows.

Your fortune she'll spey, and tell you what girl
          Is crying her eyes out for you;
You'll sing like a merle, and live like an earl,
          If her bidding you'll only but do.

She'll rail at her sex, or give, with a waff
          Of her hand, them, the devil's panade[33];
And go limping off, with a spit and a cough,
          When you your white shilling have paid.

THE PEWIT[34]

A handsome bird the pewit is
    Green above and white below:
And, running, those light shanks of his
    How fast they o'er the meadows go!
        Scare him, he'll fly, and "pewit!" cry,
           And flap his wings and speed away,
        The fields across, and o'er the moss,
           To marshy shores by dark Lough Neagh.

---

[32] Female with allegedly magic powers, including the ability to foretell the future.
[33] A rude gesture.
[34] Also known as the lapwing. It has black and white plumage and a splendid green crest.

At dusk, he to the grazing comes,
    To forage where the cows have fed;
Red worms and snails to him are crumbs,
    And slugs and beetles daily bread.
        At hush of night, see him alight,
            His toes have scarcely touched the sod,
                When soft he lifts his wings, those gifts
                      That somehow make us think of God.

Then folds he them, and running swift
    From this to that dust heap unstirred,
Lightly he pecks, nor cares to lift
    A cloud-like wing, the pretty bird!
        Scare him, he'll fly, and "pewit!" cry,
            And flap his wings in hurried flight;
        And then he'll rise, and with his cries
            Fill all the listening summer night.

The little crest, of glossy green,
    Set daintily on his dainty head
How brave it looks! How bright its sheen,
    When in the east morn blusheth red!
        Time then to fly, and "pewit!" cry,
            And with his brethren haste away
        To Lough Neagh shores, where scores and scores
            Of pewits "pewit" night and day.

THE BANSHEE'S LAMENT

You who often, often said,
    Death had left you no relation;
Lying on your dying bed,
    Hear the banshee's lamentation—

    Och anee! But I am sad,
        Leading men and women hoary,
    Souls whose aims in life were bad,
        Down to dismal purgatory
            Woe is me!
            Och anee!

What a weary lot is mine!
    Never known at birth or bridal,
Ghosts may rest when nights are fine,
    But the banshee's never idle.
        Och anee!

Peasant folk on humble beds
    Childer upon chaff ticks lying,

Sleep and dream, and hap their heads,
   In their sleep, when I'gin crying.
      Och anee!

In the drain the've drowned the cat,
   Lest your disembodied spirit,
Cold and naked, (think of that!)
   Her black carcass might inherit.
      Och anee!

So for you this night I've come
   You to take to purgatory,
There to dwell in regions glum,
   Till you're fit to go to glory.
      Och anee!

Hurry, friend, and let your breath
   Flicker out, nor keep me troubling;
Night and day so busy's Death,
   He upon my heels is doubling.
      Och anee!

In the moonlight here alone,
   Every weeping bush beside me,
Every stick and every stone,
   For my errand seems to chide me.
      Och anee.

Ha! Yon's the bandog's mournful howl!
   He, by day, so fond to scamper,
Keens, to-night, for one poor soul,
   Who'll walk no more the ould moss ramper,
      Och anee!

Save us! That was your last gasp!
   Bless us! How you shake and shiver!
Clasp me close, and closer clasp,
   While we cross this burning river.

Och anee! But I am sad
   For the souls in purgatory,
Souls that will be, oh so glad!
   When at last they go to glory—
      Closed on me,
      Och anee!

OUR BOGLAND HOME

The roof's a roof of wheat straw thatch,
    The walls white rough-cast walls,
And in the old brown door, the latch
    Soft lifted softly falls.
The floor's a rough uneven floor—
    Blue clay to black that turns,
And on the hearth, the hob before,
    A fire of brown turf burns.

Outside (and mostly 'tis outside
    The bogland native dwells)
Are heather banks that far and wide
    Are red with heather bells.
And here are lichens, pink and blue,
    Bunches of rosy ling,
And soft green pathways that renew
    Their verdure every spring.

And where no rough feet them may crush—
    Close to the brick and lime,
Bloom marigolds, and all ablush;
    Roses that clasp and climb;
And here some sturdy wallflowers, set
    In mortar and in clay,
Such fragrances yield, seemed never yet
    Red wallflowers sweet as they.

Before the door, the little street,
    The path o'er which we pass
Up to the cow-house, warm and neat,
    Is pranked with weeds and grass,
Nasturtiums burn along one edge—
    Joy of September suns!
And down the further side, a hedge
    Half thorn, half privet runs.

Beyond the house, a fairy dell,
    With bird-song never dumb;
And here are graftings loaded well
    With apple, pear and plum,
Here, too, is Mary's flower-knot sweet
    And rich with mint and rose;
Fond woodbine climbs about the seat
    In which she sits and sews.

And all around the place are plots
    Of praties, oats and rye,

And rough-dug riggs o'er which the chats
    Delighted flit and fly.
And where green linnets come and go,
    And dallies many a breeze,
Behind the house, a darling row
    Of tufted rowan trees.

A sonsy poplar at the gap
    Keeps rustling night and day;
And when some birken boughs o'erlap
    They shade the gravelled way,
A row of stones, new limed-washed all,
    The dingiest white as foam,
Leads us down into what we call
    Our little Bogland Home.

BONNIE MARY OF DRUMCREE

Tell me not of nymphs whose glances,
    Arrow-like, transfix the heart;
Modest beauty me entrances
    More than any trick of art.
Moonlight cannot make her pallid,
    Sunlight cannot dime her ee;
Blithe she is as this my ballad,
    Bonnie Mary of Drumcree.

In the lanes where nothing sweeter,
    Neater than herself is dressed,
Willy wagtails run to meet her,
    Linnets greet her from the nest.
In a voice than Cupid's clearer,
    Calls the throstle from the tree,
"Nearer, nearer, O come nearer,
    Bonnie Mary of Drumcree."

When his song the yorlin raises,
    'Tis her coming to proclaim;
Wren and redbreast sing her praises,
    Every whitewing knows her name.
Single some, and some together,
    Bird and butterfly and bee
Welcome, as they do the weather,
    Bonnie Mary of Drumcree.

Blooms no bitter day can darken—
    Purple heather, heath and ling;

Flowers that in the meadow hearken
      To the melodies of Spring;
Violets blue and daisies rosy,
      Mayflower and anemone
Blossom all in Nature's posy—
      Bonnie Mary of Drumcree.

Than her ruddy lip a rarer,
      Never tempted lover young;
Than her dimpled cheek a fairer,
      Celtic poet never sung.
Than her tresses nothing blacker
      Floats abundant, wild and free—
Troth! Against the world I'd back her—
      Bonnie Mary of Drumcree.

Stand aside ye nymphs whose glances
      Move but never melt the heart;
Modest beauty me entrances
      More than any trick of art.
Sweeter than the op'ning blossom,
      More than mortal blest is he
Who at dusk folds to his bosom
      Bonnie Mary of Drumcree.

VERSES FROM THE BOGLANDS

PULLING FLAX

Their talk not all of this year's yield,
    Their aprons, crumpled sacks,
By kerchiefs bright their necks concealed,
A dozen women in the field
    Are busy pullin' flax.
        Oh, the pullin',
           The merry, merry pullin',
           The pullin' of the flax!

A level crop - light brownish green,
    The bolls brown, too, like wax,
And scarce a weed the stalks between,
Up by the roots it cometh clean,
    And straight of stem - the flax.

Cut green, to stand the strain's demands,
    And crossed nor loose nor lax,
Of rushes made they are the bands
That knotted firm by rough red hands,
    Tie up the beets of flax.

The shilty's cart, too, by doth roll,
    On which in bulky stacks,
Strap and stalk and root and boll,
The beets are piled for the bog-hole,
    Where steeped it is - the flax.

That jokes pass 'round, ye weel may ken;
    And, spite of aching backs,
That peals of laughter reach us when
A dozen women, helped by men,
    Are busy pullin' flax.
        Oh, the pullin',
           The merry, merry pullin',
           The pullin' of the flax!

Harvesting the flax crop.

IN THE TOWN OF BIRR

Surrounded are the skirts of Birr
      By boglands wide and brown,
From which great loads of peat and fir
      Are carted to the town.
And in the soldiers' barracks there
      Big fires of turf are made,
At which the Tommies sit and stare
      When not upon parade.

The town of Birr may not be rich,
      Its streets may not be clean,
But it can boast the lens through which
      The moons of Mars are seen.
And when the turf fires out have burned,
      And bunked the Tommies lie,
The mighty telescope[35] is turned
      On worlds that light the sky.

Lord Ross' telescope, Birr, Co Offaly, 1905.

---

[35] For more than seventy years, Lord Ross's reflecting telescope at Birr Castle was the largest in the world. The 72" mirror, mounted in a 56' long tube, weighed three tons. Built in 1845, the telescope was used by Lord Ross to discover the spiral nature of nebulae. The mirror of the Birr telescope is now in the Science Museum in London.

THE RAG THORN

A wondrous bush it is, indeed,
    A marvel to behold;
A thousand thorns and more 'twould need
    Its many clouts to hold.
Cow jobbers passing by in gangs,
    They meet the maid forlorn,
Who, grieving for her lover, hangs
    A rag upon the thorn.

IN DERRYLILEAGH WOOD

When the birks begin to bud
    Down in Derrylileagh wood;
When the sap begins to stir
    In the ash and oak and fir;
When the beams of April shine
    On the poplar and the pine,
The violets then their heads unhood,
    Down in Derrylileagh wood.

When the red cow chews the cud,
    Down in Derrylileagh wood;
When, wherever they find room,
    Fairyfingers blush and bloom;
When for ditches not too dry,
    Gillyflowers bless July;
Leverets then through heather scud,
    Down in Derrylileagh wood.

When the dock wears ne'er a dud,
    Down in Derrylileagh wood;
When the silence just to fill,
    Sings unto itself the rill;
When, as rough as it is brown,
    The scaly crig comes clattering down;
Then the haw looks red as blood,
    Down in Derrylileagh wood.

When asleep is next years bud,
    Down in Derrylileagh wood;
When the birch, her white limbs bare,
    Cold looks in the frosty air;
When green robed, the gallant fir
    Does his best to shelter her,
Then the rabbits' heels play thud,
    Down in Derrylileagh wood.

A BOGLAND BOY[36]

Fair haired he is and light of foot,
      And smart as smart can be,
And at the school when it's not shut—
      He's in the rule of three
Yet he can dig, or trench a fur.
      Nor will it him annoy
If you address him as "Young Sir."
      This blue-eyed Bogland Boy.

On Nature's wonders still intent,
      And using well his eyes,
He knows what drains the ducks frequent,
      And every bird that flies.
The flowers that in the hedges bloom,
      To him they are a joy,
And glad he is the earth has room
      For him - the Bogland Boy.

AT THE CROSS ROADS

"This road takes you to Maghery,
      An' that one to the Moy,
An' fairin' on by yon big tree
      Will bring you to the Foy.
An' this poor narrow windin' way—
      You say you're from Armagh—
Well, friend, you cannot go astray,
      It leads to Derryagh."

Ah! I was bothered for a while,
      The roads themselves are dumb,
And many a long and weary mile,
      By asking, I have come.
No longer loved, no longer young,
      I wander like a ghost,
Believing still the human tongue
      Is the best finger-post.

THE JACKSNIPE[37]

In muddy drains and swampy places,
      In marshes bristling with horse-pipe,
In bogs and scroggs and open spaces
      Feeds the brown jacksnipe.

---

[36] Almost certainly, the poet himself.
[37] A small, short-billed snipe with brownish plumage.

In spring, when day and dusk are meeting,
    Over wastes and wilds afar,
Tremulous we hear him bleating
    To the evening star.

At Martinmas - the weather milder
    Sometimes than it is in spring,
Than the snipe, no bird is wilder
    Couched, or on the wing.

But when winter sorely tries him!
    And worm-food is hard to win,
Roving lads full oft surprise him
    The wet heather in.

Flushed, his rapid zig-zag flying,
    Fear in every whirring quill,
Oft the fowler's aim defying,
    Foils the rustic grill.

Then once more to open spaces,
    Reedy swamp or boggy stripe,
To wilds afar, and marshy places
    Flies the brown jacksnipe.

AUTUMN IN THE BOGLANDS

A BOGLAND CUSTOM

Each afternoon, at half-past three,
      The workers on the farm
See Peggy coming with the tea,
      And on her crooked left arm
A basket in which slice on slice
      Of buttered soda bread
Makes for the men a luncheon nice,
      Though cloth there none is spread.

Whether stacking turf, or shearing corn,
      Or stocking upland wheat,
The men, all to the custom born,
      Look forward to this treat.
And still some Peggy, smart of foot,
      Comes close on half-past three,
Beside them on the rigg to put
      The bread and mugs of tea.

SLOES

Where late the misty cobweb hung,
      Where life has ceased to grow,
These greenish-yellow leaves among,
      How blue-black is the sloe!
Try-one. You'll find it sour enough
      To set the teeth on edge;
And mark the bush, how hard and rough
      It grows in this thorn hedge.

Yes! That's a sparrow's empty nest
      The knotted twigs below;
And almost every leaf at rest
      Above it, hides a sloe.
For days, when not a leaflet stirs
      On this side of the hill,
How still - the leaves and gossamers!
      The blue-black sloes - how still!

ADOWN THE LANE

Sweet-smelling herbs still fill the banks,
      Grass fringes either edge,
While from the thorns hang faded hanks
      Of robin-run-the-hedge,
And those red berries at the root

Of that white-barked woodbine,
    Unpressed by any straying foot,
        Are full of honeyed wine.

Where smooth red hips, so sweet to gnaw,
        Make known the buckiebrier
The black-specked leaves upon the haw
        Seem burnt as if with fire,
Through naked boughs, o'erhead that meet,
        Looks down the clear blue sky;
And thick below our wandering feet
        The yellow ash leaves lie.

THE WET-MY-LIP[38]

When on the bank the shearers' coats
        Lie black and grey and brown;
When on the riggs of ripened oats
        The morning sun shines down—
Unseen by e'en the brightest lads,
        The fattest bird that flies
Runs up and down the little pads,
        And loud and quick she cries
"Wet-my-lip! Wet-my-lip! Wet-my-lip!"

The stubbles matching and the mould—
        Head, back and wings and tail
All golden brown and brown and gold,
        How beautiful the quail!
And when the shearers meet at morn,
        And each his own hook tries,
Sudden from out the ripened corn
        A voice, half human, cries
"Wet-my-lip! Wet-my-lip! Wet-my-lip!"

Wet-My-Lip

IN THE POTATO PLOTS

Now, in the black potato plots,
        The bleached white stalks and dry—
White, though specked all o'er with spots—
        In straight rows, take the eye—
In rows they stand, for still in drills
        Undug the tubers lie.

And oh what weeds, what splendid weeds
        The sheughs and sheugh-sides fill!
Some with their heads red-crowned with seeds,

---

[38] The common quail - a small, plumpish bird with buff-brown plumage, that nests on the ground.

    And some in blossom still—
Neat-rooted in the clean black mould
    The weeds are hard to kill.

And here and there a head of corn
    Shakes out it tresses free;
And in that sheugh, sure as you're born,
    There's a late-blooming pea.
And crisp and green the curly kail—
    Och! Aren't they good to see?

Wee boys with baskets and big men
    With spades will soon be here
To dig the praties out, and then
    The ground of weeds to clear,
A fire they'll make, and roasted spuds
    As snacks, their hearts shall cheer.

But, let us take this graip and try
    A stalk, as we've been told;
There! pleasing are they to the eye,
    A crop a dozen fold;
And well the large potatoes look
    White on the loose black mould.

AUTUMN'S SELF

With oat-straw sandals on her feet,
    And rowans in her yellow hair,
Autumn - from uplands rich with wheat,
    Has come our bogland joys to share.
In little plots of ripening oats,
    The rustling of her homespun gown
Is heard by him whose tuned ear dotes
    On music never heard in town.

Listening herself she sometimes stands
    Where, by the scanty garnered store,
The flail, swung loose in willing hands,
    Rings on the moss-man's threshing floor.
Or, having reached some green hillside
    O'er which the white chaff flies amain,
She, by the cart shafts stands, blue-eyed,
    Watching the cleaning of the grain.

Some morns beside the pool that hears
    The dawn awakening darkly red,
Clothed on with mist, and bathed in tears,
    She mourns the other autumns fled.

Through ling and heather then she strays,
    And there so sad her footstep falls,
The curled-up orchid curled-up stays,
    And pensively the pipit calls.

Then, ere comes eve, her way she finds
    Up some lone pathway to the hill,
And there, where calmed are all the winds,
    And holy dusk is hushed and still,
She sits below the yellowing trees;
    And though her presence folk surmise,
Only the poet 'tis who sees
    The pathos in her splendid eyes.

AUTUMN IN DERRYAGH

When o'er the fields the chookies go,
Pullets, hens, and cocks that crow;
And autumn seems to Billy Roe[39]
    As good a time as any, O;
Then, the barns and haggards full,
With yellow turnips still to pull,
And not a day that's damp or dull,
    Old Derryagh looks bonnie, O.

When fierce the feeding throstle calls;
And where on them the sunshine falls,
Whitewashed and clean the rough mud walls
    Long, warm and strong as any, O;
When ash and elm their foliage shed
And all the thorns with haws are red,
And autumn's sky laughs overhead,
    Old Derryagh looks bonnie, O.

When dry turf all are in the stack,
And loud and tough whip lashes crack,
And of oat straw there is no lack,
    Sweet fodder clean as any, O;
When pratie plot and stubble rigg
Are ready all to trench and dig,
And every haycock bulges big,
    Old Derryagh looks bonnie,O.

When in the can the strippin's foam,
When o'er the fields the heifers roam,
When filled is every house and home
    Wi' bairns as blithe as any, O;

---

[39] William Roe, Ballinary, born 17 July 1836: died 9 May 1911.

When bogland banks are dry and brown,
When turfcarts make their way to town,
And bright on all the sun shines down,
  Old Derryagh looks bonnie, O.

GOD'S HARVEST

In harvest time when fields are white,
  And Love's wings wide unfurled,
Who thinks not on that other sight—
  The harvest of the world?
When all the folk we ever knew,
  And all who earth have trod,
As sheaves, shall gathered be into
  The great storehouse of God!

BOGLAND PICTURES SEVENTH SERIES

A WAYSIDE FLOWER

Where at morn Old Moiley munches
      Grass and weeds by the roadside,
A little flower, in tufts and bunches
      Blue with blossom, blooms blue-eyed.

Above the dust their faces lifted,
      Sweet uplifted to the sky,
By nature seem the darlings gifted
      To attract the passer-by.

Lovely creatures, and though tiny,
      Big enough to drink the dew;
Shallow-cup-shaped all and shiny,
      Beautiful, and oh, how blue!

Ah, how fine the little hairs are,
      That from dust protect their eyes!
Ah, how innocent their cares are,
      Every sunlit morn they rise!

Surely heaven not all unkindly
      Looks down on these wayside flowers,
That, though some folk pass them blindly,
      Little sisters are of ours.

Name them! Ah, my friends 'twere better
      Book-worms for themselves should find
The scentless page, the line and letter
      Where cold type has them enshrined.

Well it is for those who've found them,
      Where in joy by the roadside,
Weeds and dust and dirt around them,
      Beautiful they bloom blue-eyed.

AT THE HILL GAP

This is the gap, the old hill gap
      Where Billy herds the cow!
To that thorn bush take off your cap,
      And to this sally, bow.
They're old, my friend, they're very old,
      And many a windy morn,
The gale has shed the sally's gold,
      And whistled through the thorn.

These rails of stout black oak, up-propped
        By stones at either end,
Have heard the carts, at night, that stopped
        When friend conversed with friend.
Below the thorns, in that dry ditch,
        Lush green the nettles grow;
And there's the car-pad still up which
        'Twere a delight to go.

The hill itself, it slopeth south,
        Down to the moss it leads,
And many a red-lipped hungry mouth
        Its produce fills and feeds.
In that rich hollow, all the roots,
        That cow and calf require,
Luxuriant grow, forbye the shoots.
        That garnish barn and byre.

There's the old flax hole! it beside
        The turf in rickles stand;
And here's the bridge, nor high, nor wide,
        The road for years has spanned.
Does ragged Robin still blush here?
        What is this wee flower's name,
This bloom that still through thorns austere,
        Peeps out in rosy shame?

This wimpling drain that winds along
        By banks where sings the wren,
At hottest noon has still a song
        For tired and weary men,
And here's a plot, so small, indeed,
        Toil seldom visits it;
Yet rich it is, in root and weed,
        This wee three-cornered bit.

Here, where this bend in the road
        Safe, and without mishap,
Of good black turf, full many a load
        Has passed through the hill gap.
The dear old gap whose oaken rails,
        Thorn bush and sally tree
Dream, not of boisterous wintry gales,
        But of the springs to be.

THE PLANTATION

A breezy stretch of bogland, granted
    Us by some good sir,
Was drained and trenched, red up and planted
    Thick with larch and fir—
And with pine! For all cone-bearing
    Trees are 'fir trees' here;
And larch and pine, their secrets sharing,
    Smile at what they hear.

Under showers that helter skelter
    Dashed o'er lough and lea,
Soon the quicks shot up, and shelter
    Gave to bird and bee.
Under skies that sun-bright shining
    Warmed both bog and wild,
Soon young twigs spread out, entwining
    Arms, like child and child.

Their roots the red bog firmer gripping,
    The pines, by day and night,
Gained in girth, though ne'er outstripping
    The tall young firs in height.
But larch and fir and pine kept growing,
    Till the magpie's nest,
Safe beyond the wind's rude blowing,
    Boy none could molest.

And now the sun, as he goes sinking
    Down behind Mounthall—
His light the many nations linking,
    Making one of all—
Takes with him into mist and fog-land,
    And o'er purple seas,
A memory of a stretch of bogland
    Dark with dreaming trees.

BLEACHING FLAX

When steeped it has been long enough
    Root, stalk and stem and boll,
The flax; atrocious smelling stuff
    Is dragged from the bog hole
And carted to the meadows green,
    The emerald spots that lie
The green-hedged sappy hills between,
    And there spread out to dry.

In rows 'tis spread, and soon the sun,
        The bleaching air and light
Have it to a new beauty won,
        A lovely greyish white.
Hand lifted 'tis tied up again,
        Sweet after many ills,
Praised and admired and taken, then,
        On carts to the scutch mills.

BOGLAND LOVE SONGS

LOVE'S ENTREATY

Now that 'tis cold and dark December,
        And leafless is the tree,
In dreams of earth, do you remember
        The roses you gave me?
And with them such a look of feeling,
        It drew us - soul and soul —
Into that world where silent healing
        Makes gentle spirits whole.

That was a pleasant foretaste, Mary
        Of that bright world where you
Now bloom, and where if e'er they vary,
        The seasons nought undo.
June then it was - which to remember,
        Gainsay it he who will,
Makes this cold day in dark December,
        To seem more dismal still.

Your face still fair, you soul still fonder
        To meet my soul's demands,
Through heaven, now, I see you wander
        With roses in your hands.
Blue-eyed and sweet, as in the old time,
        And angel though you be,
Look down, dear love, and make this cold time.
        Like yester June to me.

LOVE IN DERRYKARN [40]

When dusk descends on Derrykarn
    Dreamy, hushed and still;
When every calf in byre and barn
    Of kail has had its fill.

When granny the black skillet cleans,
    Scraping industriously,
Teresa[41] o'er the half door leans,
    Blue-eyed, expecting me.

At once peeps out the evening star,
    And past the sally tree,
Its light comes glinting from afar,
    Her rosy mouth to pree.

But neither lip nor shapely brow
    It long upon doth shine,
For in my arms she's laughing now,
    And all her face is mine.

WEAVING AND WOOING

As on the seat-board of her loom
    Young Sarah sits and sings,
Upon her cheek the virgin bloom
    Might tempt the lips of kings.
And Tammy's but a country boy,
    His buskins tied with string,
Yet when his face is lit with joy,
    He's grander than a king.

His hands are hacked and hard and brown,
    His eyes are greyish blue,
And every day, to Portadown,
    He drives the turf-carts two.
And every night he brings them home,
    The sorrel and the bay,
Gives them besides the curry-comb,
    Their bran and oats and hay.

His own face washed, his supper done,
    He foots it down the road
To where his thoughts before him run —

---

[40] Derrykarn or Derrycarran is a sub-division of Cloncore
[41] Teresa Boyce, born in Cloncore in 1849; married Samuel Johnston Robinson, 12 May 1884. Attended Cloncore National School, c.1860.

   The little thatched abode,
Where Sarah weaves by candle light,
   Her cheeks with joy abloom,
And there he sits, night after night,
   And cracks, behind the loom.

MAKIN' HAY

Mary Black[42] of Derrykeevin
   Has a winning way!
In summer when most girls are weavin',
   Mary's rakin' hay.
Each dimpled cheek has roses on it,
   Her red lips are divine,
An' below her white sun-bonnet,
   Her blue eyes beam an' shine.
Shakin', tossin', turnin' over
   White grass mixed wi' purple clover,
This upon a day,
   I met my merry class-mate, Mary,
Happy Mary makin' hay.
   Mary Black of Derrykeevin,
Has a winnin' way
   Of holdin' down her head, an' leavin'
Lovers say their say.
   But this day - Heaven's grace upon it!
When I 'gan to woo,
   Now an' then from the sun-bonnet
Peeped two eyes of blue.
   On her rosy palm the blister
Burned not, stouned not, while I kissed her,
   Kissed her - need I say
How many times? Ere blithe I left her,
   Happy Mary, makin' hay.

Mary Black and family, c.1910.

[42] Daughter of Abraham and Sarah Black, born 1855; married Thomas Trueman, 16 March 1876; died 15 March 1937.

LOVE FOR BETTY

If - ere the swallow southward flies,
    My bride she will not be,
Her rosy lips and dark brown eyes,
    They'll be the death of me.
For, though it's only once a week,
    At Milltown Sunday school,
I get at chance with her to speak,
    Yet love doth me so rule,
Each waking hour that we're apart,
    No matter where I be,
With Betty and her smiles, this heart —
    It's down in Derrylee.

The corncrake mates among the grass;
    The red-poll on the tree
Chirps to his wife, and when I pass
    He seems to pity me.
A foolish booby, me to call
    The neighbours they begin,
But love, that melts the hearts of all,
    Ere long will surely win.
For every moment we're apart,
    No matter where I be,
With Betty and her smiles, this heart —
    It's down in Derrylee.

THE MAID OF MOYALLON

Oh fair as the morn is the Maid of Moyallon,
      A foot than hers lighter the sod never prest,
And pure as the snows on the top of Slieve Gallon—
      The lilies that blow on her linen-clad breast.

In summer the roses and blossoms around her,
      Lift up their sweet faces to catch her blue eye,
The finches and linnets a blessing have found her,
      And haste to her window when winter is nigh.

Oh, list to the tone of that voice of her's - sweeter
      Than the music by rivulets made when they meet;
It rises and falls, and it runs into metre,
      Half love and half laughter - I tell ye, it's sweet.

The lads - how they lift up their round eyes in wonder,
      And rest on their spades at the end of the rows,
When moving in shadow the green sallies under,
      As trig as a queen into Gilford she goes.

I met he one morning when love spread his banner
      Above her fair head, 'neath a crystalline sky;
And so arch was her look, and so lovely her manner,
      No lark in the lift was so happy as I.

I met her once more when the far hills about them
      The blue mists of autumn dream gathered and drew;
And so tempting her lips were - how I lived without them
      Till then is a puzzle I cannot see through.

O, fair as the morn is the Maid of Moyallon.
      Than her's a foot lighter the sod never prest:
And flushed as the heath on the sides of Slieve Gallon,
      Is the face, in the dusk, that now hides on my breast.

A DREAMING SKYLARK

When summer nights are sweet and dark,
      And fowler none his life embitters,
Oh, then it is the loved skylark,
      Happy in dreamland cheeps and twitters.
Pleasant 'tis when the dusk and stars
      Over the bogland reign together,
To startled be by a few sweet bars
      Twittered low in the fragrant heather.

Pleasant 'tis through the meadows then,
      Late in the twilight to go strolling
Far from the haunts of toiling men,
      To hear - our human souls consoling,
While the stars above him wheel and pass,
      Or stand on end the brilliant seven.
The lark, low-couched in the dewy grass,
      Dreams of his morning flights to heaven.

THE BLEATING OF THE SNIPE

When from the west the evening star
      Looks forth arrayed in light,
And to the bogland, near and far,
      Comes down the sweet spring night.
Up yonder path, O then, to stray,
      Or stroll along the stripe,
And hear, now near, now far away,
      The bleating of the snipe.

Now high, now low, through mid air
      Seemeth the sound to go
Bleating, as if the loved night were
      High heaven and home also—
Bleating, as if the wet bogland,
      Tammock and tuft and klipe
And cold brown pool could understand
      The love-song of a snipe.

"Maa! Maa!" in lengthened bars,
      Joyous and loud and free,
And yet so wild - the glinting stars
      Seem glad as glad can be,
"Maa! Maa!" in softer tones,
      As if some ready pipe,
Or magic flute the Pan-god owns,
      Did honour to a snipe.

Anon "Maa!" so dour and sharp,
        So shorn of all delight,
We seem to hear some tense-strung harp
        Snap in the eerie night.
A jealous note, a note to scare
        Fowl of a timid type—
Some Fury seems to cleave the air,
        And not a love-lorn snipe.

And now those sudden whirrs are heard—
        Those sounds that while they thrill
His list'ning mate, speak of a bird
        Whose wings are busy still.
Speak of a brown bird and his bride
        Of moonicks red and ripe,
And quaking quas where cat-tails hide
        Coveys of fledgling snipe.

Sure, pleasant 'tis when in the West
        The star of twilight burns,
And, to the brown earth bringing rest,
        The sweet spring night returns,
Lone through the peaceful dark to peer,
        Or stroll along the stripe,
And o'er the hushed wild boglands hear
        The bleating of the snipe.

DAISIES ON THE BRAE

With dew, just enough on their fringes, to wet them,
      Their hearts shining golden and gay
And all freshly opened - ah, who would forget them—
      The daises that bloom on the brae?

So lovely they look on a pleasant May morning,
      One flash of their beauty's a feast for the day;
Sweet children of Nature, they need no adorning—
      The daisies that bloom on the brae.

Green brambles beside them, tall ash trees above them,
      Soft woodbine to glance at, its leaves greenish-grey;
Long boughs of the hawthorn to bend down and love them—
      The daisies that bloom on the brae.

At sunset and dawning the yorlin sings to them,
      And wee robin-redbreast has fond things to say,
When his mate, happy-hearted, a bridie hops through them—
      The daisies that bloom on the brae.

Auld silver-haired granny, God's blessings upon her,
      Contented beside them the morn long will stay;
And head-erect granddad - he still does them honour—
      The daisies that bloom on the brae.

E'en the tousle-haired lassie, so thoughtless and giddy,
      As owre them she scampers in hoydenish play.
Thinks: (though goats fare not on them) how nice for my kiddie—
      The daisies that bloom on the brae.

The schoolboy in passing takes note of their beauty
      And them in his vision has most of the day,
Till flash they before him as bright spurs to duty—
      The daisies that bloom on the brae.

Shines fresher the grass that in green tufts around them,
      Sets off their white turbans, so silky alway;
Seems Morning herself with new joy to have crowned them—
      The daisies that bloom on the brae.

Wee barefooted bairns - ah, what if they pu' some!
      Hosts still are left blooming, nor turn these away,
When beams down the sun on each bonnie bare bosom—
      The daisies that bloom on the brae.

N'er a ray be lost of the light that comes to them,
      So wisely alert and so open-eyed they,

Not a nod, not a wink when zephyr blows through them—
      The daisies that bloom on the brae.

Ah, fondly to watch them when distant clouds darken,
      And pours down the sunlight its scorchingest ray,
See! to music aerial do they not harken—
      The daisies that bloom on the brae.

And when o'er the hilltops low rumbles the thunder,
      (The trunks of the ash trees half gold and half grey)
Oh, seem they not then open-eyed, as with wonder—
      The daisies that bloom on the brae?

Ah, nearer and nearer it comes what shall make them,
      To close their white petals, and meek to obey,
For rosebuds, red rosebuds a coof now might take them—
      The daisies that bloom on the brae.

It is but a brief shower, a glad one, that passes,
      And laughs in the sunlight as floats it away,
The happier far that it blest those sweet lasses—
      The daisies that bloom on the brae.

With rain - just enough on their fringes, to wet them,
      Their hearts shining golden and gay,
And all freshly opened - ah, who would forget them—
      The daisies that bloom on the brae!

THE INVITATION

To the wilds, the mossy wilds, with me,
      Loved one, I pray thee, come,
And for thyself the heather see
      O'er which the bee doth hum.
The red-poll there thy songs shall sing,
      And the brown pipit, she —
Sipping at every bubbling spring —
      Thy bonnie mate shall be.

Fie! Bid adieu to foolish pomp;
      And every morning fine,
Fresh iris, from the laughing swamp,
      Shall in thy tresses shine;
And this, with cattails, soft as floss,
      Love-knots of rosy ling;
And yellow orchids, dank with moss,
      Shall be thy garlanding.

Scent shalt thou have, too, never fear,
      Odour and spice and bloom,
And mossgall leaves, than which, my dear,
      Is sweeter no perfume.
The bogbean leaf, thou'lt know it, too;
      Tongue-grass and tammocks see;
And step on quas, so thin, the new
      Delight shall startle thee.

The mould upon the mossbank shines,
      Saggins their blossoms show,
And thick upon the blackberry vines
      The big red berries grow.
Oh, thou shalt walk where zephyrs cool
      Fondle the birken tree;
Thy mirror - every sunlit pool
      That catches sight of thee.

Rest shalt thou, too, at sultry noon,
      Yes, sit, and listen long
To that which soothes, nor ceases soon —
      The skylark's happy song.
Nor shall thy scarlet lips despise
      Ripe moonicks from the floe;
And tempting blackberries, tart likewise,
      Thy pearly teeth shall know.

Then though it seems a heartless sin
      To filch their hidden store,

The wild bees' nests there's honey in
   Enough for us, and more.
And what sayest thou to brisken roots?
   Seared in hot ashes, they
Than hawthorn buds, or bramble shoots,
   Are sweeter, any day.

Oh we shall love, and live somehow;
   And where thy light feet go,
The level paths, ling-bordered now,
   Like paradise shall glow.
Make haste, and barefoot come, my sweet!
   Build have I there for thee,
A summer-house of sods and peat
   Below the birken tree.

BOGLAND BLOOMS AND BIRDS

LOVE FOR THINGS OF THE BOGLAND

So little we see in Nature that is ours - Wordsworth.

Ours is the beauty of the bogs,
Of black oak stumps and drying logs;
Of running drains and dark brown rills,
And of the far-off heath-clad hills.
We've made them ours. At work or play,
They've been with us since childhood's day.
There's not a stab or stick or stone
But is indeed our very own.
The ling is ours, and where we dwell,
Each bonnie bud and heather bell,
With or without a titled name,
Each bogland flowering plant we claim.
The fewer they the more beloved,
We walk among them, and ungloved,
Despite the hedge, despite the thorn,
Kiss the wild rose as soon as born.
All Nature's sweets, to mine and me,
Are bread and wine, in them we see,
As in the shining sunlit sward,
The very presence of the Lord.

Ours! Why, all our neighbour's fields are ours,
The grass, the grain, the springing flowers,
And not a weed that blooms therein,
But doth from us some beauty win.
Yea, the poor outcasts of the field,
For us do daily something yield —
Darnel and chickweed, mint and dock,
Dying have yet the strength to knock
At our fond hearts, till even they
Admitted are, or green or grey
Blushing in hedgerows many a bud,
Its modesty misunderstood,
Below the thorns such beauty shows,
That, fair at first it fairer grows,
Unconscious of the homage we
Pay to its unrobed purity.
There, too, all innocently clad,
Doth many a white flower make us glad,
Glad! yes, and eye-wet sorry, too,
So frail they are, so drenched with dew.
These, and at times a blue-eyed bud,
Mild with the grace of maidenhood,

To us are as those prayers that reach
God's heaven, without the aid of speech.

Even in common things we see
Beauty begot of industry.
Turf sods or peat all smoothly cut,
Our best selves into them we put,
Seldom it is we them forget,
When they are soaked ourselves are wet;
With them, sun-warmed, we drip and dry,
And bless the wind that whistles by,
Fragrant with heather, heath and ling,
In creels and carts home them we bring.
And stack them up against the time
The bushes all are white with rime;
Then, when we feed them to the fire,
They burn as burns our heart's desire,
Sometimes a living coal to be,
A light in God's great family.

In buds we bless, in leaves we touch,
Thus 'tis each day we see so much
Of things that growing in the wild,
Appeal to us, as doth the child
That idly wand'ring them among,
In heaven hath it praises sung;
Till, like our kindred, they more dear
Become with every passing year;
Till, let who will reap grain and flowers,
We feel - oh joy of wintry bowers!
Their beauty was and still is ours.

RUN LIKE A REDSHANK[43]

"Run like a redshank!" that's what she said
    When she wanted her laddie to go
In a hurry to Palmer's or Mitton's for bread,
    And the boy, who never was slow,
Had his breeks rolled up to his knees, and then
    Over the rampers he sped,
Ran fast as runneth the redshank, when
    It heareth the rattle of lead.

"Run like a redshank!" might have been said
    When they wanted white Death to go,
For the mother who fell in the kitchen - dead!
    Heart-failure they called it - Oh!

---

[43] A medium-sized wading bird with long reddish legs and a long straight bill.

How the man, from a country beyond the sea,
    Sped o'er the troubled foam,
And then how slowly and sadly he
    Walked out to his childhood's home!

THE YELLOW WILLY[44]

Yellow Willy, Yellow Willy!
    Creeping every spring,
Till mistress Daffodilly
    Wakes to hear you sing;
Till Princess Dandelion
    Lifts her head of gold,
You, flashing like Orion,
    Once more to behold,
Yellow Willy, Yellow Willy!
    What news from over sea,
For mistress Daffodilly,
    The money-flower, or me?

"Swee-eet!" "Swee-eet!" O romancer!
    From the upturned sod
How apropos your answer!
    Life in lands abroad,
In Norway and in Sweden,
    In the early year
When Spring returns from Eden,
    Is just the same as here.
"Swee-eet!" "Swee-eet!" Blithe romancer,
    Charming poet, too,
In song it is you answer
    All questions put to you.

Smooth is your form and slender
    And 'neath the new-lit skies,
Sweet is your note and tender,
    And bright your bonnie eyes.
Your plumage well displaying
    To the plot's dark-brown,
Clod-perched, your long tail swaying
    Constant up and down,
And still from fife-throat slender
    The springtime note that cheers,
The song so sweet and tender
    In April's list'ning ears.

Your friend, the pied black willy,
    The shy grey wagtail, too,

---

[44] The yellow hammer.

Be Yule-time mild or chilly,
>   Stay here the winter through.
But you, O free-born rover,
>   But visit us to sing
The green of spreading clover,
>   The witchery of spring.
You come, dear Yellow Willy,
>   And love flings wide the door,
To seek the daffodilly,
>   And hear your song once more.

The Yellow Willy

HOMELY RHYMES OF THE BOGLAND

LIFE IN THE BOG PLAT

When, lying flat, the bogland plat
    Is roused some April morn
By the master, fast and faster,
    O'er it showering corn,
Gowpenfuls of white oats scattering
    On its plain black dress,
Surely then some ken or smattering
    The plat knows of its usefulness.

When this plat, still lying flat,
    The same bright April morn,
Feels o'er it skim the feet of him
    Who comes to "point" the corn,
Soon as drops of sweat run trickling
    O'er ridges Time has made,
The plat then surely feels the tickling
    Of the sharp old cutty spade.

BRINGING HOME TURF

"The Wheelbarrow take, my boy, an' go
    Up the moss for a load of dhry ones,
Turf that will burn an' blaze an' glow
    Till by their light one can see to tie one's
Brogues or buskins at fall of night,
    Or, when the clock for six gives warnin',
Pull out of the ashes, dull an' white,
    Kindlin' coals, of a winther morning."

"Put in some clinkers, too, an' clods,
    An' pang the load up high wi' marleys,
An' when you come back we'll cut some sods
    In the bit of grazin' that once was Charley's.
Then we'll put on a fire that will make the hob,
    The old back hob, sweat soot an' mortar,
A fire ere night that'll do the job—
    Heat the house to its coldest quarter."

And the boy goes off to the dreary moss,
    Trundling the barrow straight before him,
Wild with the world, displeased and cross,
    And mad that his mother ever bore him.
The wee mosscheeper he heeds not now,
    Cheep she ever so sweet and clearly;
Nor the mouse that along the ramper brow,
    Running runs into a boghole, nearly.

Yet spite of himself, both mouse and bird
      For a moment respite his angry sorrow;
And then in a trice his heart's upstirred
      By the thought of there being no school tomorrow.
So the footstick's crossed, the stack-mouth reached,
      Nor long with the prop-sticks there he tinkers,
Into the barrow of turf well bleached,
      Dry turf, hard turf, clods and clinkers.

And then by the time he starts for home,
      Cheepeth the wee brown pipit clearly;
The trinklet under its arch of foam,
      It singeth the song he loveth dearly.
And when with the load he at last returns—
      Long ere the rain makes the ramper rotten,
In the warmth of the fire that so brightly burns,
      His little hardships are all forgotten.

IN THE BOGLAND

      Oh, the glorious summer weather,
      When the peerless purple heather,
The moonicks an' the hummocks, the mossgall an' the ling
      Were not one half so happy
      As the little white-haired chappie
Whose heart was up in heaven when he heard the skylark sing.

      How oft the long day found him
      Wi' the bumble bees around him,
Yellow bees an' black bees an' belted bees an' brown—
      Heath an' heather honey sipping
      Till the golden sun went dipping—
Till a ball of fire it faded in the lough beyond Milltown.

      Oh, the tiny rill that trickled
      When the marley turf were rickled—
Where the little brown mosscheeper in the dry bank had her nest,
      How it kept on dropping, dropping,
      Never still an' never stopping,
Never silent for a moment, though it silence loved the best.

      Foggy quagmires - ne'er forgotten,
      Where the heads of wild bog-cotton
Swayed this way an' swayed that way in the gentle summer breeze,
      Were stepped so canny over
      By the little barefoot rover
That the rushes nodded to him and the cat-tails kissed his knees.

In Spring, when Nature's bosom
Is decked wi' bud and blossom
How oft he heard wi' rapture the cry of the cuckoo;
An' how oft across the heather—
Shaking every long tail feather—
The yellow willy wagtail before him flashed and flew.

An' oh, his joy unbounded
When the whiterump's chuckle sounded—
When the bird itself went flitting an' flying near an' far,
Now jinkin' through the futtins
Now careerin' o'er the cuttins
The blue an' white resplendent, an' twinkin' like a star.

Oh, there's a joy diviner,
And a breathing beauty finer
On a boundless stretch of bogland than many people dream;
The pleasant healthy places
The vast and treeless spaces
A perfect sea of glory to the soul poetic seem.

Oh, days so long departed—
Though worn an' heavy-hearted,
There's one whose lasting comfort is: that still among the ling
There are other laddies playing,
And kindly mothers saying,
"Sure their hearts are up in heaven when they hear the skylark sing."

MORE BOGLAND VERSES

HEDGEROW FLOWERS

These beautiful flowers that upspring
      Under the hedges in Maytime,
These darling white creatures that bring
      Love and delight to the daytime, —
What are their names? and why do they blow
      Where the long-jointed grass and the bramble
Hunger for light, and oft thirsty go,
      Where all for a living must scramble?

Meek virgins are they, arrayed all in white,
      And sweet, as befitteth the Maytime;
And under the hedgerows they fold them at night,
      To softly look out, in the daytime.
Beautiful! Beautiful! that's what they are!
      And the least, in her modest adorning,
Is pleasant to God, as to us is the star
      That shines on the brow of the morning.

THE CLAY ISLAND

'Tween Derrykarn and Derrylard
      The rough Clay island lies,
The bogland soft, the blue clay hard
      As any 'neath the skies.
From it, at night, one hears the surf
      Tumbling on Lough Neagh shore;
And in the isle are good black turf,
      And clay and sand, galore.

Down in the moss, the rich black moss,
      Down where the drains run low,
Down where you them might leap across,
      Cart-loads of osiers grow.
And in the clay, the 'bruckle' clay,
      With black mould mixed and marl,
Such mangolds grow, of them men say
      A few would fill a barrel.

'Tween Derrylard and Derrykarn
      This bog-girt island lies;
And straw and clay are house and barn,
      Turf roofed the dark pigsties.
Yet many a pink-faced hollyhock
      Muffled in light-green leaves,
At nightfall hears the sparrows talk
      'Neath warm Clay island eaves.

THE OLD LIMEKILN

Though now with ivy overgrown,
      In days not long gone by
The limekiln, built of rough grey stone,
      Stood big and round and high.
Here on the edge of this green hill,
      Here on this thorny ground,
In it was burned the lime that still
      Keeps sweet the fields around.

Its eye, with brambles now upgrown,
      Scarce sees the light of day;
And in its mouth the wet winds moan,
      They moan, but never play.
Neglected, or remembered not,
      Its rim no revel knows,
And where coarse lime once crackled hot,
      Uncropped the daisy grows.

Yet men still live, who with delight
      Inform the-would-be-wise,
When newly lit, how grand at night,
      It smoked against the skies—
How, from Armagh, in carts, was brought
      The limestone, all unclear,
To be, by those who in it wrought,
      Burned into white lime here.

A row of turf, a row of lime,
      Alternate row and row,
In it were laid, till came the time
      To light the turf below.
To set the whole on fire, and then,
      Aglow with mirth and glee,
Their shining faces, boys and men,
      That was a sight to see.

But all thing pass! and round and grey
      With ivy overgrown,
The hushed old kiln stands, to-day,
      An elegy in stone.
And peacefully across the moss,
      Its eye, could it but see,
Would glimmer long, and mourn the loss
      Of old-time revelry.

THE MAID OF MARKETHILL

The young leaves on the poplars laugh,
    Wi' lights the sallies shine—
I wonder if they feel one half
    The joy that now is mine.
So rich the love-trust mine in store,
    I only can keep still
An' dream, at church, I meet once more
    The Maid of Markethill.

Her full red lips mind me o' ling
    Bells wet wi' summer rain;
Her smile it makes all nature sing
    An' blossom out again.
Her softly laughin' starry eyes
    My heart wi' light they fill;
Her like is not below the skies,
    The Maid of Markethill.

Her soft brown hair, all sunshine lit,
    Or by the firelight seen,
Oh there are red gold glints in it
    Enough to crown a queen.
An' most of all, her melting voice
    Is tuneful as the rill
Whose low soft music makes rejoice
    The Maid of Markethill.

To those who question me of her,
    So deep are my replies,
The buds that on the woodbine stir
    Twinkle their grey-green eyes—
"An' is she pure as she is sweet?"
    "Go ask, and but ye will,
The flushin' rose that longs to greet
    The Maid of Markethill."

To those, who feeling still love's sting,
    Tell me in time be wise,
The birds that on the hedgerows sing
    Seem glad of my replies—
"An' is she fond as she is fair?"
    "Go ask them, if ye will,
The doves that follow everywhere
    The Maid of Markethill."

IN MEMORY OF MOTHER

At times, as a boy, if I wandered wide,
    Or late in the night would roam,
My mother would wait by the fireside,
    Good mother! till I came home.

As by her lamp she lone vigil kept,
    She many a garment made,
Or while brothers and sisters soundly slept,
    For them and me she prayed.

She never reproved me when I came,
    But softly unlatched the door—
She was not a mother to chide or blame,
    But a welcome smile she wore.

And I sometimes think, though I may be wrong,
    In her heavenly home above,
She awaits her boy, her child of song,
    By the lamp of eternal love.

For the one black sheep, of the loved eleven[45],
    Away on the wilds of sin,
That mother, at peace by the hearth of heaven,
    Will wait till that son comes in.

---

[45] Only nine Teggart children are noted in the baptismal records of Milltown Parish Church, but it is reasonable to assume that the other two died in infancy and hence their births were not recorded.

IN A QUAKER MEETING-HOUSE

(County Armagh)[46]

The windows, open to the breeze,
    Let in the scent of hay,
And bright on bowed laburnum trees
    The golden sunlight lay.

The women in their neat attire,
    The men in broadcloth all,
Sat, filled as if with silent fire,
    Waiting the Spirit's call.

Sudden uprose a maid (the hush
    Moved us, like melody):
"God spake to Moses from the bush,"
    Then softly quoted she.

Their eyes none lifted up, none turned,
    None looked, and none replied:
Yet seemed it while to speak we burned,
    Heaven's door stood open wide.

Seemed visible the risen Word,
    Seemed close the jasper sea;
Yet all so still, we heard the bird
    Tap, in a neighbouring tree.

Rose a young man (nor any hum
    Was there his voice to drown);
"The spirit and the Bride say, Come,"
    He said, and sate him down.

The place, to holy silence stilled,
    And fraught with fragrant air,
Was, like some court in heaven, filled
    With happy, silent prayer.

Anon, a woman's pleasant voice,
    Sweet voice - was heard to say,
"Let those who in the Lord rejoice,
    Rejoice in him alway."

While plain, from bush and hedgerow green,
    We heard the sparrows call,
Angels, invisible, walked between
    The pew rows dark and tall.

---

[46] Believed to be Richhill Meeting House.

Then heard we, and his head was grey
        Who spake, as speaks a Friend,
"I am Alpha and Omega, the
        Beginning and the end."

Feeling how good it was to meet,
        As out we slow did file,
Sweet were the women's looks, and sweet
        The Quaker maiden's smile.

Like incense came the scent of hay
        Across the daisied sod
And on the leaf the sunshine lay,
        Bright as a smile of God.

Interior of Richhill Meeting House, Co Armagh.
(Courtesy Bob Sinton, Mullavilly).

APRIL IN ERIN

Ho! For the glorious April Weather,
    The winds and the waves at play,
The golden shine and the shower together,
    And a rainbow every day.
Surely, surely the glad awaking
    Of other worlds than this!
The dark grey dome, like a mist, unbreaking,
    And showing us isles of bliss.

The woof of blue, the tint so tender
    Of the awning spread above!
A new earth clothed with light and splendour,
    And infinite joy and love.
Gush from the deeps the unsealed fountains,
    And every morn, anew
The near and the far and the distant mountains
    Laugh in their robes of blue.

The risen flowers, the birds rejoicing
    The incense from the sward,
The hills, the dales and the vales are voicing
    The glory of the Lord.
Earth once more is a joyous Eden!
    Man and maid and boy
Are glorious alleluias keyed in
    The highest note of joy.

Ho! For the glorious April weather,
    The winds to the waves that call,
The golden shine and the shower together,
    And the rainbow over all,
Surely, surely some voice magnetic
    Calls loud to land and sea!
Surely, surely our joy's prophetic
    Of the joy that is to be!

MARY MITTON[47]

Oh, how they fly, the hasting years!
    It seems scarce half a dozen,
Though twenty 'tis, since both my ears,
    Wi' bonnie words were buzzin',
Wi' honeyed words, so sweet, indeed,
    They may not here be written,
But the least one of which doth lead
    Me back to Mary Mitton.

A bonnie lass! I see her still!
    Nor need I stay definin'
Eyes brown as is the bogland rill
    In which the sun is shinin',
No more than may I the brown hair
    That, tangled by the zephyr,
Itself unloosed, when, in despair,
    Was sold the kickin' heifer.

An' yet, her rose-red lips, there must
    A word for them be spoken;
They're trim an' rosy yet, I trust—
    They once were Cupid's token
Of what a bonnie mou' should be,
    A bow from which the arrow,
Winged as a word, an' flying free,
    Thrills to one's inmost marrow.

But, here's the threshin' floor, where oft
    She fods of straw up-boosted;
An' this the shed, where fell the snow,
    On which the turkeys roosted.
An' here's the byre, in which the cows,
    Brindle, Bryde an' Briton,
Hard shook their heads, when bent her brows,
    On them, dear Mary Mitton.

Ah me, how all these things remind
    Me of bright days departed,
When not to kiss was deemed unkind
    By playmates, happy hearted.
Yet never did I pree her mou',
    So sweet she was an' bonnie,
Lest kissin' her it would undo
    Some flower of all its honey.

---

[47] Born 1856 in Ballinary; married 1907; died 1933. See Appendix 2 for further information.

I wonder if she minds the mare
        That lost a fore-foot hoofie,
When quick the red flames out did flare
        From rotten floor to roofie,
An' how the beast, hung in a sling,
        Her woeful loss kept ruin'?
A sorry mare, until next spring,
        Grew on her hoof a new one.

Oh, how they fly, the hasting years!
        It seems scarce half a dozen,
Though twenty 'tis, since both my ears,
        Wi' bonnie words were buzzin' —
An' yet, not half so deeply then
        Was somebody love-smitten,
As now he is - but, take this pen,
        And write to Mary Mitton.

BLUE-EYED MELIA LAPPIN[48]

Oh, have ye seen her at the well,
      Or met her in the loanin',
Her lip, red as a heather bell,
      Her looks her likin' ownin',
For sparrows' nests an' hawthorn buds,
      An', what may some day happen,
A walk wi' me in Keerin woods—
      Loved, blue-eyed Melia Lappin?

Oh, you should hear her meltin' voice,
      When me she's busy tellin'
How everything seems to rejoice,
      Now spring the buds is swellin';
And how he looks, that bonnie bird—
      The blackcap, tall and tappin';
It's me that drinks in every word,
      Saft said by Melia Lappin.

To Portadown, on Saturdays,
      I take my web, well-woven,
An' me it aye doth much amaze,
      To meet, or see, out rovin'
The crabtree loanin', or the lane,
      Her shoes without a cappin',
(She's all the purtier for the rain)
      Dear red-cheeked Melia Lappin.

Aye, after dusk, in all her bloom,
      (She weaves for Moses Nuttal)[49]
By candle-light, she's on the loom
      Pitchin' the boxwood shuttle.
An' oft, from town, when comin' back,
      The neighbours see me stappin'
To step inside an' have a crack
      Wi' laughin' Melia Lappin.

By the turf fire at Hollan'tide,
      Oh, then, some night to meet her,
An' kiss an' pree, wi' love and pride,
      Her lips, than sugar sweeter—
An' that might mean to hear old Mark,
      Loud an' angry rappin';
The light blowed out, an', in the dark,
      Just me an' Melia Lappin.

---

[48] Amelia Lappin, daughter of James and Mary Lappin of Derrykeerin, born 14 July 1851. She attended Cloncore National School at the same time as the poet.

[49] A linen buyer from Derrykeerin.

But, down the ramper 'tis that she
    In wild an' stormy weather,
Doth most, rain-warstled, startle me,
    Her cheeks, like blushin' heather,
An' then, altho' the cuttin' wind
    Her red lips may be chappin',
I stop, a moment, to be kind
    To blue-eyed Melia Lappin.

HOME

Not those who dwell within its walls,
      Though dear they are to me,
Nor home itself it is that calls
      Solely across the sea.
The banks that o'er the bogholes lean,
      The fragrant light brown loam,
The paths, the fields, the hedges green
      Are also part of home.

The cattle grazin' where of old
      The sharp green rushes grew;
The blossomed ling, the brown turf mould,
      The turfstacks, old or new;
The trinklet dark that trots along,
      Unroofed with ice and foam,
The yorlin's lay, the skylark's song,
      These all are part of home.

The barrow and the new turf spade,
      The graip whose every prong,
When wet turfs on the bank were laid,
      Still seemed to do them wrong;
The rampers, miry to the knees,
      The vast and starless dome,
The drizzling rain, the wet birch trees
      Are also part of home.

The heather, with its strong rank smell,
      Gold birken, and bracken brown,
The moss hole and the old moss well
      On which the sun looks down;
The little turf fire's morning blaze,
      The bairns that barefoot roam
About the loanin's and the braes—
      All these are part of home.

The poplar laughing in the breeze,
      The sally, seldom dumb;
The hawthorn and the young fruit trees—
      Russ apple, pear and plum;
The little street, half green with weeds,
      The cow, the currycomb;
The dozen wants, the many needs
      Are also part of home.

And singly, these, or one and all,
      Across the stormy sea,
Cry loud, with those who often call,

       In spirit, loud to me.
And oft, oh oft, my yearning soul
       It flashes o'er the foam,
And trembles there, beyond control,
       Itself a part of home.

NOVEMBER IN THE BOGLAND

Soughs are sighin', burdocks dyin',
       In the bogland now;
Brown, together, ling an' heather
       Fringe the ramper's brow.

Locks unbraided, grey an' faded,
       Ragweeds stub the sod;
Shorn of petals, dank day nettles
       O'er the wet sheughs nod.

Without strivin', redshanks, thrivin'
       Rain an' red bog on,
Still in trouble, seem to double
       Long ere they be gone.

Broom an' bracken burnt spots blacken,
       Crowlied more than half,
Sheltered barely, blighted early,
       Little 'tis they laugh.

Misnamed 'mossgall', where goats toss all
       Loosened life aside,
Rough of kirtle, ragged myrtle
       Smiles at bogland pride.

Cow an' cottar see mosswater,
       Brown as frozen kail,
Slow up-bubble where oat stubble
       Hides nor snipe nor quail.

Drains that wander bridges under,
       Rills that drumlie be,
Pained an' poutin', run withouten
       Mirth or melody.

Time's fatiguer, bright an' eager,
       Cheepin' oh, so sweet!
Chin-chaps chilly, pert blackwilly
       Skips o'er pad an' street.

Where the childer life bewilder,
        Bright-eyed, watchful, dumb,
Downward bobbin', red breast Robin
        Pecks at crust and crumb.

Songs in summer well become her,
        Sober now an' wise,
Life grown deeper, Miss Mosscheeper
        Sod-perched, seldom flies.

Song-time ended, unbefriended,
        But brave birdies still,
Moss plats over, skylarks hover,
        Chirpin' sharp an' shrill.

Cold that pinches brings the finches,
        Shy of boll an' burr,
To where sorrel red as coral
        Fills the oaten fur.

Nothin' smirches the white birches,
        Smooth-skinned bough an' stem,
Twig an' knotted bud, unspotted,
        Linnets talk wi' them.

Jay an' jintie, lark an' lintie,
        Sigh-birds, songbirds, all,
In November scarce remember
        April's darlin' call.

But where praties, still lodged gratis,
        Only darkness see,
Dry sheughs over, tufts o' clover,
        Docks an' daisies wee.

Silkweed sallow, mint an' mallow,
        Nettles saft o' sting,
Though dull seemin', all are dreamin'
        Of another Spring.

MARY M'ANALLY[50]

The boortree's burstin' into bloom,
      Is glossy leaved the sally,
An' trig an' green the bonnie broom
      Down in the bogland valley.
The hawthorn at the hillside gap
      Is fragrant blossoms showin',
An' full of mirth an' Maytime sap,
      The poplar sings while growin'.
But lone upon her linen loom
      Sits one whom naught can rally
To blithesome be, or blush wi' bloom—
      Poor Mary M'Anally!

Above dry clods an' clay balls rouch,
      In rows the spuds are peepin',
An' peas an' beans, above the sheugh,
      They hear the yorlin cheepin'.
From grey to green the rowan tree
      Has turned ere yet the linnet
Has time the miracle to see—
      Revealed divinely in it.
In leafy loanin's, hand in hand,
      Young lovers dream an' dally,
But lonesomest in all the land—
      Poor Mary M'Anally!

Are buds of gold upon the whin,
      Pink bloom on the wild apple,
An' green an' glossy love marks in
      The yellow mayflower's thrapple.
Young winds that never yet knew grief,
      They romp among the rushes;
An' through the mould her broad green leaf
      The bogbean slowly pushes,
Seems heaven to have come down to earth,
      An' while the saints keeps tally,
Is one who hears no sound of mirth—
      Poor Mary M'Anally!

In green the hedges robed anew,
      The cuckoo's cry are hailin',
An' softly over skies of blue
      White clouds in flocks are sailin'.
Upon his back a happy boy,
      His bygone years - eleven,

---

50 Mary McAnally, born in Ballinary in 1854; died 15 June 1894 and was buried in Milltown Churchyard.

Finds and feels his utmost joy
> In gazing up at heaven.
But though the shuttle through the woof
> Goes not unmusically,
Her nearest sky's a sod scraw roof—
> Poor Mary M'Anally!

A wet May morn: an' every bush
> Mist veiled stands in the valley,
Half sleepin' on her nest the thrush
> To rouse her cannot rally.
Is not a stone in the clay rood
> But seems to hear an' hearken
Lone Miltown bell, in a sad mood,
> The hours of sorrow markin',
The rain drops down, the poplar dreeps,
> Bows down her head the sally,
An' sod-happ'd in the churchyard sleeps
> Poor Mary M'Anally!

M'Anally's cottage, Ballinary, Co Armagh, c.1910.

GRANNY ROE[51]

Och dear, but it's a long, long time,
        It's forty years ago,
Since up the brae did barefoot climb
        White-haired Granny Roe.

Dotin' she was before she died,
        An 'neath this apple tree
Full often times she sat, blue-eyed
        And wrinkled as could be.

The younkers comin' home from school,
        Oft looked an' wondered how
Grey hair the fires of youth could cool,
        And make so white a brow.

Ere this, beside the spinnin' wheel,
        How oft the flaxen tow
O'er ninety year-smooth rock an' reel,
        Made tirl old Granny Roe!

That corner window, where the wall
        The clay and straw still shows,
Was where she spun, observing all
        Who sat them down, or rose.

And that white hair of hers, that hair—
        A sthraik of flax, to it
Looked dim as dull - her long locks were
        As if with glory lit.

Croonin' in her old Irish way,
        'Twould seem that head of hers,
In this white boortree bloom, today,
        Still nods and moves and stirs.

Need none to lay poor Granny's ghost,
        And never the banshee
Cried for her from that misty coast
        That marks death's sunless sea.

Gowpens of meal, full oft and oft,
        Poured from her kindly han',
Some homeless mother's face made soft,
        Or cheered the beggarman.

---

51 Mary Roe, buried in Tartaraghan Churchyard, 27 February 1886, aged 91 years.

And now, today, all thickly clad
        Wi' daisies, this ould brae
Reminds us, joyful we or sad,
        How swift time flies away.

Full forty years, och, they have sped,
        Since homeward last did go,
God's golden sunlight or her head,
        Old barefoot Granny Roe.

DOWN IN MAGHERY

Cabins of the humble poor —
        Digger, ditcher, fisherman;
An old white chapel, to be sure,
        Doing all the good it can;
A thatched white farm house, or two,
        A tavern - Oh the pity! there,
Man should bibber in the brew,
        Life belowering anywhere.

An old plank ferry, towed across
        Wan Blackwater, over it,
Some for profit, some for loss,
        Scores of jobbing bodies flit.
Men and cattle from Tyrone
        Lads and colts from Portadown,
Make the place, from nothing grown,
        Busy as a market town.

Pollen fresh, by the boat load,
        Packed and shipped across the 'say',
Care and 'luck' on them bestowed,
        Maghery trollers well repay.
Glower down may that old pile—
        Derrywarrach[52], long time named,
But the wide lough's sunlit smile,
        Seen from Maghery, far is famed.

---

[52] Site of the remains of an early seventeenth century fortified dwelling, believed to have been a stronghold of the O'Connors, and known locally as *'the chimneys'*.

The fir wood, through which folk pass,
      On their way the chapel to,
(Both the roadsides green with grass)
      Gleameth back against the blue,
Bogs there are on either hand—
      Marley turf in Maghery homes
Torch up, as in the bogland
      Swiftly blaze up fozy fombs.

Flowers abloom by stone and wall;
      Daisies in wee flower beds;
Hollyhocks, as sunflowers tall;
      Poppies lifting scarlet heads
To a sky of sunny blue;
      Oats in plots of thirsty sand,
And, in blossom, praties new—
      Pith and pride of Ireland.

A little seaport seems the place,
      Smelling times of pitch and tar,
Lough winds blowing in its face,
      Duck holes green with glut and glar—
Yet, to-day, how many hearts,
      Far across the briny sea,
Sigh, full sick of foreign parts,
      Home in Maghery to be!

THE MILLTOWN MAID

When the summer morning rising red
    Breaks o'er the bog so brown,
With a basket of pullens on her head
    She jog trots into town.
Her bare feet down the dusty road
    Do not take time to wade,
A catch of fresh fish is the load
    Laid on the Milltown Maid.

The breeze delighted dusts her toes
    And blows her blue eyes clear,
O'er five long miles of ground she goes
    Light-footed as a deer.
Her lithe, elastic, graceful form
    Is into sweet rhythm swayed,
When she the road begins to warm,
    The rosy Milltown Maid.

She has a kindly word for all
    That meet her on the way,
Her feet to music rise and fall
    They haven't time to stay.
Fresh fish she to the market brings
    And when for them she's paid,
Then like a linnet lilts and sings
    The merry Milltown Maid.

Her curly tappin looks as if
    It never knew a comb,
On shanks that never yet was stiff
    She jogs and journeys home.
Jobbers who travel many a mile
    To purchase and to trade,
Have each and all a kindly smile
    For the winsome Milltown Maid.

She meets the weaver with his bag
    The carts with turf so brown,
And the Birches boy behind a nag
    That knows the road to town.
So bright and early she was off
    That nothing her delayed,
She has no extra duds to doff
    Or don - the Milltown Maid.

She's happy as the lark that sings
    In heaven overhead,
And it's not the briny sea that brings

Her coin for daily bread.
Lough Neagh's a very mint of cash,
    And the morning star must fade,
When the silvery pullens gleam and flash
    Around the Milltown Maid.

WHEN MOTHER'S GONE

Ye little ones, and ye grown folk
    Who muse this life upon,
Oh, how much harder seems the yoke,
    When mother's gone.

A home we had, a pleasant one,
    Set in a verdant lawn;
A leafy nest, but now we've none,
    Since mother's gone.

The past, the never-dying past,
    It oft times we think on,
And down our cheeks the tears flow fast,
    Since mother's gone.

The stay she was of that loved home,
    And now - both dusk and dawn,
No more they charm us when they come,
    Since mother's gone.

So fair, so beautiful she was,
    To her all hearts were drawn;
And now, ere entering home, we pause,
    Since mother's gone.

Home! did we say? We have no home;
    The sun still shines it on,
But cold it seems, and wide we roam,
    Since mother's gone.

It's dark, pitch-dark, the windows look,
    And loveless seems the lawn;
The music's flown, and closed the book,
    Since mother's gone.

Oh little ones! Oh upgrown folk
    Who muse sad death upon;
Grows harder still life's weary yoke,
    When mother's gone.

WINTERTIME IN DERRYAGH

(Co Armagh)

Clipped hawthorn hedges, not a leaf
        Their red-brown twigs upon;
Bush hollies, all in green relief,
        Rime-hung at ruddy dawn.
Grey poplars here, white sallies there,
        And on the alder tree,
Pink sealed-up buds, the black stem bare
        And blistered as can be.

The borders of the fields along,
        Live guardians of the land,
Broad-shouldered, and as giants strong,
        Bare-limbed, big ash trees stand.
From some lone hedge a crabtree lifts
        Its round head, not so high
But boys on it can see the gifts
        Love left in passing by.

The bogland in - dry stacks of turf,
        Wee plats of kale and greens
And running drains, their foam the surf
        That icy margins screens.
Some lad, a barrow him before,
        The which he wheels along,
And up the ramper whistles more
        Than sings he pensive song.

To market crawling, lorn, and loath
        To lively step or stir,
The donkey and the shilty both
        Take panged-up loads of fir.
To lick herself the cow, turned out,
        Stands in the grazin' plat,
Or, hind legs hirpled, limps about,
        Nor deep of flank, nor fat.

The brown-eyed goat, just hear her maa
        As at the stab she pulls,
Or trails the tether on the brae
        To pick green thimblefulls!
Her parted hoofs crush vi'let leaves,
        And primrose stalks to her
Are but as plants whose verdant sheaves
        No longings in her stir.

Look! there's a birch, a bonny one!
    See how the dark brown buds
Turn purple in the noonday sun,
    Thin husks their winter hoods!
And mark the stem how white it is,
    The skin so smooth that we
Full well may think of the love His
    Who forms the birken tree.

But, turn to this low mud-wall hut,
    See, the front window in,
That wallflower, by some kind hand put,
    Warm, sunny rays to win.
And look at the wet, smoking thatch—
    A skiff of frost, and then—
Burns noonday on the old brown latch,
    And sweats the roof again.

Some foolish folk may bawl out "Bagh!
    There's nothin' here to see!"
But wintertime in Derryagh,
    A happy time may be—
If boys will but pile up the fire,
    Till shine the plates like shields,
And hardy lads seek life's desire
    Among the sleeping fields.

ON THE BANKS O' THE BANN

On the banks o' the Bann! sure, the words are enough,
    The days of my youth, like a dream, to recall!
'Mong the reeds an' the canes don't I hear the wind sough,
    As I did when a lad growin' soople an' tall.

No thought had I then, like a liltie, to roam,
    No past to sigh over, no future to plan,
Love sweetened each day, an' a heav'n was my home,
    Our little white house on the banks o' the Bann.

What would I not give for a peep round the porch,
    A keek, just a keek, at the kindled turf fire;
Or, out in the lane, make my bow to the birch,
    The leaf-tasselled birch that the folk still admire!

Once more to the well in the rood just to go,
    Some beautiful mornin' in spring when the sun
Makes to laugh the black baytons, their headriggs aglow,
    Were to feel that real life had but newly begun.

An' oh! what a joy the proud skylark to hear,
    His song shakin' out away up in the blue,
The rowlin's so lusty an' liquid an' clear,
    'Twere worth half a lifetime to hear them anew.

To see the good people once more, in the bogs,
    Some diggin', some trenchin', an' some stackin' peat,
Wi' some hardy old trooper upsplittin' fir logs,
    Were to me, as 'twas often, a summer day treat.

Then! the apple trees, grafted, to see them in bud,
    The clay-strengthened bandages, crackly and dry,
Were to feel a new force leap to life in my blood,
    An' my pulses, love-gladdened, ran happy an' high.

Inside the bit housie - oh there for a while,
    A wee while, a glad while, wi' mother to stay,
Were (an' God blest her for it) to see the moon smile,
    An' the whitethorn to smell when it blossoms in May.

The calves an' the cows on the hillside to see,
    Some switchin' their tails, an' some boundin' for joy,
Were as meat an' as drink to a rover like me
    Who in heart an' in spirit am still but a boy.

E'en the crack of a whip, plaited leather the lash,
    To hear it once more on the ould stony brae,

Were to see pumped-up water, a pail of it, splash
     On a pair of young ponies, a brown an' a bay.

An' sweeter than all - but the dear one is dead,
     Whose looks an' whose words were aye tender an' true;
Lies the rain on the grass now above her dark head,
     An' in dust are the eyes once so lovely an' blue.

Och! these things an' those things when I think them on,
     My eyelids they moisten, an' in me the man
Becomes a saft child that cries sore for the dawn,
     In some grief-darkened home on the banks of the Bann.

TOBY HOLE[53]

(An Old Burying Ground in County Armagh)

A burial place by the roadside,
    Nor hedge nor dykes enwall it,
Nor ought its old moss'd tombstones hide,
    And 'Toby Hole', folk call it.

Inscriptions here in ancient Erse,
    But few they are can read them;
Quaint line on line, and verse on verse,
    Only the lichens heed them.

What old time Irish hand here traced
    Strange signs, so deeply graven,
Not time itself has them effaced,
    Though black some as a raven?

Great artists were they in those days,
    When Erin in her glory,
Saw much to love, and much to praise
    In sculpture, song and story.

But evil days befell the land,
    Grief changed both men and manner,
And weak it grew the exiled hand
    That might have raised her banner.

Here wander cows, as if by stealth,
    Lest lush grass might be wasted,
Which some folk knowing - not for wealth
    Would these cows' milk be tasted?

Long buried here lie kings and queens
    Of days so old and hoary,
And so stern browed no wind but keens
    And harps their wondrous story.

And lonely here, in these days laid,
    Sleeps she, the outcast creature,
Who once a young and blushing maid,
    Was fair of form and feature.

---

[53] The oldest graveyard in Tartaraghan Parish with burials dating back to at the mid-eighteenth century, and probably much earlier. Allegedly named after Sir Toby Caulfield (1565-1627) who owned the townland of Eglish in which the graveyard is located.

Likewise are those who long-time held
    Opinions without number,
About the place and days of eld,
    Now peaceful in it slumber.

The same rain falleth soft alike
    On lowly grave and royal;
On him who shook aloft the pike,
    And him to Nature loyal.

The same bright sunshine lighteth up—
    Nor partial it nor crazy—
The nettle and the buttercup,
    The thistle and the daisy.

The yellow yorlin here sweet sings
    Above the dust of Dobbin,
As doth beside the tombs of kings,
    His hedge - mate, redbreast Robin.

Poor old Toby Hole! A place
    That still adown the ages,
Has puzzled much, race after race,
    Who studied have time's pages.

Thou kirkless, yet a green kirk yard
    Of Nature, the wise mother,
Hast only for thy priest - a bard,
    One to the glow worm brother.

One who beside thee loves to rest
    When peaceful stars are rising,
And sad pale ghosts glide past in quest
    Of good, and good advising.

When weeds, abundant as the lives
    That here seem to lie buried—
Dame Nature 'tis that still survives—
    Sleep in dark ranks and serried.

Strange road! where big and splendid trees
    Seem each with each condoling,
That only brambles clasp their knees
    And not hands - hardship tholling.

Strange Toby Hole! in all the world
    Are but such places seven,
Where serf and king, their life's flag furled,
    Dream side by side of Heaven.

Oh, sleep thee on, sad Toby Hole,
        While still the dews are falling:
There may on earth be some kind soul
        Whose love is thee enwalling.

There may, from heavenly courts, be those
        Who on God's errands going,
Have seen thy green at evening's close,
        And think thee worth the knowing.

Toby Hole Graveyard, Eglish.

BOGLAND STUBBLE

Stubble stirs me. Three's no denying it,
      No gainsaying but I love it well,
The linnets in it, the larks o'erflying it,
      Dreams of the ripened grain that fell.
Bowed and fell when the gleaming sickle
      Rasped as it felt upon it fall
The shining dews that down ran trickle,
      When came the shock that comes to all.

Green the herbs where the bee, a rover,
      Drones from bloom to sleepy bloom,
Clasps and clings to the honeyed clover,
      Sweet with its wealth of wild perfume.
Here is mint with its fragrant flavour,
      There is darnel, still in prime,
And here's a balm whose tints still savour
      Of Eden's bowers in the olden time.

Also see how the broom is seeded,
      Black and shining the rattling pods,
They form, they fill, and they fall unheeded
      On healthy banks where the bracken nods.
These, all these, themselves would double.
      Yea, threefold spring were they not crushed
When grinds the spade through the frozen stubble,
      And the tit-lark's song for the time is hushed.

Hither they come for the sweet seeds in it—
      The bogland stubble unknown to fame,
Brave of heart, the rose-breast linnet,
      Forbye the yorlin - a flash of flame!
In their gentle bosoms no morning trouble,
      Nor any cares their joys to drown,
When sunset burns on the oaten stubble,
      And every bramble glistens brown.

Strung with jewels this cuckoo sorrel,
      Not in vain grows ripe the seed,
Red it is as those grains of coral,
      Wet, that cling to the tropic weed.
And look, my friend, nor be thou lazy
      Pretty things rough-set to see—
Fringed with pink this wee stubble daisy,
      And gold, pure gold, her shining ee.

Bright and balmy the harvest weather,
      Wee birdies wanton on the wing;

Here on the headrigg is purple heather,
        And, blushing near it, rosy ling.
On silent mossholes - not a bubble,
        Light and the blue, blue sky above,
And, here at our feet, the white oat stubble,
        Spangled with herbage sweet as love.

A plot of rye, in this pleasant city,
        Reaped, and only the stubble left,
Moved me this morning to love and pity
        For tender herbs of their shade bereft—
Moved me till my thoughts, untangled,
        Here are set that folk may see
How new-cut stubble, herb-bespangled,
        A poem is writ, bonnily

Stubble stirs me. There's no denying it,
        No gainsaying but I love it well—
The linnets in it, the larks' o'erflying it,
        The tender herbs and their sweet, sweet smell,
In dreams once more I hear the sickle
        Rasp as it feels upon it fall
The dews that down from ripe heads trickle,
        When comes the shock that comes to all.

THE WET BOGLAND

Agh! it's poor, the wet bogland,
      Though tufts of rosy ling
And fragrant myrtle make it grand
      And beautiful, in spring.
And so much heather, sprouting green,
      In bunches, big and small,
That, in the sunbright distance seen,
      Coarse heather seems it all.

Where dreams the rush a dream profound
      And is nor ebb nor flow,
Dark little mossy pools around
      White cattails thrive and grow.
And, barely noticed 'bove the mould,
      Brown mould, so surface-dry,
It sullies not her robe of gold—
      The orchid, 'shamed and shy.

In quas are moonicks, little ones,
      That on their boggy bed,
Their cheeks, turned to the summer sun's,
      Show yellow, pink and red.
Blackberries, soggy tammocks down,
      And starring hardy stems,
Kissed by the sunlight, ripen brown,
      And glisten bright as gems.

Above the mould the green bogbean
      And plants without a name,
Long leek-like things, whose roots, when seen
      The white of scallions shame.
And oh, such mosses, many-hued,
      Yellow and green and tan,
Their tinges and their tones subdued
      To charm the eyes of man.

These sung to by the many birds
      Born in the brown bogland,
Hear all the songs as lovesome words,
      And hearing understand.
Our fay - the pipit, if she keeps
      Her songs for sunny days,
It's always sweet she chirps and cheeps
      About the mossy ways.

Negleced since the days of eld,
      Below a rainy sky,

What seas of water have upwelled!
      What loughs run turf mould-dry!
Piped to or not by some fond Pan,
      East wind or west wind fanned,
In things, that meet the wants of man,
      It's poor, the wet bogland.

AN OLD WORLD SUMMER HOUSE

Grassy sods and dry the seat
And, as shelter from the heat,
A roof of roses white and sweet!

The eye before, a little plot,
Cool when all the world was hot,
Flower-beds seven - the Flower Knot!

The delight of every breeze,
Snowy-blossomed rowan trees,
Musical with humming bees!

Red-flowering currant bushes - they
Made more odorous the May:
Dropping sweetness every spray!

Linnets trilling late and soon,
Finches still with throats attune
Leading May to leafy June!

Sweet at dewy close of day,
Sweeter in the twilight grey—
Robin Redbreast's roundelay!

Abloom below the soft blue skies,
That summer-house, to boyhood's eyes,
Was a bower in paradise!

When I think of glory fled,
At times I feel that I, loved-led,
Could die because delight is dead.

Gone, long gone the grassy seat,
Gone the roses white and sweet—
Wreck and ruin - gone complete!

WHEN THE CARTS COME HOME

Many an hour's spent o'er the fire,
      O'er the 'greeshy' red with heat,
Till the heavy eyelids tire
      Of the pictures in the peat.
Kings and queens and castles there
      Fall in ashes white as foam,
While we wait with nervous care
      Till from town the carts come home.

Often to the door we go,
      Silent stand with listening ear,
While the bitter north doth blow,
      Or the dripping night is drear;
Or great jewels - frosty stars—
      Stud the dark, metallic dome;
But no sound; save that of cars,
      Jaunting cars returning home.

Hark! A rattle on the hill!
      Yon's the rumble of the wheels!
They are coming - (Spot, be still!)
      Oh, how glad the listener feels
When, after waiting lone and long
      For the feet afar that roam,
The noise is heard, sweet as a song,
      Made by carts returning home.

Now the very blood doth burn
      And the heart beats loud and fast;
Hear them safely take the turn!
      They are on 'the street' at last!
Get each steed into his stall,
      Ply the wisp and currycomb;
The skies may now in torrents fall,
      Horses, carts and all are home!

THE OLD COW LOANIN'

A rough old lane it was, I vow,
        Half-hid by hawthorn hedges;
Grass so unclean, nor calf nor cow
        Would even clip the edges.
The dingy ditch still full of old
        Tin-pots and pans and kettles;
The bank, a hedgehog's back unrolled,
        Bristling with briers and nettles.
The place where midnight waif might hear
        A ghostly banshee moanin'—
The drizzling night, indeed, fell drear
        Adown the old cow loanin'.

The boy had been a hardy wight,
        Who with his wattle only
Had ventured on a winter's night
        To walk that lane so lonely.
Yet many a lad to meet his lass,
        Or see some hillside posy,
At mirk came up from the morass
        To crack at firesides cosy.
A bogle in each thorny bush
        All gruesome might be groanin'—
Past it he slipt, and past the thrush
        That slept in the cow loanin'.

The lass herself was not afeard
        Adown it to go roamin'
What time the yellow primrose peered
        A pale star in the gloamin'.
A weaver boy she there might meet,
        Or hear the warblin' robin;
The swain aye found the tryst made sweet
        By smiles, or sighs, or sobbin'!
Fine sure it was within that lane
        To hear the rosebud ownin'
"She had no sweetheart," - while the swain
        Kissed her in the cow loanin'.

O rough old loanin', wheel-rut scarr'd,
        Hard as the path of duty;
In thy green banks the rustic bard
        Discovers buds of beauty.
There, safely sheltered 'neath the thorn
        That withers not nor winces,
In spring the blue-eyed violet's born,
        The primrose blooms - a princess!

And brave o'er their unbroken sleep,
    The redbreast chirps condonin'
When winds of winter howl and sweep
    Adown the old cow loanin'.

THE BONNIE BOGLAND GIRL

Sing loud, O skylark, over
    Red heath and thymy ling;
Sing clear above the clover,
    And o'er the grazin' sing.
What though a shower is fallin'
    Each shinin' drop - a pearl;
She hears thee to her callin',
    The bonnie bogland girl!

Old Dick the weaver's daughter,
    Her tresses black as coal;
A 'go' of brown moss water
    She brings from bogland hole.
Sylph-like, in barefoot beauty,
    A mate for knight or earl;
To 'do the turns' - her duty,
    The bonnie bogland girl!

If busy windin' bobbins.
    The wheel run swift or slow,
Her voice, soft as a robin's
    Is sweet and rich and low.
Oft of her ploughboy thinkin',
    Wi' tunes she mocks the merle,
Love-note to love-note linkin',
    The bonnie bogland girl!

Again, the cow outdrivin'
    A birch switch in her hand,
Her soft blue eyes enliven
    All space not rainbow spanned,
Her lips out-bloom the clover,
    Her teeth are pearl and pearl;
And blithe the lark sings over
    The bonnie bogland girl!

LOVELY ANNIE BARR

I left her - with her tresses brown;
      Her blue eyes - star and star;
And as I journeyed home from town,
      My coach a jaunting car,
I fondly said, "Of life the crown
      Is lovely Annie Barr."

The mosses - oh, but they looked drear,
And beauty seemed so far,
      I said, "Her presence is not here,
But where young lovers are;
      They yearn the doorstep to be near
Of blushing Annie Barr."

Oh beauty, thy bewitching charms,
      Bewildering are to me;
In vain I stretch out empty arms,
      In vain I sigh for thee!
The lily of the Bannside farm
      Scarce knows the withered tree.

The heather in the Montiaghs' moss
      Blooms sweet in early spring,
Pink honey bells all rich emboss
      The little sprigs of ling;
But when a drain I jump across
      They bow in sorrowing.

Irreverence, my intruding there;
      My footsteps they but mar
The beauty - oh, sweet heaven, how fair!
      Of blushing blooms that are
Awaiting with a modest air,
      The smiles of Annie Barr.

She draws me with her tresses brown,
      Her blue eyes - star and star—
Light memory back to Portadown,
      Where bonnie lasses are;
But none so fit life's hope to crown
      As lovely Annie Barr.

GORSE

*Lines to a lovely bit of whin, or gorse,
a-bloom on the edge of a moss ramper.*

My blessings on thee, bonnie gorse,
        By meddling fingers unmolested!
How often, when we had no horse,
        I wheeled the load to thee - and rested.

Here by the ramper's bristlings brow,
        In the noonday sunshine basking,
Bestowing gladness still art thou,
        And bits of gold without the asking.

To look at thee a joyance is,
        Firm-rooted where is fading heather;
Wee birds fly o'er thee with a whiz,
        And, like thyself, enjoy the weather.

The nannie goat thee meddles not,
        Serene in thy secure dominion;
The browsing donkey seeks some spot
        Where bristles not thy thorny pinion.

Yet, by the roadside gladly shine,
        A poet is there, no bard master,
One who adoring blossoms thine,
        Would grieve to see thee meet disaster.

The yellow blooms - oh, they to me
        Are gold and sunshine blent together;
And in they sharpest thorn I see
        Nor donkey's teeth, nor nan-goat's tether.

Here as the 'whin' thou art, indeed,
        A gem among the bogland blossoms;
Yet women they'd term thee a weed,
        Though placed thou wert upon their bosoms.

But bloom thou on, thou bonnie whin,
        Thy gold buds, this November weather
Are more to me than - oh, the sin!
        Any slaughtered peafowl's feather.

Sweet! Let me look at thee again,
        So taken am I with thy beauty;
An' hour beside thee I'd remain,
        But, bless me, yon's the call to duty.

Gorse.

Yet oft in memory, dear, shall I
      See thee shining where the ramper
Lone and loveless here doth lie,
      A road no heather sods can hamper.

As 'furze' thou'rt also widely known,
      And yet whatever name they call thee,
Still may thy glory be thine own,
      And never ill mishap befall thee.

LINES TO A SKYLARK IN WINTER

Though song none from thy splitten tongue,
      These frosty days, dost fall,
Yet these wild heaths and bogs among,
      How rich thy winter call.

A gurgle is there in it, sure,
      A lullaby right loud,
Both fit for one - her home the moor,
      Her curtain - yonder cloud.

Brave bird! the music is not lost;
      The treble of the young
Sires in it, though this chilling frost
      Has dulled the tuneful tongue.

Skirl on, skirl on, thou bonnie bird!
      I'd grieve to hear thee sing
These wintry days, though still I'm stirred
      When thou art on the wing.

A gurgle is to me and mine,
      Sure promise of the song,
The rich full notes, the notes divine,
      These bogs shall hear ere long.

BOGLAND PICTURES II

TURF SMOKE

When the fire is newly kindled,
    And the chimney's drawing well,
The blue smoke o'er the low, thatched cabin
    How sweet it is to smell!
Not to those who live among it,
    But to those who from afar
Bring their friends to see the Montiaghs
    And what like our hand-looms are.

Oh, how lovely, soft up-curling
    In the breathless air,
Is the turf smoke! never banner
    Blue was half so fair.
And they tell us - those who journey
    O'er old ocean's swell —
How they pace the deck, delighted,
    When they Ireland smell.

THE HOME OF JENNY WREN

You may search the banks that seem designed
    By nature and by men
To hide soft nests before you find
    The home of Jenny Wren.

Below the bridge where sand and silt
    Drop through a briery den,
'Tis there you'll find - of foggage built—
    The home of Jenny Wren.

A big brown ball - it looketh such,
    Compared with jinking Jen;
A wee side door - but who would touch
    The home of Jenny Wren?

Within the nest - all feather lined—
    Are egg-pearls, nine or ten,
Any may the robbers never find
    The home of Jenny Wren.

Her winter house and summer burb,
    Just look at it again!
What frost can fret, what storm disturb,
    The home of Jenny Wren.

TO A BOGLAND ORCHID

Child of the bogland! Wealth and rank
        And joy are not for thee!
Thy birthplace is the cold moss-bank
        They portion - penury.
And yet God's air and light are thine!
        Nor can the watery globe
Show any star that can outshine
        Thee in thy saffron robe.

For wizard, too, thou has the lark,
        One brush of whose brown wing
Scatters, like mist, the summer dark,
        And morning in doth bring.
The wee mosscheeper - pretty bird!
        Running the banks along,
See thee and starts, and then, soul-stirred
        Bursts into joyous song.

For thou are fair as is the star
        That of itself doth shine;
Lovely and fair, as all things are
        Whose hearts to good incline.
Upcurled while cold the night dews fall,
        At the first breath of morn,
Thy fresh unfolding gladdens all
        The bank where thou wast born.

Uprising from they peat-mould bed
        Thy sweetness all thine own,
Too oft, alas, on they meek head,
        Wet turf and cold are thrown.
For though he does not wish thee harm
        Nor cruel mean to be,
Thy beauty and thy bogland charm
        The native cannot see.

Yet when bloom-lovers wand'ring here,
        Sing sweet of rose and rue,
Pray, tell them, through they beauty, dear,
        Thou'st had thy poet, too.
That one whose birth was poor as thine,
        One wed to penury,
Was proud in metre to enshrine
        Thy bogland home and thee.

THE BANSHEE[54]

When the old man, sick to death,
      In his crib quits groanin';
When the fay-wife "Himh himgh!" saith,
      And up the cow loanin'
Freezing on our lips the breath
      Comes the banshee moanin',
Filled with terror, then we know
      Some one soon, feet out, must go.

A witch-like something all in white,
      It commences moanin'
Near the house at middle night;
      Then from lane to loanin'
Whisks about as whisks a light,
      Groanin', goanin', groanin',
Till with terror filled, we know
      Some one soon, feet out must go.

MONTIAGHS' MARY

Barefoot she runs about the bogs,
      Free to the winds her form!
Until the frost comes, then in clogs
      Her feet are dry and warm.
Glinting like polished cairngorm—
      Her blue eyes laugh at toil;
Nor can rough winter's rudest storm
      Her cheek's red rose despoil.

The lark may sing his songs of joy,
      But she in cold retreats,
Full often with the servant boy
      Must help to rickle peats.
Unused to this world's cloying sweets,
      Born to the harsh and wild,
Still in her guileless bosom beats
      The soft heart of a child.

---

[54] Female spirit in Gaelic folklore whose wailing in the night is thought to presage a death.

BREAKING-IN BOGLAND

Soddin' praties on the heather,
      Oh, the poor return!
Even fowl of coarsest feather
      Oft the product spurn.

Droppin' peas among the praties,
      Seems a contract small,
But we get the blossoms, gratis,
      And they're worth it all.

Dibblin' curleys in the edges,
      Apart - about an ell;
Seems like planting woeful pledges,
      But the sprouts look well.

Even when we dig and ditch it,
      Pound and beat and burn,
And with heated clay enrich it,
      Poor is the return.

Yet 'tis thus the bogland farmer,
      Belted must begin,
Ere he can the golden charmer,
      Ceres, hope to win.

A FAREWELL

Farewell, ye cold black bogs and moors!
      Goodbye, ye gold-bloomed whins!
Ye teach me how the love endures,
      That in friendship fond begins.
Goodbye ye little redbreasts all
      That sing so sweet at dawn,
At dusk I hear your pensive call,
      And shall when I am gone.

Ye joyous lark that in the blue
      Already carols loud,
I know your song is sweet and true
      Though I'm with sorrow bowed.
A home across the western wave
      Once more I go to seek,
Beside your song, so loud and brave,
      This dirge sounds worn and weak.

Farewell, ye kindly people all
      In bogland and in town,
Your friendship I esteem, and shall
      Till I this head lie down.
In that last sleep o'er which the dawn
      Of heaven some morn will rise,
When I, fond hope! though some time gone,
      Shall join you in the skies.

APPENDIX A

FAMILY TREE OF THE TEGGARTS, BALLINARY, CO. ARMAGH

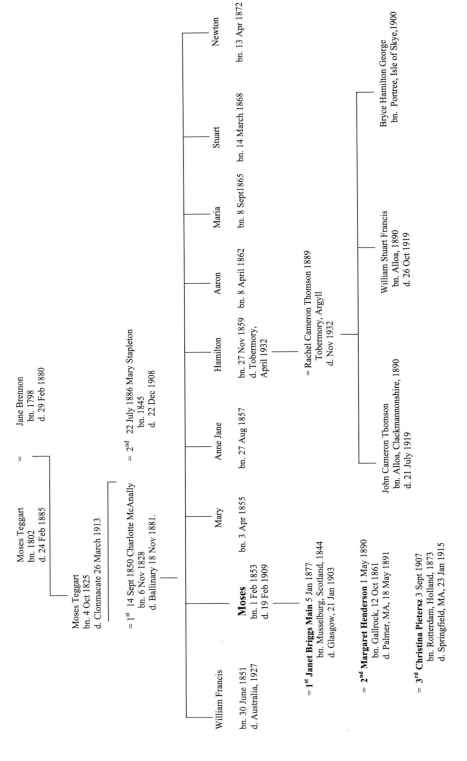

APPENDIX B

FAMILY TREE OF THE MITTONS, BALLINARY, CO. ARMAGH

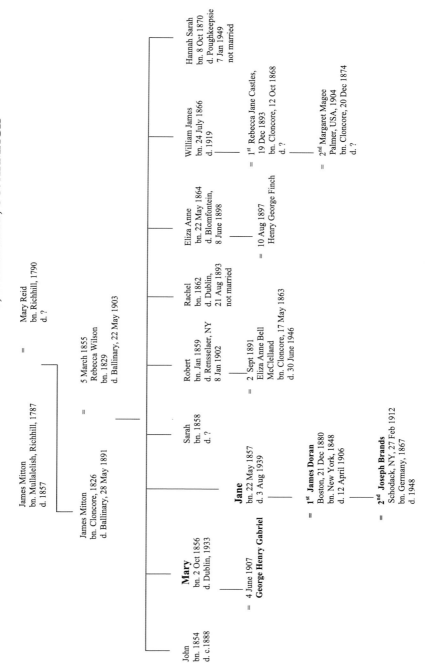

407

SELECT GLOSSARY

aiblins:	perhaps, maybe
anee:	cry of lamentation
ava:	at all
bab:	bunch
balkin:	eccentric, strange, odd
bandog:	large guard dog
banshee:	female spirit whose wailing outside a house is believed to portend death within
baytons:	patches of rough ground used for growing vegetables
ben:	in, into
biggin:	buildiing
birk:	birch
birkie:	smart young fellow, lively, spirited, harbinger, herald
blate:	bashful, shy
blinkerdom:	source of evil influence
bloodroot/bloodwort:	herbaceous plant, flowers from March - May, native to eastern USA, white petals with yellow stamens
bog mist:	bog cotton
boogles:	ghosts, phantoms
boor tree:	the elder, in particular the black elder
boxty/boxtey:	a kind of bread made with raw potatoes, grated and mixed with flour or meal
bruckle:	broken, brittle
buckiebrier/buckybrier:	wild rose

burdocks:	biennial thistles
but and ben:	to and fro
buts and bens:	rooms in a house, resting places
carles:	old men
carlie:	fellow, man of the common people, peasant
cary:	clouds, sky
chappit:	knock, tap, strike
chay/chegh:	name by which a cow is called when at a distance
chits:	saucy girls, gossips.
chiel:	fellow
chookie:	a hen
clachan:	a village, hamlet
claiver:	clover
clinkers:	extemely hard, slow-burning, top quality turf used for fuel
clipe:	a large piece or area
coaties:	skirts, petticoats
coof:	a foolish person
coom:	soot
corries:	armchair shaped hollows found on sides of hills
couthie:	friendly, sympathetic, pleasant, agreeable
cowped:	overturned
crack/craic:	animated conversation, entertaining chat, general merriment
croupy:	wheezy
crouse:	proud

crowlied:	stunted in growth
cuckoo sarl:	sorrell, perennial herb, grows in meadows and often cultivated as a root vegetable
curleys:	cabbages, kail plants
cutty:	short
danner/darmer:	to wander, saunter, walk aimlessly
darnel:	weedy annual grass often found in grain fields
dinnels:	tingles
dool:	distress
dree:	slow, tedious, wearisome, weak, lacking in energy, drooping
drumlie:	muddy, turbid
dubs:	pools
duds:	clothing, usually of inferior quality
dull:	a noose or snare
dunders:	loud knocking, thundery noise
dwamy:	sad, tearful, temporary onset of nausea, feeling faint
fairy fingers:	foxgloves
fash:	trouble, annoy, anger
fause:	false, deceitful
fay-wife:	female with supernatural gifts, credited with ability to foretell the future
ferlie:	stranger, busy-body, person of no account
flytes:	barges, scolds, upbraids
fods:	bundles

footy:	ineffectual, powerless, unimportant, pointless, foolish
freen:	friend, usually a blood relation
freets:	superstitious observances, rites or ceremonies
futtens:	turf stacked up for drying
gear:	property, goods, money
gillyflowers:	wallflowers, carnations, gold marguentas
glaiks/glakes:	a lever attached to churn-staff by use of which the churning is made less laborious, content of churn
gomerel:	simpleton, fool
gorsons/gosoons:	young boys
gowans:	yellow or white wildflowers, especially the mountain daisy
gowpenfuls:	double handfuls
graip:	garden-fork, usually with three or four prongs
hackle:	board with spikes for dressing flax
hangrail/hangerel:	a coarse rafter generally cut from bog oak
hart's tongue:	evergreen fern with leathery, glossy leaves
hasky:	dry, rough, harsh, ill-natured, churlish, rude
haugh and shaw:	low lying land and wooded dells
heddle:	one of a set of paralllel cords or wires in a loom, used to separate and guide the warp threads and make a path for the shuttle
hum-humin:	chewing small piece of food (often for weaning infant), low muttering
ilka:	each
jinty:	a wren
jaloused:	inferred, deduced

keeks:	glances
kimmer:	young girl
kirtle:	women's dress, petticoat or skirt
klipe:	a tell-tale
kye:	cattle
laigh:	low
laverock:	skylark
leal:	faithful
lift:	the sky
linn:	waterfall, pool below waterfall
litten:	lit up
loe:	love
loof:	palm of hand
loups:	leaps, springs, vaults
merle:	a blackbird
mim:	demure
mirk:	dark
moonicks:	red berries, often cranberries
moily/moiley:	cow without horns
mosscheeper:	titlark, meadow pipit
mossgall:	bog myrtle
muckle:	large, big
muirfowl:	the red grouse
my certes:	exclamation of surprise, assuredly
nobby:	stylish, well-dressed

osiers:	long rod-like willow twigs, often found in wetlands
paidles:	walks slowly with short steps, paddles
panade:	rude gesture, abusive language
panged:	fill to over-flowing, crammed
pilgarlic:	sneaky unpopular fellow, bald man often regarded with humorous contempt
plaidle:	shawl, woollen tartan, mantle
pluckstick:	stick used by handloom weaver to propel the shuttle
pollen/pullen:	Lough Neagh fresh water herring
praties:	potatoes
pree:	taste, have experience of, sample
prig:	haggle, wheel and deal
quas:	marshy patches of ground, abbreviation of quagmires
ragged robin:	greater stitchwort, robin-run-the-hedge, goosegrass
ramfoozle:	muddle, confuse
rasp:	raspberry
rickle:	small mound or clump of turf
rigg:	broad drill
ringgle:	wall-eyed, having white ring on iris of eye
saggans:	species of iris with triangular leaves, waterflag
sark:	women's shift or chemise
saugh:	willow
sconce:	wall-light fixture

scollops:	bent wooden pins to keep bundles of thatch in position on a roof
scroggs:	rough ground with stunted bushes
sheugh:	ditch, usually with water in it
shilty:	pony
shoogie:	shakey, unsteady, wobbly, turning back and forth
siller:	silver, money
siskins:	finches
skey/skay:	rudely constructed loft, generally laid with loose or round timber, built over hearth area of jamb wall house, usually used for storage and occasionally for sleeping
skirling:	shrill crying
sley:	instrument used in weaving to beat up the weft
snedding neeps:	cutting the roots or foliage off turnips
sonsie/sonsy:	attractive, comely, friendly, fortunate, full of life, skilful
soople:	the striking part of a flail
soughs:	sound of a soft mumuring wind
spad:	a spade
stouned:	violent throbbing, short jabs of pain
stoups:	mug, tankard of alcohol
strath:	river valley
stripper:	cow or pig from which the young are being weaned
styme/stime:	speck, very small particle
tammock:	small hillock

tholed:	put up with, endure
tine:	lose
tirl:	sing loudly, make a rattling sound
towmond:	twelve months
trig:	tidy
turf bummer:	one who goes round town or countryside selling turf
twait:	a finch, usually a red-poll
unco:	extraordinary
vetches:	weak-stemmed, semi-vining plant with pinnate leaves, often used as green manure for soil improvement
wakerife:	sleepless
warstle:	wrestle, contend with, struggle with
waur:	worse
weel-kent:	kind-hearted, generous
wet-my-lip:	a quail
whitewing:	a chaffinch
whinchat:	stonechat or stonebreaker, small bird with yellowish rump and white tail with black terminal band
wimpling:	winding, meandering, twisting
yorlin:	yellow-hammer

SELECT BIBLIOGRAPHY

Barrows Charles H, *The Poets and Poetry of Springfield, Massachusett From Early Times to the End of the Nineteenth Century*, Connecticut Valley Historical Society (Springfield, Massachusetts, 1907).

Cunliffe Marcus, *The Literature of the United States* (London, 1954).

Fenton James, *The Hamely Tongue*, Ulster-Scots Academic Press (Belfast, 1995).

Fleming Rev W E C, *Tartaraghan Precinct North Armagh* (Dundalk, 2006).

Hewitt James, *Rhyming Weavers* (Belfast, 2004).

Lutton William, *Montiaghisms: Ulster Dialect Words and Phrases*, 2nd edn. (Armagh, 1924).

Macdonald Hugh, *Rambles Round Glasgow* (Glasgow, 1854).

Milford Humphrey (ed), *Poems of William Cullen Bryant* (London, 1914).

Robinson Mairi (ed), *The Concise Scots Dictionary*, Aberdeen University Press (Aberdeen, 1985).

Tower James E (ed), *Springfield Present and Prospective* (Springfield, Massachusetts, 1905).

Whiting Charles Goodrich, *Walks in New England* (New York, 1903).

Wilson Leslie Perrin, *Thoreau, Emerson and Transcendentalism*, (New York, 2000).

ALPHABETICAL INDEX OF POEMS

A Birches Boy	251
A Black Frost	304
A Bogland Boy	335
A Bogland Custom	337
A Change	295
A City Rowan Tree	143
A Dreaming Skylark	350
A Farewell	405
A Fine Crop of Turf	322
A Giant's Hemlock	146
A Little Thorn	295
A Lough Neagh Lament	293
A Lover's Song to Spring	156
A Monody for Mary	317
A November Hepatica	163
A Wayside Flower	342
Aboon Ben Lomond	83
Above the Bogs in Ireland	269
Adown the Lane	337
Aella Green	139
Ailsa Craig	85
Ames Hill	167
An Exile	215
An Old World Summer House	394
Anither Year	84
April in Erin	369
Arrow-Wounds	113
At Dewy Dusk in August	132
At New-Year's Time	102
At Sunset	162
At the Birthplace of Burns	71
At the Cross Roads	335
At the Hill Gap	342
At the Mouth of the Old Turf Stack	237
Aurora to Tithonus	184
Autumn	173
Autumn in Derryagh	340
Autumn's Self	339
Bella	302
Ben the Thatcher	264
Bilzy	207
Bleaching Flax	344
Blue-Eyed Melia Lappin	372
Bog Fir	298
Bogland Stubble	391
Bonnie Mary of Drumcree	330
Brannon's Brae	290

Breaking-in Bogland	404
Bringing Home the Cows	187
Bringing Home Turf	360
Burn's Great-Granddaughter	87
By the Banks of the River Wey	94
Caged Skylarks in Forest Park	140
Campsie Glen	73
Cast Down	121
Childhood	199
Columbkill	324
Coney Island	256
Crowned with Glory	110
Daisies on the Brae	352
Dawn	111
Dead at the Birches	228
Distant Hills	161
Divided	300
Down in Maghery	380
Down the Long Road	319
Enduring Love	248
Fate	114
Fine Grosbeaks	321
Five Unhappy Song Birds	142
Flora: A Lady Tree	130
For the Last Time	175
Forebodings	119
God's Harvest	341
Gorse	399
Granda's Laburnum	321
Granny Roe	379
Hedgerow Flowers	363
Helen's Gift to Telemachus	183
Her Lover's Lass	78
Hero to Leander	176
Home	374
Home Thoughts from Abroard	192
How They Manage in Derryagh	325
Humility in Song	134
In a Quaker Meeting-House	367
In Carlo's Company	155
In Dear Old Ireland	276
In Derrylileagh Wood	334
In Memory of Mother	366
In Milltown Churchyard	298
In the Big Moss	305
In the Bogland	361
In the Potato Plots	338
In the Strathavon	106
In the Town of Birr	333

Innocence	169
Jenny Gow	104
Jenny Wren	122
Jenny's Hazel Een	80
June	172
Keepin' Tryst	81
Lenora	158
Life in the Bog Plat	360
Light and Darkness: or The Birches Boy's Fate	282
Lillian Martin	281
Lines to a Skylark in Winter	400
Lines to a Lonely Pine	153
Listening to the Lark at Sunrise	171
Liza	297
Liza and her Ploughboy	240
Lizzie Wall	272
Loch-na-Gar	99
Love for Betty	348
Love for Things of the Bogland	356
Love in Derrykarn	346
Love in Spring	206
Love in the Kail-Plat	213
Lovely Annie Barr	398
Love's Entreaty	345
Lulworth Cove	96
Makin' Hay	347
March in the Boglands	246
Mary M'Anally	377
Mary Mitton	370
Memories of the Wee Mosscheeper	236
Mirren	77
Montiaghs' Mary	403
Morn	312
Morning Song of the Wood Thrush	133
Mounthall	242
My Father's Birches	306
My School-Girl	190
Ned and Mary	245
Night	313
Night and Morn	248
November in the Bogland	375
O Fresh and Fragrant Roses	194
On the Banks O' the Bann	386
On the Lord's Day	160
On the Wee Green Ramper	303
Our Bogland Home	329
Our Dumb Animals	136
Over at Mitton's	299
Pulling Flax	332

Remembrance	120
Rowanberries in Campsie Glen	89
Run Like a Redshank	357
Sloes	337
Snowbirds	147
Solicitude	247
Spring in Ballinary	218
Summer Nights	319
Summer's Come! Summer's Come!	252
Sweet-Brier	191
Tartaraghan	200
The Banshee	403
The Banshee's Lament	327
The Bard Greet Himsel' on New Year's Eve	91
The Belle of Ballinary	238
The Belle of Clonmacate	309
The Belle of Columbkill	258
The Belle of Derryagh	285
The Belle of Derrykeevin	225
The Blackcap	297
The Blackthorn Blossom	274
The Bleating of the Snipe	350
The Blue Cornflower	325
The Blue Jay	145
The Bluecap	303
The Bogland Farmer to his Wife	229
The Bonnie Bogland Girl	397
The Bonnie Rose O'Airlie	75
The Bonny Scotch Bluebell	79
The Boor-Tree	214
The Boys an' the Bird-Creel	216
The Braes of Ballinary	233
The Bullfinch	325
The Cattle Come from the Hills	267
The Chay Lady	262
The Chickadee	148
The Clay Island	363
The Crabtree Chair	254
The Crabtree Loanin'	235
The Daffodils	174
The Dog Argos	181
The English Starling	126
The Fisher Girl	314
The Flower of Derryane	222
The Go-Ahead Yankee	109
The Harebell	160
The Home of Jenny Wren	401
The House at the Head of the Town	231
The Invitation	354

The Jacksnipe	335
The Jaguar in Forest Park	127
The Lily of Lough Neagh	226
The Little Sprig of Green	129
The Lough at Derryadd	295
The Loved One	308
The Luggie	90
The Maid of Markethill	365
The Maid of Moyallon	349
The Meadowpipit	306
The Milltown Maid	382
The Montiagh Moss	188
The Moon and the Soul	117
The Music of Sorrow	166
The Music of the Crows	164
The Old Cow Loanin'	396
The Old Foot-Stick	323
The Old Limekiln	364
The Old Moon and the New	112
The Old Stone-Breaker	315
The Old Stripper	186
The Ould Straw Stack	271
The Peabody Elm	141
The Pearl of Portadown	220
The Peasant Folks' Hallowe'en	211
The Pewit	326
The Plantation	344
The Rag Thorn	334
The Red Pines	160
The Redbreast's Vesper	154
The Reply to Mr Frank Burns, Rural Postman, Portadown, Ireland	193
The Rose O'Rochsilloch	108
The Sally Tree	270
The Sands of Troon	70
The Scarlet Tanager	123
The Shovel and the Spade	311
The Skay	223
The Sky	118
The Spey-Wife	326
The Stonechecker	302
The Turf Bummer	302
The Turf Cutter	277
The Vision and Penelope	179
The Voice of Mary	280
The Water Wagtail	196
The Welcome of the Fields	149
The Wet Bogland	393
The Wet-My-Lip	338
The Whiterump	275

The Wimplin' Luggie	98
The Wind and Brown Oak Leaves	165
The Wind and the Leaves	157
The Wood Thrush and His Song	162
The Woods in Winter	115
The Yellow Willy	358
'Tis all for Thee	247
To a Bogland Orchid	402
To be a Boy Again	318
To James Duncan	172
To Spring	171
To the City of Homes	137
To the February Wind	141
To the Robin Red Breast	287
Toby Hole	388
Treasure-Trove	306
Turf Smoke	401
Under the Elms	124
Up the Ramper	286
Upon the Sally Tree	197
Upon the Stubble Rigg	297
Ursa Major	152
Weaving and Wooing	346
Wee Jerry	305
When Mother's Gone	383
When the Bud is on the Thorn	249
When the Carts Come Home	395
When the Skylark Soars and Sings	198
Where Blue-Eyed Mary Dwells	260
Where Darling Sally Dwells	289
Where the Bog Bean Grows	279
Where the Bonnie Kelvin Winds	100
Where Yellow Poppies Blow	135
Wintertime in Derryagh	384
Woodland Clover in March	151
Working and Dreaming	318
Yellow Broom	307

MOSES TEGGART
Bard of the Boglands

1853 ~ 1909